Publisher's Acknowledgments

This book was produced by a team dedicated to excellence; please send your feedback to Editors@ForTheGENIUS.com.

Members of the team who produced this book include:

Editors

Acquisitions Editor: Amy Eisenstein

Comprehensive Editor: Stephen Nill

Copy Editor: Jill McLain

Production

Book Design: Deborah Perdue

Illustrations: Kimberly O'Reilly

Layout Editor: Jill McLain

Administrative

For The GENIUS Press: Stephen Nill, CEO, CharityChannel LLC

Marketing and Public Relations: John Millen and Linda Lysakowski

About the Author

Marc S. Freedman, CFP®, is president and CEO of Freedman Financial and has practiced financial planning and investment management out of his office in Peabody, Massachusetts, since 1992.

Marc's high-energy storytelling skills make him a highly-sought-after speaker to both the financial planning community and the consumer public at large.

Over the past few years, Marc has been the radio host of *Dollars & Sense*, where he delivers "financial advice in a language you can understand." He has been quoted in national media outlets, including the *Los Angeles Times, The Wall Street Journal, Money* magazine, *Bloomberg Businessweek*, and multiple industry publications. He has appeared on *CBS This Morning*, FOX Business Network, CNNMoney, and local television affiliates in Boston.

His first publication, *Oversold and Underserved—A Financial Planner's Guide to Serving the Mass Affluent*, has been recognized by the industry as a blueprint for building a better relationship between financial planners and the mass affluent baby boomer marketplace.

A 1989 graduate of Babson College, Marc is married to Laura and has five children. He is an avid fan of the Boston Red Sox and the Wonderful World of Disney. It is his lifelong dream to dress as a Disney character in the Magic Kingdom for just one day. After that, he would like to happily retire as a guest relations cast member.

thanks for visiting our office today!

Marc Freedman

Retiring with Confidence

for the GENIUS®

Your Blueprint for Planning a Successful Retirement

Not affiliated with or sponsored by T. Rowe Price Group, Inc.

FOR THE GENIUS IN ALL OF US™

Marc S. Freedman, CFP®

Retiring with Confidence for the GENIUS™

One of the **For the GENIUS®** books

Published by
For the GENIUS Press, an imprint of CharityChannel LLC
30021 Tomas, Suite 300
Rancho Santa Margarita, CA 92688-2128 USA

ForTheGENIUS.com

Library of Congress Control Number: 2014910711
ISBN Print Book: 978-1-941050-06-4 | ISBN eBook: 978-1-941050-07-1

Printed in the United States of America
10 9 8 7 6 5 4 3 2

This and most For the GENIUS Press books are available at special quantity discounts for bulk purchases for sales promotions, premiums, fundraising, or educational use. For information, contact CharityChannel, 30021 Tomas, Suite 300, Rancho Santa Margarita, CA 92688-2128 USA.
+1 949-589-5938

Dedication

To my mother, Phyllis Freedman. You taught me the importance of being resourceful—or, as you said it, "figuring out ways to do things differently." You said it built character. And, Mom, what a character you were. I love you so much and miss you more each day.

Author's Acknowledgments

Building a book is no easy task. It takes concentration and commitment each and every day (despite having a real job too). I would never have been able to complete this book on deadline without the "genius-like" guidance provided by my editors and publisher at **For the GENIUS** Press.

But there are also others whose patience, encouragement, inspiration, and perspiration allowed me to deliver a book that I'm proud to share.

Thank you . . .

. . . to my father, Barry Freedman. Without your mentorship, I might still be selling Chinese food takeout containers.

. . . to the mass affluent baby boomer population—those of you over fifty with a net worth of between $500,000 and $2.5 million. You are the inspiration for this book.

. . . to our clients, the greatest clients in the world. You are the inspiration that allowed me to share stories, examples, and lessons. I remain so incredibly honored to provide comprehensive financial planning advice to each and every one of you.

. . . to my peer reviewers—Ray Ferrara, CFP; Bill Carter, CFP; Marci Lerner; Rick Kagawa, CFP; Mark VanDrunen, CFP; and Timothy Wyman, CFP—for your invaluable and honest insights.

. . . to my incredible staff at Freedman Financial and, of course, my business partner, Marion Gilman, for allowing me to keep my hands on the keyboard when my head could have been in client meetings. Trust me, my heart was in both places.

. . . to Judy Parisella, my marketing and social media expert. Thanks for always keeping me on my toes, delivering fresh content, and working so diligently to promote this book.

... to my family and neighbors for having to watch me type every weekend on my front porch. I promise to stop wearing my pajamas outside.

... to my daughter Mindy Freedman and our friend Hannah Gray, who spent hours and hours editing a book that was of little interest to them. Though, in the end, they admitted that they actually learned something!

... most of all, to Laura, my beautiful wife of twenty-two years, and my five children, Mindy, Ilana, Jerry, Noah, and Corey. The gift you've given me has been the opportunity to try to be the best husband and dad ever. I love you all very much.

Contents

Summary of Chapters

Foreword

Thomas Edison famously said, "Genius is 1 percent inspiration, 99 percent perspiration," and that person lies within each individual now reading this wonderfully written book on retirement by my good friend Marc Freedman, CFP®. When Marc first asked that I review the book, I thought to myself, "What? Another book on retirement? Just what the world doesn't need."

But Marc, as always, comes through with an instructional, thoughtful, and entertaining book on retirement planning for the mass affluent baby boomer, who generally is someone with a net worth of between $500,000 and $2.5 million. He recognizes that each one of us has the ability to be a genius—if we take the time to accept responsibility for our financial life. *Retiring with Confidence for the GENIUS* is a great tool to start you on that journey. This is the first book, to my knowledge, specifically written for mass affluent baby boomers. They represent a significant portion of the ten thousand baby boomers turning age sixty-five each day.

If you're looking for an easy way to plan for your retirement, you may as well stop now, as Marc recognizes the significance of the tough journey upon which you are embarking. If this was easy work, everyone would be doing it successfully, and that simply is not the case. But Marc, while giving you solid advice built on over two decades of serving clients, tries to make it fun, because the work you are about to do is just too important for you and your family to not complete. Some won't make it to the end, but those who do will have a great beginning in understanding the financial and personal implications of retirement.

Doing this work is a lot like starting exercise. It's something you know you need to do, and you are always going to start tomorrow on a regular basis. Don't try to consume this book quickly. Rather, like enjoying a good meal, savor the great advice and let it digest in your own mind to extract the rich nutrients most important to you.

Marc's firm, Freedman Financial, has been serving its clients since 1968, and it takes great pride in the fact that 90 percent of its clients live and/or have roots in New England. Marc didn't write this book to get new clients, but that may happen in spite of his desire to make sure that readers can find CERTIFIED FINANCIAL PLANNER™ professionals in their local areas. The CFP® mark is the highest financial planning standard recognizing competent and ethical financial planners. This book is written with those same objectives.

May you find the same honest, no-nonsense advice from Marc in planning your retirement that I have enjoyed from calling Marc my friend for many years. Now it's time to take the next step in your journey toward retirement. I wish you much success in finding a retirement that fulfills your hopes, dreams, and aspirations.

V. Raymond Ferrara, CFP®
2014 Chair
Certified Financial Planner Board of Standards Inc.

Introduction

Congratulations on your purchase of *Retiring with Confidence for the GENIUS*. Don't worry. You need not be an MIT graduate, a Rhodes scholar, or a child prodigy. That's because *this* book is written in a language we can all understand.

The truth is that millions of baby boomers lack the basic confidence to make rational, informed, personal financial decisions. It's those pesky emotions that get in the way. They create a haze of indecision contributed by social circles, Twitter feeds, and media talking heads—and if you're Jewish, like me, guilt.

What Should You Expect?

In *Retiring with Confidence for the GENIUS*, you'll find timeless strategies, information, and thinking cues, making this book an everlasting reference manual for retirement. After all, you're likely to live in retirement for as long as you've worked. Yikes!

Let's face it. Retirement planning books on the shelves today are boring. Instead of offering true stories, real-life examples, and/or thinking scenarios that apply to people like you, they are crammed with academic facts, statistics, and definitions. How does that help you make heads or tails of *your* financial situation?

If there's one thing I've learned in my more than two decades of practicing financial planning, it's that academic studies and Excel spreadsheets on retirement projections make for great research papers, but they fall short when tested individually in the real world.

You deserve authentic advice for *your* personal retirement needs (not advice that serves the masses). With more than ten thousand people turning sixty-five years old every day for the next ten years, there is an abnormal collection of salespeople, marketers, and television personalities with marketable systems designed to help you achieve success. Most don't do it out of the goodness of their hearts. They see an opportunity to make money, and they prey on your vulnerability and lack of confidence.

This is a "go-to guide." Prepare to explore *your* retirement, on *your* terms. You're about to gain a better understanding about what you've accumulated so that you can decide how to use those resources effectively throughout your retirement years. After all, if you don't know how every piece in your financial puzzle fits into your life, how can you build confidence about your financial future?

Be prepared. Once you have some answers, you'll really be feeling like a genius.

Are "Genius" Skills Required?

Can you add, subtract, multiply, and divide—with a calculator? If so, you can master the most basic financial principles surrounding money.

Lack of intelligence is *not* the reason you might struggle with achieving your personal financial goals. It's the difficulty in trusting the information you've acquired and having conviction to implement that knowledge into action.

A retirement plan should never leave you so confused that you're relegated to a state of paralysis. After all, who wants to feel like an "idiot" or a "dummy?"

I believe that retirement is more than a destination. It's a multidecade life experience, and it's up to you to craft your own personal journey.

But the truth is that retirement is different for everyone. You are in charge of your decisions. You are the boss, and no one will be reporting to you. What's worse is that you may not be reporting to anyone else either (with the exception of, perhaps, your spouse).

You have no work routine. Your schedule is your own. You can do whatever you want.

As long as you have the ability to think, you'll be in the position to plan your own retirement.

Scary, isn't it?

Why You'll Love This Book

No one wants to buy a guidebook and learn two chapters into it that the book isn't for them. If you can answer affirmatively to some of these questions, you're in for a real treat:

- Do you expect to retire someday?
- Are you currently retired but believe there's a better way to manage your financial resources in an effort to help you achieve your goals?

Pure Genius!

Are You among the Mass Affluent Baby Boomers?

Mass affluent baby boomers are a segment of the population that represent more than twenty-two million people in America.

Let's see if the bullets below begin to describe you.

- You are over the age of fifty.
- You are a homeowner.
- In retirement, you seek to spend between $4,000 and $10,000 per month. (You'll learn how to calculate this in **Chapter 4**.)
- You have investable assets of between $300,000 and $2 million.
- You have a *total* net worth (including your home and other personal property) of between $500,000 and $2.5 million. (You'll learn more about this in **Chapter 3**.)
- You have multiple financial accounts and feel a need to get better organized.
- You worry about taxes, medical costs, and how to take distributions from your accounts. (You'll love **Part 2** of the book.)
- You are seeking validation on whether you have enough money to retire. (Check out **Chapters 15–17**.)

- Do you worry about how you'll replace your paycheck in retirement and support the life you want?
- Do you feel that your financial life is scattered and in a state of disarray?
- Are you finally at a point in your life where you feel it's time to get serious about planning for your financial future?
- Do you want to be among the geniuses who understand financial planning in retirement?

Why Might This Book Frustrate You?

If your expectation of retirement means relying on government assistance programs and subsidies because you haven't accumulated enough personal money to support life in retirement, then this book won't provide answers.

As such, don't buy this book if any of the following describe you:

- More than 80 percent of your retirement income will come from Social Security.
- You are in need of credit counseling.
- You are seeking a way to "beat the system."

If you're still reading, and I hope you are, let's start learning.

How the Book Is Set Up

Retiring with Confidence for the GENIUS is organized with your retirement in mind.

Part 1

Part 1 handles the toughest part of retirement planning: getting your financial house in order. You will better understand what you own, how much money you spend, and how your overall investments will impact your retirement. You'll also get an education on how investments play an important role in a retirement plan. You'll learn about risks, stocks, bonds, mutual funds, and many other common investments held by mass affluent baby boomers.

The first few chapters will require some work on your part. I'll provide you with steps and guidance, but you'll be responsible for gathering your data and beginning to explore your goals and dreams. Hopefully when you're done, you'll want to celebrate because it's work you know you needed to complete but just haven't known how to get started.

Part 2

Part 2 begins with the emotional moments leading up to a retirement decision. We'll explore the typical conversations you'll have with your employer—and the decisions you'll need to make concerning retirement plans and pensions. We'll review your Social Security options, discuss the impact of taxes—and, most importantly, show how you'll replace your paycheck with your own customized income strategy in retirement.

Part 3

Part 3 deals with some of the toughest conversations and realities of life.

Aging—especially in your eighties, nineties, and beyond—is hard. You'll read real stories and life experiences that serve as guides on how best to position your assets, have conversations with your children and loved ones, and make sure that you squeeze the most out of each precious moment. In addition, we'll talk about uncomfortable subjects, such as life after losing a spouse, and offer ideas on how best to honor the wishes of loved ones.

Part 4

Finally, in Part 4, you'll get to put what you've learned into action. You'll be given practical ideas, tools, templates, and questionnaires that I've accumulated over the years. Whether you're a do-it-yourselfer or you're considering having a financial planner help with your retirement plan, you'll be equipped with resources that will position you as the genius you've always wanted to be.

Plus I've thrown in a bonus chapter that discusses the nonfinancial issues that I see retirees facing every day.

About Sidebars

Throughout the book, you'll find sidebars designed to add texture and bring attention to a topic at hand. You just saw an example of one that describes the mass affluent baby boomer. We refer to them as sidebars. There are ten different ones used in this book, each with its own cute little icon.

Pure Genius!

This sidebar brings attention to something of significant importance that will serve as a lifelong lesson or reminder.

Inspiration

Here you'll find stories and examples that share hope, inspiration, and success.

Perspiration

There are times in the book where some work is necessary to get results. These sidebars offer additional exercises or stories about work that was needed to achieve success.

Uninspired

How often do find yourself making decisions that sound good at first but leave you regretting them afterward?

Definition

Sometimes it's easier to pull out a word in a story and then add a definition and some added color.

Example

Sometimes a story can explain a concept so much better.

Important!

This will draw your attention to aspects of the chapter that are of importance.

Pure Genius!

Following the Rules

The road to a successful retirement can be achieved on your own. Yet every day, thousands of baby boomers and retirees seek advice from professionals. Throughout this book, I'll make reference to CFP® professionals and CERTIFIED FINANCIAL PLANNER™ professionals. I believe this designation represents the gold standard in the industry. That's because CFP professionals must abide by the four Es:

- A code of **E**thics
- A comprehensive **E**xamination
- Ongoing **E**ducation
- Relevant work **E**xperience

CFP Board, the licensing body for the CFP® mark, has very clear rules on how planners can promote its designation to the public. If an individual holds the CFP® designation, the registered-trademark symbol must appear after the three letters. If the word mark CERTIFIED FINANCIAL PLANNER™ is used, it must appear in all capital letters and be followed by "™."

Now that I've explained this to you, the ®, the ™, and the capitalization need not be a nuisance to your readability for the remainder of this text. The authorities at CFP Board have granted us a waiver if we provided this explanation up front: When you see CFP, we are referring to CFP®. When you see Certified Financial Planner, we are referring to CERTIFIED FINANCIAL PLANNER™.

And so now, with the lawyers smiling and my footnotes shared, we can begin a journey that will help you rise from the clutter and find happiness in a retirement plan that lies ahead.

Observation

Sometimes there's a moment in the book when it's important to add a personal reflection or offer some time to pause to think about a topic.

Quote

There are a lot of smart people in the world who have given us nuggets of wisdom that add even more clarity to a topic.

Watch Out!

These are hints about roadblocks to avoid or tread upon carefully.

Ready to Get Started?

Everyone needs retirement planning advice. But more than anyone else, the mass affluent baby boomers need genuine advice in a language that serves their needs—not the needs of the super wealthy or those who'll need state-sponsored care. The mass affluent baby boomer needs to understand that retirement planning should be about flexibility. It is about allowing yourself to live in the world of gray rather than believing that a black-and-white solution is always the answer. Retirement planning should be fun and easy to understand. It's with that spirit that I'm pleased to invite you to explore *Retiring with Confidence for the GENIUS*.

BANK ACCOUNT
MUTUAL FUNDS
INSURANCE POLICY
IRA
401k
PENSION
STOCKS
CASH
FLOW
JOINT
ACCOUNT
BONDS
NET
WORTH
ANNUITIES

Part 1

Building the Foundation for a Successful Retirement

For at least the next decade, ten thousand people will turn sixty-five years old *every day*! Each one of them will have a different perspective on how to live life in retirement. Some will plan well, and others will deplete their money faster than they ever imagined. Some will be surprised by how large a retirement they can live, and others will have to cut back and succumb to a dramatic lifestyle change. Which will you be? Would you like to know before it's too late?

Chapter 1

What Is Retirement Planning Anyway?

In This Chapter...

- The art and science of retirement planning
- How old is old?
- Should you do this on your own or hire someone?
- Defining financial planning

Retirement means something different to everyone. It's not about achieving a "number," and it's most certainly not about an investment or insurance solution.

There isn't a software program or a smartphone app that can deliver all the answers to your retirement issues. What it takes is a little time, an honest conversation, and desire to keep your financial house in order. But geniuses like you already know that!

The Art and Science of Retirement Planning

How many times have you contemplated answers to the following questions?

- At what age do I plan to retire?
- What will I do with my time when I'm retired?
- How much money will I need to support my life in retirement?

These questions are pretty common, and you likely already have some answers in mind. If only retirement planning was that easy. Just imagine if planning for your retirement was as easy as plugging figures into a software program and relying on outputs as the answers to your problems. There are lots of software vendors, financial institutions, and television gurus that seem to think it's that simple. But you're smarter than that. You know that retirement planning isn't that easy. Life consists of uneasy questions—and even more unknown answers.

When planning your retirement, you're faced with emotionally charged questions that are tough to answer. This book guides you through rational strategies to address them. But it will take time. The answers to your retirement questions aren't hidden in a quick-and-dirty smartphone app. After all, no one understands your financial life better than you.

Throughout this book, you'll be encouraged to toss out rules of thumb. You'll learn that the old wives' tales your parents taught you may not be as relevant in your life as they were in theirs. That's because you're about to look at retirement planning from a whole new perspective.

Here's an example of what is meant by a whole new perspective.

Below you will find a list of new retirement questions. Are there easy answers to these questions?

- How long do you plan to live?
- How much money will you spend each month in retirement?

- What does retirement feel like to you? (To your spouse?)
- How much longer can you save money for retirement?
- Are your investments allocated in alignment with your goals?
- Will your children/grandchildren need financial support during your retirement?
- Will you be burdened with helping out your aging parents?
- Will you run out of money in retirement?
- Will you outlive your spouse? Are you prepared to manage finances in your spouse's absence?
- How will your health impact your retirement lifestyle?
- How will you manage health insurance issues, especially if you choose to retire prior to age sixty-five?

Financial planning software can be a great starting tool—but it's not the finish line. Trying to plan for retirement with financial models can be a dangerous endeavor, especially if there isn't a place to factor in your personal job security, your health, your living arrangements, your lifestyle, and more. Finding solutions to uncertain answers isn't easy. Retirement planning involves both facts and feelings. *Your* facts and *your* feelings. No one else's.

Retirees Will Soon Rule the World

Did you know that more than 80 percent of all people who ever lived to the *young* age of sixty-five are still alive today? In fact, every day for the next ten years, ten thousand people will turn sixty-five years old. The business world sees this demographic changing. It's creating products and solutions to fulfill the needs of an aging population. Take a look around you. The number of disabled parking spaces is growing. Adult living communities are sprouting up in every neighborhood in America. The future for the retiring community is brighter than ever. The services, fashion trends, employment opportunities, travel options, and more will be far more diverse and accessible than ever before. If you want to see more about what the future holds for retirees like you, visit AgeLab at MIT (agelab.mit.edu).

Inspiration

Retirement planning software solutions can't do the heavy lifting for you. If you really, truly want to build a retirement plan that's yours and not a copy of someone else's, you'll need to be prepared to weave an imperfect tapestry. That's right—an *imperfect* tapestry.

Living in retirement isn't a single irrevocable decision. It's filled with ongoing decision making, and it rarely produces simple answers. If you're an engineer, mathematician, scientist, or architect, you might (correction, you *will*) struggle at first with planning for your retirement. You see, retirement planning is about living in the gray. It doesn't come with exact answers. Your life in retirement will be faced with hills and valleys, cherished moments and periods of sadness. You'll encounter new surprises, embark on adventures, address health challenges, and even face the loss of a spouse or loved one. Unfortunately, spreadsheets, algorithms, quadratic equations, and research studies won't solve your retirement planning puzzle. In retirement, the financial answer may not always be the best solution. Sometimes you'll have to trust your heart.

There is as much art as there is science when developing a retirement plan. Financial assets and income streams can be plotted on a spreadsheet. You can make assumptions for growth, inflation, income, and taxes. But how do you plan for changes in job status, the cost of helping out a child or parent, changes in your personal health, or perhaps a dramatic shift in economic policy? Often financial planners include a paragraph like the one below in preparing a retirement plan.

"Financial planning is a fluid activity that requires adjustments and monitoring throughout your life. Changes in employment, spending, marital status, lifestyle, family size, inflation, economic conditions, and tax rates are just a few of the issues that will have an impact on the recommendations we make today. Your ability to achieve your goals will more than likely be a moving target; therefore, is it critical to view your financial plan as a living document and a blueprint that requires continual review."

Some people might view the above paragraph as a financial planner's CYA (cover your ass) disclosure statement. In reality, it is a paragraph that reflects both my experience as a financial planner and the realities of watching hundreds of clients live in retirement.

Honestly, it doesn't matter whether you are twenty-five years from retirement or preparing to collect your gold watch at a retirement party tomorrow; your retirement life will need to be flexible. In the chapters that follow, you will be introduced to several concepts on projecting how spreadsheets and software programs can help you better envision your retirement goals. Yet I promise not to stop there. We'll do a reality check. You will be asked questions and be given situations to consider. You're going to need to become comfortable with the fact that mathematical projections used to plan your retirement will serve as *very* broad guidelines only. If someone tells you otherwise, *run*! Life will get in the way. That is an absolute promise!

How Old Is Old?

A couple of years ago, Prudential Financial rolled out an ad that asked a very simple question: "How old is the oldest person you know?" Think about it for a minute. Of all the people you know who are still alive, how old is the oldest? Now ask yourself how long you think you'll live. With significant advances in medical science, we could all live longer than we ever imagined. Just think, Mick Jagger is still performing at seventy years old, The Who is back on tour, and even Betty White made a superstar-esque comeback at the age of ninety!

How Will Willard Scott Keep Up?

The increase in one-hundred-year-olds has exploded. Over the past thirty years, the number of centenarians is up 65.8 percent. In 1980, there were 32,194 people living to age one hundred and beyond. In 2010, that number increased to 53,364. By the time you retire, that could be more than 100,000 people over the age of one hundred.

Source: U.S. News & World Report, *January 7, 2013*

Inspiration

Chances are, you are going to live longer than you ever imagined. People in their eighties and nineties are more active than ever. It's likely to be even better for you.

Living Life on Your Terms: Meet Alice and Herman

Alice and Herman were among the first clients in our firm. My father, Barry Freedman, who started our firm in 1968, met with Herman when he was forty-three and a distributor for a produce company. Alice was a stay-at-home-mom raising two great kids. At the time, Herman was beginning to make some money and knew that saving for his retirement would be important. Barry talked with Herman and Alice about their goals and dreams. They briefly discussed planning for retirement, but at forty-three, this couple was too busy thinking about work, paying for college costs, and buying their next car. Nevertheless, with each review meeting, Barry would revisit conversations that kept them living with one foot in the present and one in the future.

Fast-forward forty years. In 2008, I went to visit Alice and Herman in Florida. They were now enjoying retirement at the ages of eighty-four and eighty-one. I met with them at Abe and Louie's for dinner for an annual review of their financial plan, but in all honesty, our visit was mostly social. Herman pulled up to the valet in his Cadillac. Alice perked out of the car with a zest for life that had become her trademark. At dinner, Herman ordered his "regular," the king-cut prime rib. "Make sure it's on the bone," he said to the waiter. Alice had the shrimp.

While we enjoyed our second glass of cabernet, I asked them to reflect on a question my father had asked almost forty years ago. I said, "When you met Barry [my father] in 1968, you were both in your forties. You came to our firm with hopes of us constructing a financial planning strategy that would allow you to maintain the lifestyle to which you had grown accustomed and also build a longer-term plan so that you could continue it well into retirement. Now think back. Do you remember how old you thought you'd live?"

Herman laughed, "Marc, I think about that question every day. You see, as far as I'm concerned, I'm on borrowed time. I never imagined I'd live beyond seventy. Both of my parents died in their early sixties. I cherish each day. Alice and I have been married for sixty-one years, and I love her more each day." It was a touching moment. But for me, it was another reminder of how important it is to plan for your future. After all, it's tough to estimate your own longevity.

Herman did.

After the waiter brought Alice her baked stuffed shrimp, he placed Herman's prime rib in front of him. It was cooked to perfection. Herman had already tucked the white cloth napkin into his shirt in preparation for his feast. With his left hand, he grabbed the exposed rib bone, and with his right hand, he lifted the heft of meat to his mouth. He salivated and then tore a bite off like Fred Flintstone would have attacked a brontosaurus steak. Herman was living his life on his terms. Who was I to play Emily Post?

Are You Ready to Begin Planning for Your Retirement?

Retirement can be what you want it to be. But without a plan, without foresight, and without confidence, it will be a challenge. In the chapters that follow, you'll be guided through several scenarios, questions, and circumstances. You will be able to choose *your* path, explore *your* options, and make informed decisions that make sense for *you* and *your* family. When you're done, you'll feel smarter. In fact, you might even feel like a genius.

The Truth about the Green Line

Fidelity Investments deserves a lot of credit for developing a fabulous collection of recent advertisements. They used a slogan that read something like this: "All our lives, we were told about the importance of saving money for the future, yet no one ever taught us how to spend our money in retirement."

They nailed it. And their "Stay on the green line" ad is one of the most memorable and effective campaigns in the industry.

But here's the truth: No one ever stays on the line forever. Both before and during retirement, you will have events in your life that will take you off the "green line." You will. And you know it. Ad campaigns are most effective when they touch your heart and create an artificial experience that seems to connect with your real life. That's what creates impulse purchases. When you place that in the context of retirement planning, it can lead to a fragmented collection of investment relationships, bank accounts, tax uncertainties, and more. When people

How Long Will Retirement Last?

It's possible you'll live in retirement longer than you will have worked.

Inspiration

visit a financial planner for the first time, they often have a laundry bag full of stuff, and they simply want the financial planner to help them get their financial house in order.

Working with a Financial Planner or Doing It on Your Own

Let's get something out of the way really early in this book. Retirement planning is *not* rocket science. If you can add, subtract, multiply, and divide, you're more than halfway toward understanding how to structure a retirement plan. You're not recreating the atom. You're not putting someone on Jupiter. You're not turning trees into automobiles. Retirement planning simply requires some dedicated time—and it doesn't have to happen all at once.

The Do-It-Yourselfer

Perhaps you've elected to manage your financial life on your own. You pay your bills online. You use programs like Quicken and TurboTax. You maintain spreadsheets and use a brokerage firm like Schwab, Fidelity, or an online trading outfit. To save more money, you purchased insurance through an online service, drafted your will through a "DocuPrep" type solution, and elected to manage your own 401(k) plan at work.

If you've been able to manage your retirement plan on your own and you're very pleased with everything you've done, perhaps you're a genius already. Congratulations!

But how did you react when the markets tumbled in 2008–2010? Where did you turn for guidance? Did you lose sleep? Were you rational?

You Can Do This

The first key to achieving retirement success is to have confidence in yourself.

Inspiration

Staying Rational in Emotional Times

As long as the financial markets perform well, your job remains stable, and everything goes as planned, you're a hero. But what happens when things take a turn for the worse? What do you do when an economic downturn strikes?

From 2008 through 2010, the uncertainty of the housing market, the credit crisis, the stock market, and a fragile economy weighed heavily on conversations around the kitchen table and among your peers. Perhaps it caused some friction in your marriage because you each wanted to respond differently to the risk in your overall financial plan (or lack thereof).

You soon realized that you not only needed to get serious about your investments or insurance accounts but that you also needed advice that addressed the bigger picture. You needed a rational voice when times became emotional. And today you are searching for something that will help you address everything in your financial life: taxes, expenses, risk, inflation, debts, health care, investments, and so much more. It's time to get serious. Whether you choose to be a do-it-yourselfer or consult the services of a financial professional, you're going to need to do some financial planning.

Why Financial Planning Appears Complex

If the public has trouble defining financial planning, and the professionals who deliver it can't agree on a definition either, how do you know whether you've actually received financial planning advice in the first place?

Uninspired

Getting Retirement Advice from a Financial Planner

Financial planners come in all shapes and sizes. Trying to pick an adviser who fits your needs isn't all that easy. Some are specialists and some are generalists. Some are independent and some are affiliated with large firms. There are those with thousands of clients and some with fewer than a hundred. Finding the adviser that fits your situation takes time.

Feeling Stuck with Your Financial Adviser?

It's possible that you were initially drawn to your financial adviser because:

- she sounded nice on the phone;
- he invited you to a free dinner and his presentation seemed sincere;
- it seemed like everyone in the community worked with that firm; or
- you won a free consultation in his office—he said he'd give you advice for no charge.

Initially, you may have thought that you were going to receive financial planning advice. But is it possible that all you received was an investment idea—or a solicitation for an insurance product? Did you hope that your financial adviser would deliver lifelong advice but soon realized after you made an investment purchase that the "financial planning" part of the relationship would be very short lived—or perhaps it was just a sales gimmick to get you in the door?

Perhaps you've grown frustrated but assumed that moving your accounts would produce a similar relationship elsewhere. Have you left that money with the existing adviser but chosen to meet with another adviser when you had new money or a new financial issue to discuss? Is it possible that you've now accumulated a lot of accounts, a lot of relationship with advisers, and a whole lot of confusion?

Finding a Financial Planner Isn't Like Buying a Snickers Bar

Hiring a financial planner should never be an impulse purchase.

You should interview at least three professionals. Arrive prepared. Come equipped with questions. Notice whether they spend more time listening to you than talking about themselves and their firms. Most importantly, don't make any decisions or sign any documents in the first meeting. This is a big life decision—and not an impulse purchase. Want to find Certified Financial Planner professionals in your area to interview? Visit letsmakeaplan.org.

Perspiration

Hopefully the above scenario doesn't describe you. But if it does, don't worry. You're not alone, and you are certainly not an idiot or a dummy.

There is a select group of financial planners all around the country who deliver outstanding financial planning advice. If you've got one, stick with your adviser. You're very lucky.

What Is Financial Planning?

If you ask the next one hundred people you meet to describe "financial planning," how many of those definitions will be the same? The answer, more than likely, is none.

Don't feel bad. When financial planners are asked this same question, their answers are just as varied.

Financial Planning

Financial planning is the long-term process of wisely managing your finances so you can achieve your goals and dreams while at the same time negotiating the financial barriers that inevitably arise in every stage of life. Remember, financial planning is a process, not a product. See Financial Planning Association, fpanet.org.

Definition

Let's be clear. Financial planning isn't about establishing an investment account. It isn't about trading a few stocks. And it most certainly isn't about buying a life insurance policy. Financial planning starts with a serious conversation about your future, your goals, and your dreams.

In the next chapter, you will be introduced to a formula that helps people just like you make financial planning seem more tangible. It's the first step in giving you the keys to your retirement kingdom. The goal of a successful retirement plan is to incorporate all the elements of personal finance into a blueprint that's embossed with your DNA. The time is now, so let's go for it. Your retirement plan is closer than you think. Are you ready to be the genius of your own retirement plan?

To Summarize...

- Planning for your retirement is more than achieving "a number."
- Planning for your retirement will require flexibility. If your plan is strictly attached to spreadsheets, you could be in trouble.
- You're likely to live a lot longer than you ever imagined. You need your money to last longer than you.
- It's important to act rationally during emotional times. A financial plan will help you keep your eye on the horizon—and away from the choppiness of the ocean.

Chapter 2

Crafting a Successful Retirement Plan

In This Chapter...

- What is the financial planning formula?
- Critical conversations when planning for retirement
- Protecting your retirement
- Calculating your wealth

Building a retirement plan that relies on the hopeful performance of your investment accounts is a strategy fit for dummies. As a genius, you know better.

To build a sensible retirement plan, you need to assess your financial situation through a much larger lens and think hard about how financial decisions will impact your life.

When thinking about your retirement, getting comfortable with how financial planning fits into your life will be a major key to your success.

Is It Possible to Define Financial Planning?

> **Taking Care of Number One**
>
> *You are in charge of your happiness. Plan your dreams. No one else will do it for you.*
>
> Haitham Elsaadany
>
> Quote

Have you ever met a "quant"? These are people who salivate over the opportunity of taking another calculus class in college. They are the teacher's pets in probability and statistics sessions, and they generally believe that a mathematical formula is the single best way to find answers to a problem. Anyone who knows me would agree that I am far from a "quant guy."

Rather than focus exclusively on mathematical principles, I've layered the elements of the human condition along with the realities of personal finance. Someday, just maybe, it will be viewed as the benchmark for "financial planning done right." I'll leave it to the geniuses who read this book to help me come to a conclusion.

Examining the Financial Planning Formula

In order to successfully achieve financial planning, you need to focus on the trifecta of personal financial principles:

- Discovery. Conversations about your goals, challenges, successes, and opportunities.
- Capital protection. Protection for your life, your family, your wealth and your legacy.
- Wealth management. Understanding your net worth and cash flow.

Discovery

Financial planning should always start with a conversation around goals. It doesn't matter whether you're married, a same-sex couple, divorced, a polygamist, or happy being single all your life. Understanding the relationship that you and your loved ones have with your money is a critical conversation. No, I'm not talking about dating your money, but let's be realistic. Without connecting your money with your life, you'd be heartbroken. Financial planning starts with examining, discussing, and pursuing your goals. As the saying goes, "If you don't know where you want to go, how will you know when you get there?" Think about it. Is it really possible to make investment decisions without fully understanding how they could affect your overall financial life? Sometimes yes. But when it comes to preparing for your retirement, the answer is likely no.

Discovery questions always address at least these basic issues:

- Long- and short-term goals
- Personal and financial successes in life
- Challenges you have faced and those you may expect to encounter in the future

The Six-Step Process for Building a Financial Plan

The list below defines *the steps a financial planner must follow* to prepare a financial plan (as defined by the Certified Financial Board of Standards):

1. Identify goals and objectives.
2. Collect data.
3. Analyze data.
4. Present recommendations.
5. Implement strategies.
6. Review the plan.

Definition

If you're a couple, it's more than pillow talk. It's about truly sharing feelings, hopes, and dreams. Beginning to develop a framework around what you hope to accomplish in retirement can never start too soon. In fact, after more than two decades in this business, the number-one comment I hear from our clients is "I only wish I had started planning for my retirement sooner."

If you're uncomfortable engaging one another in a "discovery" conversation, it may be worth a visit to a Certified Financial Planner professional. You can find a financial planner in your community by visiting CFP Board's website at letsmakeaplan.org. These professionals are among the best equipped to provide you with authentic financial planning advice. They are skilled in asking open-ended, exploratory,

The Gold Standard in Financial Planning Advice

Certified Financial Planner professionals are among the nation's best-trained financial planners in the country. Not only do they have a fiduciary responsibility to place your interests first when doing financial planning, but they also must abide by a strict code of ethics and practice standards.

Inspiration

and sometimes provocative questions that ultimately lead to uncovering your true financial goals and dreams.

Dig Deep: Do the SCOG

Here's an exercise you might try to do at home. It's an adaptation from an MBA technique taught in business schools worldwide. It's designed to help businesses illustrate a current snapshot of strengths, weaknesses, opportunities, and threats (SWOT). However, in this example, let's use **S**uccesses, **C**hallenges, **O**pportunities, and **G**oals (SCOG).

I want you to think about your current financial situation as it stands right now. Try not to think about what you hope it could be—or what it was like in the past. Think about today. Right now.

Write down answers to the following questions and plot your answers in the appropriate box below. It's an even better exercise if you and your partner (if applicable) do this exercise separately.

Here are the question(s):

- When thinking about your current financial situation, what are your **S**uccesses?

  Some examples might be:

  - Raised a good family
  - Paid for and sent all my kids to college
  - Married for thirty-one years
  - Reached partner status in my firm

When thinking about your current financial situation, what are your **C**hallenges?

Some examples might be:

- Not sure if I have enough money saved for retirement
- Feeling compelled to continue supporting adult children
- Can't make heads or tails of all my investment accounts
- Worried about the health of my parents

When thinking about your current financial situation, what are your **O**pportunities?

Some examples might be:

- I know I can save more money for the future
- Just four more years until the mortgage is gone
- I'm on track for a big promotion
- I know I could sell my business for a big profit

When thinking about your current financial situation, what are your **G**oals?

Some examples might be:

- Purchase a second property in Florida
- Retire on an income level no less than what I bring home today
- Ensure my kids get the best education possible
- Take a two-month vacation to Europe

Here's a template of a SCOG chart. Go ahead. Try filling it out with your information.

Successes	Challenges

Opportunities	Goals

The completion of a SCOG is a notch in your belt. You have just addressed a critical step in your retirement plan. Congratulations! Feeling like a genius yet?

Capital Protection

One of the most overlooked and misunderstood areas within the financial planning formula is capital protection. It's oftentimes referred to as risk management or, more likely, "insurance."

Insurance isn't a bad word. You and I both know that insurance protection is a necessary evil. Yet it's one of those products that comes with all too many unknowns. It's kind of like buying a car. You always wonder whether you could have found a better deal, whether all the extra features are worth the extra costs, and whether the promises of the warranty will really come true if you need them. Nevertheless, your need for life insurance, disability insurance, auto insurance, homeowners insurance, long-term-care insurance, etc., needs to be part of your financial planning conversation. To me, this is the rubber cement that connects your goals and dreams to all your hard work and investments. This is an important component to that comforting term "peace of mind." You can sleep well knowing that if you die, if you became disabled, if your house burns down, or if you lose your job, resources would spring into action to support your family.

Here's a fact. Too many people are underinsured. That's because in America, we've been taught to build wealth first and *then* protect it.

Dating All Over Again

In retirement, you're likely to spend more time with your spouse than you have in years. When you were working, you might have seen each other for a few moments in the morning, enjoyed each other's company periodically at dinner, and perhaps spent some weekends together. But on your first day of retirement, you're not going back to the office. Instead, you'll spend the whole day with your spouse. You'll do this again on Tuesday, Wednesday, and so on—for perhaps the next thirty years. What will you do to keep the spark alive?

Inspiration

Lessons from the Dutch

I do a lot of speaking around the world, and one of my favorite places is Holland. On several occasions, I've had the good fortune of being a keynote speaker at Holland's largest gathering of financial advisers.

I was presenting to them in February of 2009. It was a time when the economic crisis in America was at a low point. The Dow Jones Industrial Average was preparing to dip below seven thousand, and the unemployment rate was approaching double digits (but nowhere near as high as the 25 percent during the depression). It was a depressing time and one of the most difficult in my career. Surprisingly, though, the angst and worry didn't appear on the faces of people I met at the Amsterdam meeting.

"How could that be?" I wondered.

After all, the European markets were stumbling, and banks worldwide were being called into question for their lending practices, just as they were in the United States. So where was the depression? Why was the conference center buzzing with activity? Here's what I learned:

According to the Dutch, Americans work hard, reward themselves, and spend more money than they should. In fact, it is their belief that Americans focus on wealth accumulation first and then, when there's finally enough money left over, look to buy insurance to protect what they've gathered. This approach, in their opinion, is very risky. If early on in life you leave yourself exposed without insurance, your family's financial lifestyle could change dramatically in the event of death or disability. That's not the case in Holland.

The Dutch have a different approach. Protecting their families, themselves, their legacies, and their property is of primary importance. The Dutch will elect to buy insurance prior to amassing wealth. When they invest, they choose highly conservative banking instruments like certificates of deposit (CDs) and fixed annuities. They build the cost of life, disability, homeowners, and automobile insurance into their budgets before ever allocating money for savings. As they become more successful, they begin investing. They understand that stock-and-bond investing comes with risks, and they are willing to invest only with money they can afford to lose.

Imagine for a minute if you approached your life through the lens of a Dutch person? Would it work here in America?

Perhaps. Perhaps not.

We need to provide for our own financial well-being. Social medicine, low-cost college education, and pensions are a big part of the Dutch system—though it is changing. We can learn so much from other countries and the way personal finance is managed in households there.

Protecting Your Life, Your Family, Your Wealth, and Your Legacy

By understanding how insurance planning and risk management integrate into your financial plan, you can begin to achieve some peace of mind. It is not the most exciting stuff to talk about, but having the right insurance in place allows you to focus on the stuff that you can control. No one wants to discuss how one might prepare for a death, a family tragedy, or long-term disability.

Let's examine some of the risks that you might want to protect as you plan for your retirement:

- Life risks. Premature death, long-term disability, or even having to care for a family member could have drastic implications on your ability to achieve your life goals. Protecting your life so that the people you love can continue living their lives without financial burden is your responsibility. In **Chapter 11**, we'll discuss some of the different types of insurance options that may be worth considering.

- Family risks. Divorce, second marriages, children with special needs, and unpredictable in-laws can all prevent your dreams from being achieved and can also affect how your money will be used well after you've died. Are you prepared to create provisions that would protect your family, and/or perhaps your wealth, from spendthrifts and those who may not have the ability to manage money on their own?

- Wealth risks. Changes in inflation, personal spending, employment, market conditions, tax law, and more will impact your ability to achieve your financial goals. What risk-minimization techniques are you employing to smooth out the choppiness when detours in your planning occur? In **Chapter 8**, we'll focus on various investment strategies that are part of many retirement plans.

- Legacy risks. Unless you plan to spend your last dollar on the day you die, it is imperative that you prepare for the transfer of your wealth, your personal property, and—if you have young children—your offspring. Visiting with an estate planning attorney is a crucial component of a sound financial plan. In **Chapter 21**, we'll discuss what you need and what you don't need to purchase from an estate attorney.

As always, it is critical that you continually review and revisit your ability to protect your family, your health, your wealth, and your legacy.

Wealth Management—Is It Just about Picking Good Investments?

The final component of the financial planning formula is the one that seems to get all the attention, yet it's very misunderstood. Wealth management is the combination of multiple components that impact your financial well-being. In a sense, it's the analysis of all the financial moving parts in your life. It's the continual monitoring of your income, your expenses, your assets, and your liabilities so that you can be prepared during changes in the economic environment.

Net Worth

The most critical component of wealth management focuses on your collective net worth. It's determined by adding up *everything* you own and subtracting out *everything* you owe.

Items that you own are often referred to as assets. These include items like property, automobiles, bank accounts, investments, retirement plans, businesses, etc. When you owe money, it is referred to as a liability or debt. These include mortgages, student loans, credit card debt, auto loans, etc. Yes, your mortgage is still a debt. I can't tell you how many people visit my office and tell me that they are debt-free, but I later learn that they have nine years remaining on their mortgages. In **Chapter 3**, I'll share an illustration of a net worth statement so that you can build one for yourself.

We Are But Mere Mortals

Death, disability, medical costs, and long-term health care are delicate subjects. Usually someone in the room is always willing to change the subject when the topic comes up. If you want a financial plan that works, you owe it to yourself and your family to address these issues with honesty and seriousness. After all, can your financial planning goals be achieved without implementing capital protection strategies?

Observation

Net Cash Flow

You've probably heard the term cash flow, but perhaps not *net* cash flow. Every dollar that enters your household—through employment income, a gift from a relative, a dividend from an investment, or rental income from a property—is all considered income to you. Yes, some of these income streams are taxed differently than others, but let's not worry about that for now. Generally, it's pretty easy to gather all the sources of income you receive in a given year. It's a lot tougher to calculate the collective expenses that offset your income. Expense items can include all taxes, debt payments, household expenses, vacations—and so, so, so much more. Your *net* cash flow represents any money that remains in your household for savings or investing during a given year. As such, any excess money that is used for savings or investment should be added to your net worth each year.

A Tale of Two Clients

The Brimstones

A few years ago, we met two couples who had been referred to our office by a mortgage broker. Neither couple had ever worked with a financial adviser before but felt that now was the time to begin getting their financial houses in order. The first couple, the Brimstones, arrived on a Wednesday afternoon around two o'clock. Dr. Brimstone was a well-regarded surgeon throughout the New England area and had built a successful practice over the past twenty years. His wife was a popular socialite and enjoyed spending her time at the country club.

At fifty-eight and fifty-six, they both wore the finest clothes, drove the nicest cars, and lived in a well-appointed home in an upscale suburban community. For the past several years, Dr. Brimstone had earned around $650,000 a year. Their two children were grown and out of the house with successful jobs of their own. At the suggestion of their accountant, the Brimstones visited our office to ensure that they were on track to meet their retirement goals. They had hopes of living a similar lifestyle in retirement and just wanted to know what year Dr. Brimstone could stop working. After all, they thought, with an impressive income of $650K, retirement should be easy.

After reviewing their tax returns, analyzing their investments, and reviewing how they spent their money, we were able to give them a very quick answer. Retirement would be impossible if they continued spending money at the same pace they were today. You see, even though the Brimstones had an envious income, they had a net worth of $450,000. And most of that money was because of an inheritance they had received a few years before. We learned that their $1.2 million home had a mortgage of $950,000. They also carried credit card debt in excess of $80,000. They leased both of their cars, and they were still paying off student loans for their children.

Essentially, they spent much more than they made. While they talked about drinking fine wines, eating at gourmet restaurants, and traveling to exotic destinations, the Brimstones had not stopped to think that the value of their net worth would be far more important to their retirement planning success than their income each year.

Your Real Net Worth

I'm not sure which marketing guy came up with the term "investable net worth." This phrase seems to have replaced the term "net worth" that is taught in business schools around the country. Your net worth is the total of everything you own (your home, vehicles, investments, cash value of life insurance, personal property, etc.) minus everything you owe (mortgages, credit card debt, auto loans, and more). However, the financial services community has created this term "investable net worth." It describes assets that can be potentially managed by them, such as cash, stocks, mutual funds, IRAs, annuities, old retirement plans, and more. It generally doesn't include your home, your personal property, and other illiquid assets. Simply stated, if it can't be managed by them, they have little interest in learning about it. It's a shame. You deserve better!

Uninspired

The O'Haras

The O'Haras (aged fifty-five and fifty-four) came to visit us on Friday of that same week with a much different story. Mr. O'Hara was an engineer at a local factory in town. He had been there for more than twenty years and earned a salary of $85,000. His wife worked twenty hours a week as a bank teller making $15,000 a year. They had three children—one who joined the Army, one who was a junior at a state college, and another who was a senior in high school. The five of them lived in an 1,800-square-foot home in a north-of-Boston suburban community that they bought when they got married. Each year, they planned family vacations to the mountains in New Hampshire or to Cape Cod. They lived a modest lifestyle. They owned their cars for ten years at a time and had only three years remaining on their mortgage. They each contributed the maximum allowed into their company 401(k) plans—and even made Roth IRA contributions as well. They put money aside each week from their paychecks to build a college fund for their kids. They told their children that they would pay 50 percent of the cost of a state education. The rest was up to them.

The O'Haras were hoping to retire at sixty-five. They thought they'd need about $5,000 a month ($60,000 a year) in after-tax income to support their life in retirement. Their biggest fear was that they hadn't done a good enough job preparing for their own retirement. In our first meeting, we learned that at age sixty-seven, they would likely collect about $2,500 collectively from

Social Security. Assuming Mr. O'Hara stayed with his employer until sixty-seven years old, he'd be entitled to a pension of $2,000 a month. They'd also accumulated $420,000 in their collective investment accounts. Their retirement certainly appeared a lot more promising.

Let's review. The O'Haras earned $100,000 a year, and the Brimstones earned $650,000 a year. Do their salaries have any relevance on their ability to achieve their retirement lifestyles? Do their respective occupations suggest that one will be guaranteed a better retirement than the other? Definitely not!

Pure Genius!

What's a Lot of Money?

If someone were to ask you how much money you make, chances are you wouldn't tell them. That's private information, right? The amount of money we earn has become a taboo subject for dinner conversations, among our family (especially our children), and in most social settings. It's impolite to brag about how much money you make, but you'd probably love to learn what everyone else is making.

If you earn $75,000 at your job, is that a lot of money? Only you hold the answer to that question. There are some people who would give their right arm for that salary and others who would lift their noses and turn the other way. Whether you earn $75,000, $150,000, or $750,000, the answer to the question "What is a lot of money?" is clearly in the eye of the beholder. Yet, interestingly enough, studies say that if you were to have the opportunity of doubling your salary, that's when you think you'd be making a lot of money. Here's the truth, though: The amount of money you make is irrelevant to your retirement plan. What matters is how much you keep.

Measure your financial wealth by determining the value of your total net worth, not the amount of money you make each year. If your employment earnings aren't enough to create a positive cash flow each year, then you don't make a lot of money. It's that simple.

What Is "Real Growth," and How Does It Fit into the Financial Planning Formula?

Like every good formula, adjustments are needed to keep the results honest. Imagine if you had a total net worth of $500,000. Would you think that was impressive? After all, you'd be worth one half of a million dollars. But what if you had a $500,000 net worth in 1960? Would you think of that number

WATCH OUT!

Beware of Investment Projections

If you elect to use investment planning software as a tool to project the future growth of your investment accounts, beware of the default projections that are built in to the software.

If your primary assets are in cash, it's fair to assume that your growth rate will be close to zero. Yet many software programs rely on long-term historical data when providing projection rates (thus, potentially *over*estimating the potential value of your accounts).

Err on the side of conservatism.

Below is an example of projected growth rates on a very popular financial planning software program. I'll leave it to you to decide whether you'd feel comfortable using these rates when projecting your money.

Asset Class	Current Growth Rate	Asset Class	Current Growth Rate
Large US growth stocks	7.58%	Long-term municipal bonds	5.86%
Large US value stocks	9.13	Short/intermediate, high-quality bond	4.20
Mid-cap value stocks	11.67	Cash	3.64
Small-cap growth stocks	7.09	REITs (real estate investment trusts)	9.30
US balanced funds	9.54	Alternative Investments	1.06
Large foreign funds	4.11		

differently? Of course, you would. According to my parents, you could go to the movies back then for a quarter, get a steak dinner for $5, and purchase a house for $10,000. The cost of goods has increased over the decades. It's important that your plan has triggers to keep your numbers honest and realistic.

When building financial plans, it's typical for a planner to incorporate a 2.5 percent inflation factor. No, inflation hasn't been nearly this high for several years, but I think we can all agree that the likelihood of inflation remaining low is as possible as Britney Spears returning to the Mickey Mouse Club.

In addition, depending upon the overall allocation of your investments, you might consider using a 6 percent growth rate on assets. Some might say this is high; some would argue it's too low. But when you combine a 6 percent growth rate with a 2.5 percent cost-of-living adjustment, you net a real return of 3.5 percent. Too low? I don't think so, but then again, I'd prefer to see people overachieve their financial planning projections than come up way too short.

How Can Inflation Impact a Retirement Plan?

Unlike your working years, retirement doesn't typically provide you a bonus, incentive compensation, or cost-of-living adjustments. Yes, Social Security does factor in a cost-of-living increase, but it's typically pretty minimal. And I can't imagine that you believe Social Security income alone will adequately support your retirement needs. The reality is that the price of goods and services will increase each and every year you live in retirement.

Take a minute and think back to what a postage stamp cost in 1980. How much was a gallon of gas or the price of a house? You've got a great chance of being alive twenty-five years from now. What do you think the cost of goods will be then? If you haven't doubled the number in your head, you're more than likely underestimating.

	Cost in 1980	Cost in 2014	Cost in 2039
Postage stamp	$ 0.15	$ 0.49	?
Gas	1.03	3.91	?
Milk	1.60	3.67	?
House	86,159.00	281,000.00	?

Are your financial resources positioned so that your retirement lifestyle can keep up with the pace of inflation? If not, the value of your assets could erode without you even recognizing it.

Why Aren't Taxes Factored into the Formula for Financial Planning?

Taxes are an incredibly important component in every retirement plan. Yet they are just another expense line on your cash flow statement. The term *taxes* gets a lot of attention in the press, on your pay stub, and on many purchases you make each day. What's uncertain about taxes, though, is what they will be both as you approach retirement and during your retirement. Later in the book, I'll tackle how the impact of taxes is a significant (and highly misunderstood) element with your retirement plan, but for now, let's agree that taxes are just another item that's part of your overall cash flow.

Wrapping It Up

All right. In this chapter, you were introduced you to a formula for financial planning. It included the trifecta of financial planning principles: discovery, capital protection, and wealth management. Each of these principles had some subcontext so that you could capture a better flavor for each item. Collectively, these elements deliver the formula for financial planning.

To Summarize...

- A proper financial plan must include an examination of discovery, capital protection, and wealth management.
- Attempting to build a financial plan with just investments in mind discredits a real financial plan.
- What you earn for a living is far less important than what you keep.
- You need to have a deeper, more realistic conversation with those you love so that your retirement plan can be achieved.

Chapter 3

Getting Your Financial House in Order

In This Chapter...

- How to build a net worth statement
- What are you worth—right now?
- Why hiding information is dangerous

Getting your hands dirty and really examining every piece of your financial life is crucial. If you don't know where everything is and what it's all worth, how can you start planning for your financial future? In this chapter, you will build a snapshot of your financial life.

When's the last time you cleaned out your garage or your bedroom closet? If you're like me, you've probably thought about cleaning it for a really long time, but something always comes up. Perhaps you've made cursory attempts, but the genius in you knows that you'd never be completely satisfied until you pulled everything out, sorted through it all, and then put the rest of it all neatly back in order.

Over the years, I've met with thousands of individuals and families. Each person has shared a unique answer to the question "What does financial planning mean to you?" Topping the list would be "Getting my financial house in order." But preparing to get your financial house in order requires courage, thought, and action. You can't be a victim of your own *Fear Factor*.

> **What's Your Net Worth?**
>
> *Your net worth to the world is usually determined by what remains after your bad habits are subtracted from your good ones.*
>
> Benjamin Franklin
>
> Quote

Are you ready to get to work?

Gathering the Goods

In **Appendix A**, you'll find the comprehensive questionnaire that I provide to all new clients.

If you want to be the genius of your own retirement plan, you'll need to *work with purpose* to gather all the items. Pace yourself. It *will* take some time. But after following the instructions in this chapter, you're going to feel so much more confident about where you stand financially.

Building Your Personal Net Worth Statement—The Right Way

If you're like most people, you've got statements, online accounts, stock certificates, and savings bonds scattered all around your house. Some are in file folders, others are stashed in an underwear drawer, in a safe, or stored on your computer. Some records are old, and there are likely some you don't even remember. Don't forget the accounts that you maintain exclusively online with firms like E*Trade, Capital One 360, etc. You'll need to account for these too.

Getting your financial house in order starts with *you*! Gathering everything in an organized manner so that you (or a financial planner) can help make sense of all these accounts is your critical first step for success.

A Simple Approach for Organizing Your Financial Life

Here's an easy idea that will help make the first step in organizing your financial life simple. Find two accordion folders (preferably different colors) and a black permanent marker.

On one of the folders, write "Stuff I/We Own" in big, bold letters. On the other folder, write "Stuff I/We Owe."

These folders will hold "on paper" your financial life over the next few months.

As bank, investment, and retirement reports arrive over the next ninety days, place them into the folder marked "Stuff I/We Own."

Likewise, when you receive bills/statements for items that you've purchased but are in the process of paying off, i.e., mortgage, student loans, auto debt, credit cards, etc., place these statements in the file marked "Stuff I/We Owe."

Important: Be sure you pay your bills before placing the statements in the folder!

At the end of the quarter, you will have many of the items needed to build a quick net worth statement. All the stuff you *own* is your "assets," and all the stuff you *owe* is your "liabilities." Your net worth is equal to the difference between your assets and your liabilities.

Pure Genius!

Data Gathering—Better Known as "Organizing Chaos"

You're about to get a crash course on data gathering. It's a logical approach for building your financial snapshot and how I train paraplanners and other financial professionals.

Let's start by creating a file folder for each category listed below. As you review a statement, insert it in the appropriate file. After all, when you leave your statements lying all over the house, it's exposed for family, friends, and CUTCO knife salespeople to review.

Here are the categories:

- Bank statements
- Retirement account statements
- Nonretirement account statements
- Personal property documentation
- Other property/businesses owned
- Life insurance
- Mortgage and other debt

Gather All Your Bank Statements

Whether you do your banking at one institution or at a variety of banks, it is important to account for every dollar. Your monthly statement will list amounts for your checking account(s), money markets, and certificates of deposit (CDs). If you have a passbook savings account, update the balance by bringing the booklet to the teller at the window.

Do you maintain banking relationships online? Make sure to print out a current statement for each of those too. (Just don't tell the environmentalists.)

Now, with a yellow highlighter, circle the current balance in each account.

Don't include bank retirement accounts—such as IRA CDs, IRA money markets, or other retirement investments purchased at the bank—in this folder. These are best placed in the retirement accounts folder.

What about FDIC Insurance?

The Federal Deposit Insurance Company (FDIC) protects all types of bank accounts (such as checking, savings, and CDs) at insured banks. As of 2014, you can maintain up to $250,000 in accounts of similar registration and have coverage (it used to be $100,000). Remember, FDIC does not insure the following:

- Safe deposit boxes
- Investments purchased through bank investment representatives
- US Treasury securities
- EE savings bonds

What's With All the Bank Accounts?

Do you have multiple bank accounts at a variety of financial institutions? Why?

Chasing high-interest certificates of deposit, receiving a toaster oven for maintaining a minimum balance, or simply keeping an account at a local bank because you've always had one there are no longer legitimate reasons for having multiple bank relationships.

For most, maintaining one checking account, a savings/money market account, and perhaps a CD or two at *one bank* makes the most sense.

Perspiration

Retirement Account Statements

Retirement statements come in all shapes and sizes. They may be CDs and money market accounts at a bank, but it's even more likely that they include traditional IRAs, Roth IRAs, 401(k)s, and other retirement accounts held with brokerage firms and/or mutual funds companies. Don't be surprised if you've got a few retirement plan statements still sitting with previous employers. The average sixty-year-old couple has between five and ten different types of retirement accounts scattered all over the place.

Organizing these accounts may seem daunting. It's not. But remember, you're the best person to know where all the accounts reside. Just think. Who would find this money if you weren't around to let your family know? Each time you move or your former employer changes 401(k) providers, you run the risk of moving farther and farther away from *your* money. It's no wonder states have billions of dollars in unclaimed property accounts. Don't let that be you.

Gather as much current information as you can, and don't dismiss something because it's too hard to find. With access to the Internet and the cost of a phone call running only pennies by the minute, you can work at digging deep to uncover accounts that you may have forgotten about.

When you've got all the statements together, circle all the values and place them in the retirement accounts folder.

All Investment Account Statements

Just like retirement accounts, your investment accounts may be dispersed all over the place. You may have brokerage accounts, mutual fund statements, annuities, etc. If you own individual stocks and the certificates are in the safe deposit box, go get them. That's the worst place to keep them. I'll explain why later on. If you do own certificates, make a copy of each one and then return the originals to the safe deposit box (for now). In addition, if you have dividend reinvestment plans held with a "transfer agent," such as Computershare or BNY Mellon, you'll want to account for those shares as well. And don't forget to print out statements from your online accounts. Once you've got it all—well, you know what to do next.

Personal Property

If you own a home or piece of real estate, you can obtain a reasonable estimate by looking at the "appraised value" on your property tax bill or by visiting zillow.com. The Zillow "Zestimate" offers an independent estimate of your home's value by comparing it with others in your neighborhood. I rarely find someone who agrees with the zillow.com estimate, but remember, your house is worth only what someone's willing to pay for it.

Other personal assets include the appraised value of your jewelry, any of the valuable contents in your home, the Kelley Blue Book value for your automobile, the resale value of other real estate investments, and other collectibles. These values are generally subjective, yet they do belong on your net worth statement. Don't worry if you can't nail down a value on everything in this category.

Other Property or Businesses Owned

If you don't own a business or rental property, you can skip right past this section.

If you were to sell your business today, how much could you get for it? Perhaps you have inventory, goodwill, a strong customer base, etc. If you think your business holds value *and* you anticipate the proceeds from your business creating an income stream (or a lump-sum amount of money) in the future, hire someone to appraise your business. It's the only way you'll get an objective value. When you get a value, record it as part of your net worth. This number is likely subject to negotiation.

Cash Flow

Income (salary, pension, rental income, dividends, interest, etc.) is *not* part of your net worth. It is part of your cash flow. I'll address this in **Chapter 4**.

IMPORTANT!

Investment Property

If you own an income property, a vacation home, or family cottage, you'll want to calculate a value for your share of ownership. For instance, if you have a family cottage valued at $300,000 owned evenly between you and your two siblings, your share would be $100,000. Record that amount for your net worth statement.

Life Insurance

The death benefit of a life insurance policy should not be listed on a net worth statement. Why? You're not dead! If you were, your net worth wouldn't belong to you any longer. It would be owned by your estate, or some other person or entity. However, the cash value in a life insurance policy should be counted on your net worth statement. That's because you can generally borrow against it, or even take it out for keeps. Identify the cash value, if any.

Mortgages and Other Debts

You are not "debt-free" if you still carry a mortgage. While there is good debt and bad debt, *it's all stuff you owe*, so it's still debt.

For this folder, gather the following:

- Your most recent mortgage statement
- Equity lines/loan statements
- Current credit card statements
- Student loans and auto loans
- Promissory notes owed to friends and family

If you're going to be true to yourself, it's imperative that you declare *everything* you owe and *everything* you own.

It's emperor's-new-clothes time. Hide nothing.

Turning Chaos into Organization

The next step is to prepare your data into an organized manner. I've provided an example questionnaire in **Appendix A,** "The Fact Finder." Using the

Sample Net Worth Statement
Name: Ilana and Noah Fredrickson
As of : ____________

Assets	Noah	Ilana	Joint	Total
Bank Account(s)				
Crown Bank checking	$	$	$ 16,000	$ 16,000
Crown Bank CD (due 10/18/15)	22,000			22,000
National Bank savings		28,000		28,000
Babson Credit Union	71,000			71,000
Subtotal	93,000	28,000	16,000	137,000
Nonretirement Account(s)				
LPL Financial			360,000	360,000
Charles Schwab			87,000	87,000
US EE bonds		10,000		10,000
Subtotal		10,000	447,000	457,000
Insurance Assets				
MetLife (cash value)	6,200			6,200
Subtotal	6,200			6,200
Business Assets				
Jerrycadabra Enterprises	80,000			80,000
Subtotal	80,000			80,000
Retirement Assets				
Majestix 401(k) plan	481,000			481,000
City of Peabody 403(b)		46,000		46,000
Pineapple Bank and Trust Roth IRA		57,500		57,500
Topix 401(k) (previous employer)	62,000			62,000
Bank of Kansas IRA CD (due 1/6/17)		37,000		37,000
Subtotal	543,000	140,500		683,500
Personal Assets				
54 Corey Circle (home)			400,000	400,000
2104 Acura MDX		36,000		36,000
2010 Honda Accord	18,000			18,000
Jewelry and personal property			45,000	45,000
Subtotal	18,000	36,000	445,000	499,000
Total Assets	$ 740,200	$ 214,500	$ 863,000	$1,862,700

Liabilities (the Stuff You Owe)	Noah	Ilana	Joint	Total
Mortgage—54 Corey Circle	$	$	$ 160,000	$ 160,000
Home equity—Crown Bank			35,000	35,000
Auto loan—Acura			25,000	25,000
Credit cards	2,000			2,000
Total Liabilities	$ 2,000	$	$ 220,000	$ 222,000
Net Worth				$1,640,700

Add additional rows or columns as needed.

information you've gathered and what you already know, begin to fill in the sections that apply to your personal situation.

Remember, the goal here is to help you visualize a snapshot of your financial life as it stands right now.

The Final Step

There is just one more step before the net worth statement is complete. When you're done, you will, without a doubt, feel like a genius.

From the fact finder in **Appendix A**, transfer the numbers onto the one-page net worth template (**Appendix B**, "Net Worth Statement"). A sample net worth statement is printed on the facing page.

Be sure that you categorize each asset and liability in the proper ownership column. In doing so, you'll be able to see not only what you're worth but also who owns what. As you begin planning for your retirement, it will be important to understand who owns what, which account should be touched to produce income, and what, if any, estate implications could be caused by owning your assets the way that you do.

Time to Celebrate Your Genius-*ness*!

If you've followed the steps, you should feel a huge sense of accomplishment. Was your net worth greater or smaller than you imagined? Did anything jump out that surprised you? Was your net worth over a million dollars? Do you feel like a millionaire? No? Don't worry. Most people don't feel that way either.

However, I trust that you're pretty darned proud of yourself. Feeling like a genius yet? There still is a lot of work to do, but some of the hard, hard stuff is behind you.

The next step is learning about how you use money each month/year. It's called cash flow. As Professor Richard Bruno, my accounting professor at Babson College, used to say, "Happiness *is* positive cash flow." In **Chapter 4**, we're going to get dirty one more time and uncover where all the money's going. Are you ready? You're more than halfway through the tough stuff. Let's keep going.

To Summarize…

- A net worth statement is equal to everything you own less everything you owe.
- By building a net worth statement, you can learn where everything is and what it's worth.
- Knowing who owns each asset and liability is a critical component of a net worth statement.
- Prior to making any investment decisions, you need to have a solid sense of your net worth.

Chapter 4

Where Does All the Money Go?

In This Chapter...

- Determine how much money you spend
- Happiness is... positive cash flow
- How you own stuff matters
- Preparing your assets for emergencies

Most people entering retirement don't have the slightest understanding of where their money goes each month. For many, it's an uneducated guess. It's among the primary reasons individuals procrastinate on planning for (or even enjoying) their retirement. Let's change that.

The secret to understanding spending habits isn't hard. Nor is knowing what you'll need to spend in retirement. In this chapter, you will learn a few easy tricks so that you understand what it takes to run your lifestyle now—and what those costs might look like in the future.

Building Your Cash Flow Statement

The second most important financial statement that every retiree should maintain is the cash flow statement. This document provides, in broad strokes, how money flows through your household.

Cash Flow

The formula for determining how money flows in and out of your household is as follows:

Cash Flow = Income - Expenses

Income

- Employment income and bonuses
- Non-reinvested interest and dividends
- Rental income
- Other income (capital gains, inheritances, pension, Social Security, etc.)

Expenses

- Fixed expenses. Items that are typically the same each month. These are financial commitments you've made and are relatively inflexible to change. If you did need to change these expenses, it would require significant time and energy on your part. Examples are mortgage, rent, utilities, clothing, groceries, medical copayments, prescriptions, and auto payments.
- Discretionary expenses. These expenses are ones that you've selected as part of your personal lifestyle. They can be modified rather easily—but not necessarily without pain, as they often represent "quality of life" items. Examples are dining out, travel, pocket money, entertainment, charity, etc.

If your net cash flow is negative, it is time to access where you *must* cut back. When entering retirement, you simply can't afford to spend more than you have in income, especially in the early years of retirement. If you still need to save for retirement, you must consider what retirement will look like if you don't save enough. It isn't a pretty picture.

Keeping Up with the Smiths

The amount of money you spend each month should never be measured against anyone else—though this happens all the time. One of the most typical questions I hear is "How does my spending compare with other people in my situation?" Like with many answers in financial planning, the honest response is "It depends." The way you spend money can't be compared with others. Rule-of-thumb charts are overgeneralizations and in most cases focus on the median. Chances are you're doing better than the median.

Each year, the Bureau of Labor Statistics produces a public report that attempts to capture how the average household (referred to as consumer unit) spends money. These numbers are typically used by the media to illustrate "the state of the American consumer." The table below shares some of those figures. How does your financial situation stack up? Take a look at the numbers and compare your current lifestyle. Would you now consider yourself "average"? My guess is that the answer is no!

Snapshot of the Average American Household (as of 2012)	
Number of consumer units surveyed	124,416,000
Average age of primary consumer	50
Average number in consumer unit (household)	2.5
Percentage who are homeowners	64%
Pretax earnings	$65,596
Annual expenses	$51,442

Consumer units include families, single people living alone, those sharing households with others who are financially independent, and two or more persons living together who share expenses.

Based on the numbers above, would you consider yourself average?

How Much Money Do You *Think* You Spend Each Year (and Month)?

It's time to pull back the curtain and reveal what you typically spend over the course of a year. I know—you don't want to know. But in order to manage your retirement "like a genius," you *need* to know how much money is required to cover your month-to-month expenses. It is critical.

Let's start with this simple question.

How many checking accounts (or online bill pay accounts) do you use to pay your bills? It's probably one or two.

While you likely use an ATM card to grab cash from the bank and rely on a few different credit cards to pay for purchases, it's probable that you have one bank account (or just a few) that records all the money that goes out of your household. All too often, I see people lose sight of this very simple fact.

Think about it. When you take $100 from the ATM or use your debit card at the supermarket, it is immediately recorded to your bank account. If you use your VISA card to spend $150 for dinner or drop $1,250 for a laptop computer using your MasterCard, the amount you pay to VISA each month gets recorded to your bank account(s) the moment the check clears. While you might think your spending is erratic, inconsistent, and/or unmanageable, *tracking* what you spend each month might not be all that hard after all.

Test Time: What Do You *Think* You Spend Each Month?

> **I Can See Clearly Now!**
>
> The most successful retirees have a clear, ongoing understanding of how much money they spend on both a monthly and an annual basis.
>
> Observation

Grab a piece of paper and a pen. Now imagine, just for a moment, what you *think* it costs, on average, to cover all the expenses in your home on a monthly basis. Don't forget about the quarterly bills such as property taxes and/or annual payments such as life insurance.

Go ahead. Take all the time you need.

How'd you do? Was it tough? Do you think you captured everything? Honestly, unless you are a walking budget calculator, this exercise is really hard. It's the reason most people have no idea how much they spend each month. It's just too darned hard to figure out!

That's because there are some months where more expenses are due than others. And I'll bet as you're reading this paragraph, you're thinking, "Oh yeah, I forgot about birthday gifts, eating out, the money I take from the ATM each week," and so on. So what do you say? Let's try something a little easier.

Wrapping Your Arms around Your Expenses

In **Chapter 3**, I asked you to gather all of your bank statements into one pile. What I'd like you to do now is grab just the statements that reflect the checks you write to pay your bills and the ATM activity that puts cash in your hands. My guess is that you've got one or two checking accounts that hold the answers to 90 to 100 percent of your spending activity.

Remember, each time you pull money from the ATM, make a credit card payment, use your debit card, pay a bill online,

The Finished Product

There will always be months when you spend more money than others. The timing of when you pay your bills might be indicative of when your paycheck is deposited or bonuses are received.

You may also be thinking, "But this year was different." It probably wasn't. Unless you paid for a wedding, purchased a home, or finally spent a large chunk of money that you had been accumulating for a number of years, your expenses can generally be normalized. There will always be ancillary, high-cost expenses that throw off your normal spending pattern. Items such as home improvement costs and vacations are just a couple of expenses that might fall into that category. Trust in the fact that this will always happen—and that it's just a part of your personal spending lifestyle

Here's an example of a monthly expenses report:

Month	Amount
January	$ 6,245
February	5,320
March	5,763
April	7,489
May	5,860
June	9,085
Six-month total	$39,762
	× 2
	$79,524
	÷ 12
Average monthly expense	$ 6,627

The example above would suggest that, on average, you spend $6,627 per month.

Example

or write a check, it's reported on your bank account. In most cases, your checking account is your single access point to viewing your spending.

A Secret Recipe for Identifying Your Monthly Expense Needs

The recipe below offer a step-by-step approach for capturing your estimated monthly expenses. It won't take all that long, but the results may have a long-lasting effect on how you begin thinking about your own retirement.

Recipe: Monthly Expenses

Prep time: 15 minutes
Calculation time: 10 minutes
Genius level: Easy
Financial planning time: Priceless!

Ingredients:

1 calculator

1 piece of paper

1 pencil (preferably sharpened)

6 consecutive monthly checking account statements (If you have more than one statement, you'll need to collect 6 months' worth of statements for all the checking accounts.)

Good lighting (If you're like me, your eyes aren't what they used to be.)

Directions:

1. Create two columns on your piece of paper. At the top of one column write "Month," and at the top of the other, write "Amount."
2. Find the term "Total Withdrawals" on one of your checking account statements. It's usually on the front or back page.
3. Write the name of the month (i.e., January) that represents the statement in the month column of your paper. In the amount column, write the corresponding "total withdrawal."
4. Continue this step with all 6 of your checking account statements.
5. Total the 6 amounts using your calculator. (This isn't school; calculators are allowed!)
6. Now multiply this number by 2. This will give you an estimated annual amount spent. (If you want a more accurate depiction of the annual amount, use 12 previous statements rather than 6.)
7. Divide the number by 12. You're now looking at the approximate monthly amount that you need in order to maintain your current lifestyle.
8. Contemplate... What did you just create?

Note: If you spend money from more than one checking account, you'll want to do this exercise for all of them. Be sure to add up all the accounts to produce a more complete and accurate measurement of how much you spend each month.

Adjustments to the Spending Report

Oftentimes, and in good practice, you may have money that transfers *out* of your checking account and into another account as a means of "forced savings." If any of the following items occur on a monthly basis, subtract these amounts from your previous results. This is money you *save*, not spend:

- Any transfers of money scheduled for other bank accounts
- Automatic investments to a mutual fund, brokerage account, IRA, or long-term savings program
- Additions to cash-value life insurance or annuity policies (don't subtract the cost for insurance, though)

Do not, however, subtract money that transfers to another savings account but is used later in the year to fund an expense, such as a vacation.

Happiness Is… Positive Cash Flow

While you're in the "accumulation mode" of your life, you need to save more money than you spend. If you do that successfully, you're much happier than times when your expenses exceed your income.

One quick way to measure whether your household's cash flow is positive or negative is to simply go back and grab the checking account statements you used in the previous exercise. This time you'll want to capture both "total withdrawals" *and* "total deposits." Hopefully you already know the solution to this exercise, but if you want to see the actual numbers, go ahead and fill in the chart below.

Month	Total Deposits	Total Withdrawals	Positive/ Negative Cash Flow

So, what did you learn? Are you bringing in enough money to cover your expenses each month? If not, you're going to want to spend time digging deeper into your expenses to see where you might be able to cut back. It's not easy, and reducing expenses so that you can save money for the future is generally *not* a long-term solution. It's like agreeing to go on a diet. You'll work hard for a while, and you may even see some results. But, ultimately, most people go back to *their normal*—they return to their comfortable habits.

Another way to improve your cash flow is as simple as adding more revenue. While reducing expenses might sound easy, perhaps one of the following options is worth consideration:

- Seek a better-paying opportunity.
- Add a second source of income to the household.
- Turn one of your hobbies into a new business opportunity.

A Preview to Planning Your Cash Flow in Retirement

Once you understand how you spend money today, it becomes a baseline for understanding how you'll use money during retirement. Some expenses that you pay for today may not be items that you'll pay for later in life. Below are some expenses that may diminish or disappear altogether:

- Mortgage payments
- Home equity loan payments
- College expenses (hopefully those expenses are done)
- Life insurance payments (will you need life insurance in retirement?)

Then, of course, there are items that could be new, increase, or never go away, despite the fact that, in some cases, you want them to:

- Medical costs
- 401(k) contributions
- Social Security and Medicare taxes

- Long-term care insurance
- Second home/vacation home expense
- Supporting adult children
- Caring for aging parent(s)
- Travel
- Gifts, entertainment, eating out

Items such as automobile costs will likely not go away. You're still going to purchase cars during your retirement.

Using Credit Cards

Another danger that often gets lost in managing expenses is the amount of money you might place on your credit card.

One way that people lose control of their monthly spending is when they accrue balances on their credit cards. If you're not inclined to pay off the balance on your credit card each month, you are spending money unwisely. Interest costs that accrue on outstanding balances have a multiplier effect that can destroy your financial plan.

WATCH OUT!

Comparing Yourself with "Everyone Else"

While you may experience similar expenses and life events as your social circle changes, it's misguided to think that your life mirrors the rest of the world. It doesn't. I highly caution you against thinking that any "Report on America" attempting to capture "the average life" of Americans is a good representation of you. These reports are *over*generalizations.

Preparing for Emergencies

Will you and your loved ones be ready the next time disaster strikes? Often there isn't much time to act, so it's important to be prepared now for a sudden emergency. By planning ahead, you can protect yourself and alleviate some of the confusion, fear, and loss.

When you are caught in an emergency situation, you will not have much time to retrieve information. Organizing contact phone numbers, financial records, medical and property insurance policies, and personal identification information will make it easier for you to access resources quickly. While your net worth statement contains financial values, it doesn't typically include contact information and other important "emergency details."

Here are some other items to think about.

Medical Information

Before a medical emergency occurs, have all your vital medical information for yourself, your family, and your pets in writing. Some examples of important medical information are physicians' numbers, blood types, current medications, and insurance identification numbers.

Emergency Contact Information

If someone needed to contact your family and/or trusted professionals in your life, who would they call?

Consider making contact information for the following people readily available:

- Immediate family
- Primary care physician
- Lawyer
- Financial planner
- Accountant

In **Appendix C**, "Preparing for Emergencies," you'll find a detailed worksheet where you can begin documenting this information.

The Retirement Expense Rule of Thumb

Perhaps you've heard the rule of thumb that says you'll spend about 70 percent of your current expenses in retirement. Don't trust it.

That rule worked decades ago, but in my experience, you are likely to spend in retirement quite close to what you spend now—and maybe even more. Money will be spent in different ways.

Oh, and that rule of thumb that suggests you'll be in a lower tax bracket in retirement? Don't count on that one either. It's very possible it will be the same—if not higher.

Pure Genius!

Putting It All Together

While it's important to know what you're worth and how money flows through your household, your wealth and well-being can be decimated if someone can't gain access to critical contacts and information in the event of an emergency. Don't be in the "I wish I'd done that" category.

To Summarize...

- It's important to know how you spend your money.
- The way you spend money in retirement will be different from how you spend it today.
- Happiness truly is positive cash flow.
- Your financial situation doesn't likely mirror the "national average." Chances are that you are doing better, have more resources, and can more easily escape the financial pitfalls of the "average American."
- Document an emergency contact and information list.

Chapter 5

Are Your Assets Owned Properly?

In This Chapter...

- What is an account registration?
- The importance of owning assets properly
- Knowing the difference between personal investment accounts and retirement accounts
- The value of trust accounts
- Beneficiary designations

Before you build any type of retirement planning strategy, you need to know the rules of the game. It generally starts with making informed decisions on how you will own your various assets. Whether it's an IRA, a personal investment, a 401(k) plan, or a piece of property, how you register the ownership of these assets can have tax and legal implications.

With more than two decades of experience in the financial planning business, I've seen too many people make improper assumptions about account ownership and then find themselves in a pickle when it's time to begin drawing money from their accounts—and, even worse, after they've died.

Account Ownership—What's the Big Deal?

Unlike your childhood, when "calling it" was enough to secure ownership of an item, the titling of valuable assets is critically important in real life. When you were young, your bike, your baseball card collection, or your Leif Garrett/Farrah Fawcett poster may have been your most valuable possession, but today it's different.

A Quick Way to Identify Account Ownership

Take a look at one of your bank statements. There may be some acronyms or funny-looking expressions after your name. Those descriptors help explain the actual guidelines regarding the ownership of that particular account.

Retirement versus Nonretirement Accounts

You may recall back in **Chapter 3**, I had you separate each of your account statements into two piles (retirement assets and nonretirement assets) to build your net worth statement. You're about to find out why.

Sometimes retirement assets are referred to as "qualified assets," and nonretirement assets as "nonqualified assets."

Types of Ownership—Nonretirement Accounts

Assets, for purposes of this discussion, consist of anything tangible that can be fairly valued. Assets can be owned by individuals, couples, or multiple groups of people. Each type of ownership carries its own particular characteristics.

Individual Ownership

When you own an asset in your name alone, it's referred to as *individual ownership*. You have complete and total control over the account. You can add money, withdraw money, and make changes to the holdings in your account without consulting a spouse, family member, friend, etc. While it comes with the most control, it may also come with the most questions upon your death. Individual ownership doesn't indicate who will receive these assets when you die. These accounts are typically subject to probate and are then distributed to heirs via your will. Don't have a will? We'll discuss that later in **Part 3**.

Can You Use a Nonretirement Account in Retirement?

Absolutely. Just because an investment is classified as a "retirement" or "nonretirement" account, it doesn't preclude the owner from drawing upon either account during retirement years. Conversely, if you elect to take money from a "retirement account" prior to turning 59½ years old, you may be subject to income taxes and an IRS penalty.

Observation

Joint Tenancy with Rights of Survivorship (JTWROS)

This form of ownership is created to ensure that in the event of an owner's death, the deceased's share is automatically transferred to the remaining owners. For instance, if you owned an account with your two brothers as JTWROS and you died, your share would automatically transfer equally to your two brothers. In a JTWROS account, each owner has a respective share (in the case above, each owns a third), but any owner can take action with respect to the account, such as deposit or withdraw money. It may not take an agreement of all the owners.

Joint Tenancy by the Entirety

This form of joint ownership is reserved for married couples. Typically the account cannot be terminated without the consent of both parties. It simply states that if you die, the account immediately transfers to the spouse.

Tenants in Common

Generally two or more (unmarried) people who hold undivided interest in an asset are listed as tenants in common. The interest of these assets doesn't have to be fifty-fifty. Let's say you own an account with your sister. You both agree that this account is owned equally. Your account may be set up to require both signatures to make changes, write checks, withdraw money, etc. However, a tenants in common account means that you may not be entitled to the other owners' shares upon their death. In fact, upon the death of one of the owners, the remaining owners could find themselves with a new tenants in common owner (perhaps your brother-in-law). *Yikes*!

Community Property

If you're married in certain states (Arizona, California, Idaho, Louisiana, Nevada, New Mexico, Texas, and Washington) and you earn or accumulate individual assets during your marriage, your spouse can automatically assume one-half of the assets in the event of your death.

Using a Revocable Trust for Nonretirement Assets

A revocable trust is often referred to as a "living trust."

There are three categories of interested parties associated with a trust. Sometimes they can be the same person. They are known as the grantor, the trustee, and the beneficiary.

Generally the grantor is the one who initiates the establishment of the trust and is typically the one who funds it. The trustees, who can sometimes be the same as the grantor, usually have access to the money in the trust. A revocable trust is generally established using the Social Security number of one of the trustees. As such, this trust operates as if it is one and the same with the person named as trustee.

Finally, the beneficiary is designated by the grantor. During the grantor's lifetime, the beneficiary is often the grantor. Then, after the grantor's death, the beneficiary is the person who will receive the proceeds in the trust.

A revocable trust is typically established to provide the following benefits:

- Remove assets from probate.
- Assign the beneficiaries in detail upon the termination of the trust.
- Provide trustees with control over assets.
- Address who will manage money on behalf of minor beneficiaries.

The Empty (Unfunded) Trust

More often than not, we meet people who have visited with an estate planning attorney to have a trust drafted but have failed to *fund* the trust. Just because you pay an attorney to write a trust doesn't mean that your assets are actually *in* the trust. That's your job. Failing to fund a trust means that you paid money for a legal document that is not yet serving a purpose.

Uninspired

A revocable or family trust is most commonly used by individuals. Several other trusts can be established for purposes of protecting assets from creditors, protecting assets from estate taxes, passing assets by skipping a generation, and more. The world of trusts (especially irrevocable ones) is very complicated and is worthy of its own **For the GENIUS** book.

We'll discuss more about probate, trusts, and estate planning in **Part 3**.

Most mass affluent baby boomers don't need anything more than a revocable trust—if for no other reason than to avoid probate. A living trust also has the benefit of providing for a backup trustee in the event of your incapacity and/or inability to act. However, if your estate is in excess of $5 million or has the potential to approach that level, I'd encourage you to visit with an estate planning attorney to explore some of the more sophisticated tools available.

Other Common Account Registrations

Following are a few other ownership arrangements that are typical for readers of this book:

- Payable on death/transfer on death (POD/TOD)
- Custodial accounts—Uniform Gift to Minors Act (UGMA) or Uniform Transfer to Minors Act (UTMA)

POD/TOD

Payable on death or transfer on death is becoming a very common addition to nonretirement accounts. Unlike an account that names a beneficiary (such as an IRA, life insurance, or an annuity), an individually owned account doesn't have a listing for who inherits the money upon your death. Instead, as said above, an individual account is subject to probate.

By adding a POD or TOD designation to your account registration, you "name a beneficiary." In doing so, you can avoid probate. It's easy to do too. Visit the financial institutions that hold your accounts and ask them to add a POD or TOD. (Institutions use one acronym or the other). There should be *no cost* to do this.

Custodial Account—UGMA/UTMA

It's very common to see preretirees find old stock certificates, savings bonds, brokerage accounts, and bank statements that list: "[Parent's Name] as custodian for [Child's Name] UGMA/UTMA."

Uniform Gift to Minors Act or Uniform Transfer to Minors Act is a common form of ownership when parents want to open an account for a minor child. If you have one of these accounts, it was opened under your Social Security number and listed perhaps your mom or dad as the "custodian."

Money that your parents placed in these accounts needed to be used for your health, maintenance, and support. Your parents may have opened these accounts to help pay for college or to put money aside for your future without realizing that upon reaching your age of majority, you could change the registration into your own name—and cash it out.

Today, many people in their fifties, sixties, and seventies still own old UGMA/UTMA accounts that were purchased by their parents. If you have one, this money is rightfully yours. You don't need to ask Mom or Dad for permission to use it. You should visit the financial institution that holds this account and have your name listed as the sole owner.

Types of Ownership—Individual Retirement Accounts

Retirement accounts come in all shapes and sizes. They come with limitations and rules, thus making distinctions between each type a bit challenging. But for geniuses like you, I'm confident that with your thinking cap tightly secured, you'll pick it up pretty quickly.

To start, let's dispel one of the biggest myths about retirement accounts: There is *no such thing* as *joint ownership* on *retirement accounts*.

Individual retirement accounts were first made available to Americans in 1974 when Congress passed the Employee Retirement Income Security Act. Over the past forty years, the IRA has evolved. It now consists of several different offerings:

One Account, One Owner

There can only be *one* owner per retirement account. That's right. There's no such thing as a *joint retirement account*. There are no "sharesies."

IMPORTANT!

- Deductible traditional IRAs
- Nondeductible traditional IRAs
- Roth IRAs
- SEP IRAs
- Simple IRAs
- Rollover IRAs

Traditional IRAs

Traditional IRAs are commonly owned by investors. They are investments that allow the earnings on your investments to grow tax deferred until the dollars are distributed from the account. When you contributed to your IRA, you may or may not have been eligible to take a tax deduction.

Deductible IRAs

If you took a tax deduction for the contribution you made to your plan, it is classified as a deductible IRA. All the proceeds are considered pretax. Up until you take money out of the account, all your contributions and earnings will grow tax deferred. But when you remove money from your IRA at retirement, every dollar you take will be subject to income tax.

Nondeductible IRAs

There are some instances where you may have contributed to an IRA account but weren't eligible to take a tax deduction. In this case, you'll want to be sure that you keep very careful records. That's because despite the fact that all of the earnings on your contributions will grow tax deferred, only the earnings (and not your contributions) will be subject to income tax when you take a distribution.

> **Retirement Planning for Nondeductible IRAs**
>
> If you don't want to pay tax twice on some of your nondeductible IRAs, you need to record your nondeductible contributions on IRS Form 8606 each year. In doing so, only a percentage of the distributions from this account may be taxable—rather than all of it.
>
> IMPORTANT!

Roth IRA

The Roth IRA was established by the Taxpayer Relief Act of 1997. It said that eligible individuals could invest a certain amount of posttax money each year into an account that would grow tax-free. That's right. All earnings and distributions would be tax-free.

Any account with a Roth designation in the registration is eligible for tax-free withdrawals in retirement.

Traditional IRA versus Roth IRA

Two of the most popular retirement accounts are traditional IRAs and Roth IRAs. The main difference is that when you withdraw money from a traditional IRA, you will likely be subject to income tax on all the earnings (and even perhaps your contributions).

In a Roth IRA, any money you take from the account during retirement is *free* of tax.

SEP IRA

SEP stands for simplified employee pension. If you are a sole proprietor and wish to establish a retirement plan for your firm, you have an opportunity to put away a larger sum of money than with a traditional IRA. In 2014, business owners who have SEPs can contribute up to 25 percent of their compensation—up to a maximum of $260,000 in earnings. That means you could put up to $51,000 into your SEP IRA plan. Sounds good, right? Hold on; there's a catch. Whatever percentage of your pay that you decide to place into the plan must also be placed into the plan for all of your employees. That's right. If you put 10 percent of your pay into the SEP IRA, you need to write a check for 10 percent of every eligible employee's compensation. That could sting a bit—so be careful before you sign on to one of these.

Simple IRA

Another more popular form of a retirement plan for small-business owners is the simple IRA. In this case, employers are generally required to match up to 3 percent of an employee's compensation. In addition, both you and your employees can invest up to $12,000 ($14,500 if over age fifty) on a pretax basis into the plan.

Yes, there are many other types of retirement accounts, including 401(k), 403(b), 457, and more. We'll discuss these employer retirement plans in greater detail in the next chapter.

You Are the Owner of Your Retirement Account

Whether you own an IRA, Roth, SEP, simple, or other retirement account, you are the sole owner. The account is registered under your Social Security number, and it can be managed only by you. Unless under court order (divorce), you can't just give your IRA to someone else. If you felt so inclined to give someone money from your IRA, you'd still be responsible for the tax liability for taking money from an account that had yet to be taxed.

Calculating Taxable versus Nontaxable Share of Distributions

Imagine you made nondeductible IRA contributions of $2,000 each year for ten years. You're now in retirement, and the value is worth $50,000. You want to take $5,000 from your account. How much of your distribution is taxable?

$2,000 x 10 years = $20,000

Total value of the account is $50,000.

The portion of the account that represents nondeductible contributions is 40 percent ($20,000 ÷ $50,000).

Since you want to take $5,000 from the IRA, $2,000 of the $5,000 (40 percent of the value) represents a return of your nondeductible contributions; thus only $3,000 (the earnings) would be subject to tax.

Example

Naming Beneficiaries to Your Accounts

Have you ever given thought to how money would be passed to the next generation? Are you certain, or might you be going on some false assumptions?

Contribution Limits for IRAs

In 2014, participants in traditional IRAs and Roth IRAs can add money as follows.

IRS Contribution Limits	Standard Limit	Catch-Up Provision (Over Fifty Years Old)
Traditional IRA	$ 5,500	$ 6,500
Roth IRA	5,500	46,500

Subject to income limits.

Although you can make a contribution any time during the tax year, the deadline for adding to a traditional IRA or Roth IRA is either the date you file your taxes or April 15. Both the contribution amount and AGI limits are adjusted for inflation.

Definition

If you own life insurance, an annuity, a retirement plan, or an IRA, the new account form you signed to establish the account had a place to name a beneficiary. If you left it blank (tsk, tsk, tsk) and you die, your estate will inherit this asset. That may not be what you intended. It's one of the biggest estate planning mistakes I see today.

If you're married, you've likely named your spouse as your primary beneficiary. In fact, if you're married, most states will require this—unless the spouse signs a letter disclaiming any interest. Yes, even if you don't like your spouse, you still have to name your spouse as beneficiary.

But what happens if your spouse predeceases you? Will you have named contingent beneficiaries on your accounts? The contingent beneficiary receives the money if the primary beneficiary is not alive at the time of your death. If not, guess where the assets are going? To your estate. It will then be up to the will to determine how to pay out these accounts.

Cobeneficiaries

Below is an example of a traditional beneficiary designation for someone seeking to leave a retirement account to three children. The two sons and one daughter are considered cobeneficiaries, and unless otherwise indicated on the beneficiary form, they will receive equal shares of your account.

33% Share	33% Share	33% Share
Son	Son	Daughter
Three grandchildren	One grandchild	Four grandchildren

Is Mommy Still Your Beneficiary?

Many retirees forget about old life insurance policies and very old retirement plans that still sit with former employers. Additionally, if you've been working with the same company for more than thirty years, you may also find yourself with this dilemma.

But here's something that might get the hair on the back of your neck to stand up. When you initially established your life insurance, retirement account, or annuity, who was your beneficiary? If you weren't married yet, you may have named Mom. And if you haven't made changes to the beneficiary designation since your wedding, it's *still* Mom!

Even worse, what if you're divorced and remarried and still have your former spouse listed as beneficiary?

Perspiration

Passing Retirement Accounts and Insurance Proceeds to the Next Generation

If you are a surviving spouse, it's very possible that your children and then your grandchildren could be beneficiaries of your estate.

If you've identified your children as equal beneficiaries on your accounts, the money will be split evenly and distributed to them. But what happens if one of your children predeceases you? What happens then? Will your grandchildren receive your deceased son's share? Will it be paid to your daughter-in-law (the spouse of your deceased son)? The answer to all these questions is "It depends."

A Per Stirpes Designation

Let's say your first son predeceased you. Would it be your intent to have his share of your retirement accounts pass to his children (your grandchildren)? If so, this is called a per stirpes designation. The diagram illustrates per stirpes.

33% Share	33% Share	33% Share
Son predeceases	Son	Daughter
Three grandchildren receive father's share	One grandchild	Four grandchildren

Per Capita

But what if your son predeceased you and the designation on your beneficiary election was "per capita"? This would mean that the remaining children would split your accounts and your grandchildren from your son who has passed away would receive *nothing*. The illustration below is an example of per capita.

0% Share	50% Share	50% Share
Son predeceases	Son	Daughter
Three grandchildren	One grandchild	Four grandchildren

IMPORTANT!

Confirm Your Beneficiary Designations

Most beneficiary designations list "per capita" as the default election. This means that if one of your children predeceases you and you had hopes that your child's children (your grandchildren) would receive that child's share, your family might be in for an alarming experience.

Visit with your financial planner, insurance agent, human resource department, and anyone else who oversees one of your accounts where there are beneficiaries named. Make sure that you confirm, with your own eyes, the designation of per capita or per stirpes on the account.

How Does Your Daughter-In-Law/Son-In-Law Factor into Beneficiary Designations?

Per capita and per stirpes designations generally skip over the surviving spouse of your deceased child. Instead they follow blood lines. If it is your intention to include a surviving husband/wife of a deceased child, you need to distinctly document that on your beneficiary designation form.

Owning your assets properly is critically important to your retirement plan. Making a mistake can be far more damaging than selecting the right or wrong mutual fund for your portfolio.

To Summarize...

- The way you select to own your assets can have varying implications. Make sure you're clear on why you selected a particular designation.
- Never make an assumption on how assets will be split in the event of an owner's death.
- You can protect individually held accounts from probate by adding a transfer on death designation—and it costs you nothing.
- Reexamine beneficiary designations, and make the paperwork align with your wishes.

Chapter 6

Making the Most of Your Retirement Plan

In This Chapter...

- Why you should participate in the company retirement plan
- Selecting the right investment mix
- Understanding performance in your plan

Chances are that you've worked for a few different companies and have participated in various retirement plans. Maybe it's a 401(k), a SEP, a TSP, a simple IRA, a 403(b), or something else. The investment options are different, and the amounts you can contribute vary—and there are rules for matching, taking loans, vesting schedules, and whether you can roll your old company's retirement plan over to the new plan.

In retirement, you need to know how each of these accounts integrates into your plan.

What Is a 401(k) Plan?

A 401(k) plan is an investment opportunity provided by many employers that allows employees to put money aside on a pretax basis—and, in some cases, on an after-tax basis in the form of a Roth 401(k)—for their retirement. Designed as a more flexible, less expensive alternative to employers than a traditional pension plan, this investment program places a portion of an employee's financial future on their shoulders. Neglecting to participate in a 401(k) plan could mean that you have little money other than perhaps Social Security to rely upon when you retire.

How Does a 401(k) Plan Work?

401(k) plans become eligible to employees when they achieve certain employment requirements. This might include a minimum age of twenty-one, a minimum of one year's employment, more than one thousand hours worked during the year, etc. Each plan will has its own eligibility requirements.

> **What Do You Get to Keep?**
>
> All pretax contributions made by *you* into your 401(k) plan are yours. If you leave the company, you retain the rights to your contributions and any earnings that have accumulated on the funds.
>
> IMPORTANT!

Once eligible, you will complete an enrollment form and make two selections:

- Indicate the percentage of pay or the dollar amount you'd like allocated to your 401(k) plan each pay period.
- Indicate which investments, and at what percentage, you'd like your money allocated.

Money is deducted from your paycheck on a pretax basis and deposited into your plan.

Saving money on a pretax basis is highly advantageous. In doing so, you allow your money to grow free of taxation—until you remove the money from your account. It's assumed you will take this money in your retirement years.

Should You Participate in Your Company's 401(k) Plan?

Yes, so long as you can afford it.

What Is a Company Match?

Oftentimes employers encourage employees to participate in the 401(k) plan by incentivizing them with a company match. They may, for instance, match 100 percent of the first 6 percent of your contributions. It is generally advised to participate in the plan over at the minimum contribution from your paycheck in order to get the maximum amount of the match from your employer. It is almost like getting a guaranteed return the first year.

What If your Employer Doesn't Offer a Match? Should You Contribute?

Absolutely. While it would be nice to pick up some "free money" from your employer, you actually pick up "free money" by participating in the 401(k) plan regardless of whether your employer matches or not.

How to Make an Immediate Return on Your Money in a 401(k)

Let's assume you make $104,000 and you're in the 25 percent federal tax bracket. Every two weeks, you are paid a gross income of $4,000. You are debating whether or not to contribute 10 percent of your pay to the 401(k) plan.

Gross Biweekly Pay	401(k) Contribution	Taxable Amount of Paycheck	Federal Taxes Due at 25%	Net Take-Home Pay	Annual Taxes on Pay	Annual Deposit to 401(k) Plan
$4,000	10%	$3,600	$ 900	$2,700	$23,400	$10,400
4,000	0	4,000	1,000	3,000	26,000	0

As you can see from the table, by contributing 10 percent of your pay to the 401(k) plan, you'll save $10,400 on a pretax basis and pay $2,600 less in taxes. What's even more important is that you're putting money aside for the future—and not depositing it into your checking account. Because if you do, there is a tendency to spend it.

Could you find the immediate 25 percent return on your money? Consider this. Even if you deposited your $10,400 into the money market account of your

401(k) plan and it earned 0 percent for the year, you'd still be ahead 25 percent for the year. That's because you didn't have to pay $2,600 in taxes that ordinarily would have been due had you *not* participated in the 401(k) plan.

The IRS does limit the amount you can contribute to a 401(k) plan on a pretax basis. In 2014, it is $17,500. If you're over age fifty, you can invest an additional $5,500, for a total of $23,000.

What's the Tax Liability When You Withdraw Money from Your 401(k)?

Generally, you don't ever want to touch money from your 401(k) plan while you're working. In fact, some employers have very stringent limitations on how you can access your 401(k) money while you're an employee. They often let you take money only for a hardship, first-time home purchase, or a medical necessity—or as a loan.

Doing the Math

Let's assume that you earn $100,000 per year. You elect to place 10 percent of your earnings on a pretax basis into the 401(k) plan. Your employer offers a matching program of 50 percent on the first 8 percent you allocate to the 401(k) plan.

The math would work like this:

Your 401(k) contribution = $10,000 (10 percent of $100,000).

Employer contribution = $4,000 (100,000 x 8 percent x 50 percent).

Total money allocated to 401(k) plan for the year = $14,000.

Example

Once you leave your employer, or if you're retired and want to access funds, you may do so without a 10 percent IRS penalty—if you're over the age of fifty-five and withdraw from a 401(k). But an IRA cannot be withdrawn from without a penalty until age 59½. But beware, when you take money from your 401(k) plan, it is counted as ordinary income. That's because you never paid income tax on your contributions.

What about a Roth 401(k) Plan?

The Roth 401(k) plan was established several years ago as a means for placing money into a retirement account on a posttax basis. But when money is removed from the plan, it is paid completely tax-free.

It's important to note that employer contributions to the Roth 401(k) plan are still done so on a pretax basis.

Don't Get Double Taxed!

There are many 401(k) plans still in existence that are composed of both pretax and posttax contributions made by employers. It is imperative that you discuss these differences with your employer prior to taking any money from the plan. Here's why:

Any money you contributed with "after-tax" money would be a return of your own money. That's because you already paid tax on it. Of course, any of the earnings on the money would be subject to tax.

If you worked for your company in the seventies and eighties, it's very possible that some money in your plan could represent dollars that have already been taxed. You don't want to be taxed twice!

Pure Genius!

While I'm a fan of the Roth 401(k) plan for people under age fifty, I find that it's a rare situation when a preretiree establishes one.

Should You Pay Off Your Outstanding 401(k) Loan Prior to Retirement?

If you still have an outstanding loan on your 401(k) plan following retirement or separation of service, you will no longer have the ability to pay it back. Instead, it will be counted as a taxable distribution to you—and thus subject to federal and (if applicable) state income taxes during the year you leave employment. It may also be subject to the 10 percent penalty. Make sure you pay it off in full, or you may be surprised with a tax hit.

What Should You Do If You Have Multiple Retirement Plans?

You may hold a 401(k) plan with one former employer, a SEP IRA with another, and a 457 plan with another one. I strongly recommend that you take the time to consolidate all of your pretax retirement accounts into one rollover IRA by doing a direct rollover, which means the money is sent directly from your employer plan to your new IRA. That way, nothing is withheld for taxes. They are easy to set up, and they will most certainly simplify your life when it's time to make retirement income decisions. Here are just some of the major advantages of doing so:

- Preservation of tax benefits. All investments remain in a tax-deferred status until you take physical possession of your money.
- More investment options. Chances are that you have limited choices in each of your plans. By rolling the money into an IRA, you have a full universe of investment options.
- Better asset allocation, diversification, and rebalancing opportunities.
- Potentially lower fees. Now you have control over the fees, commissions, and charges associated with your retirement assets.
- A consolidated statement. Wouldn't it be nice to have all your retirement assets reported on one statement? Just think how easy it will be to calculate your required minimum distribution when you reach age 70½.

Structuring the Investments in Your Retirement Plan

With any luck, you can select from an array of investment choices to build your retirement plan portfolio. Make sure you include a selection of investments based in stocks and bonds. In later chapters, we'll discuss asset allocation in greater depth. But for now, let's agree to ignore the old rule of thumb that suggests the percentage of money you invest into bonds should be equal to your age. It is an old wives' tale worthy of the furnace.

If you're sixty-two years old, does it make sense to have 62 percent of your money in bonds and 38 percent in stocks? The answer is "It depends."

Furthermore, when you approach age eighty-five, there is likely no need to maintain 85 percent of your money in bonds.

Your retirement account is likely just one piece in your overall net worth. You need to overlay the asset allocation of this money with the rest of the assets that will contribute to your retirement. In fact, neglecting to allocate a larger sum of money in your retirement account to equity-based based investments (stocks) could lead to much more risk than you wanted. Inflation risk and interest rate risk are just a couple that come to mind.

Why Asset *Location* Matters

One advantage of retirement accounts is that earnings are not subject to tax until distributed from the accounts. As such, consider including income/dividend-paying investments in your retirement account rather than in your personal investment account. Sometimes the location of where each investment sits (retirement account versus nonretirement account) can be a benefit to you. Also, if you have a propensity to trade in your account, or if mutual funds you own typically pay large capital gains distributions, a retirement account may be a good location for these investments.

Danger Signs in a 401(k) Plan

While 401(k) plans are an attractive investment for employees, there are many dangers and traps. Here are some cautionary points:

- High concentration of investments in the company stock. You may feel a tremendous sense of loyalty to your company—but so too did employees at Enron, Lucent, General Motors, Kodak, and more. Generally, you shouldn't hold more than 10 percent allocation of company stock in your 401(k) plan.
- High concentration of investments in one asset class. Many investors look at past performance reports and then shift poor-performing funds into ones that produced better numbers. Beware. Doing so may position too many dollars in one particular asset class.
- Mistaking diversification for asset allocation. Having several funds in your 401(k) plan doesn't mean you have good asset allocation. Many mutual funds own the same stocks—and have tendencies to move in similar fashions. Your investments should cover several different asset classes.
- Neglecting to buy low and sell high. Is your current retirement plan's asset allocation reflective of the allocation you had originally intended? If not, it may be time to rebalance.

Selling from your best performer and adding money to a fund that underperformed may seem counterintuitive. It's not. Neglecting to rebalance could be dangerous to your retirement plan. Think of it this way: Sell (part of) your winners (sell high) and buy more of your losers (buy low). In future years, your best fund may become your worst and your worst may become your best. Over time, rebalancing works.

Your 401(k) Statement Can Be Misleading

Assume that at the beginning of the year, your 401(k) statement was worth $200,000. At the end of the year, it is worth $250,000. Was your gain 25 percent for the year?

If you're employed and an active participant in your plan, my guess is that you didn't earn 25 percent. Confused? You're not alone. Many people consider the percentage increase/decrease in value from January to December as their annual performance rate. It's just not true.

How's *Your* 401(k) Performing?

The performance numbers from your company 401(k) report are generally *not* reflective of *your* personal performance. Instead, the company report shares how the fund has done during various periods of time when no money was added or subtracted from the fund. If you were adding money, exchanging money from one fund to another, or taking a loan against your funds, you aren't earning the same rate of return that appears in the report. Chances are, your performance for that given year was *less*. Some progressive reports and/or websites will calculate your personal return for the year.

Pure Genius!

Using the example above, let's say that you contributed $10,000 over the course of the year via payroll reduction. Then your employer made matching contributions of $5,000 throughout the year, for a total amount of $15,000. Did you make 25 percent? No, you didn't. $15,000 of the $25,000 increase in account value was due to new money. In this example, you actually made only $10,000.

So now what's your return? It's not so easy to calculate now, is it? Calculating a rate of return on a 401(k) plan is difficult. It requires an internal rate of return calculation that is best simulated through computer software. A standard calculator can't do this type of computation.

What about Fees in 401(k) Plans?

You have the right to examine your 401(k) plan and learn about the fees that are paid by you and those that are paid by your employer. Most 401(k) plans have come under tremendous scrutiny over the past years. A recent PBS *FRONTLINE* episode expose tried to belittle the value of 401(k) plans, but I beg to differ with their conclusions. Most mutual funds are fairly priced as compared with their respective averages. 401(k) plans, or any retirement plans for that matter, aren't free. Someone is paying for the following:

- Your access to top money managers
- Your ability to save money on a paycheck-to-paycheck basis
- Your ability to view, change, edit, and report on your investment portfolio
- Your assurance that the trustee is providing fiduciary compliance to your plan—and more
- A continued reporting to the Department of Labor, IRS, and other regulatory bodies
- A commitment to meeting ERISA guidelines

Nothing's free—especially when it comes to money. Geniuses know that. But geniuses also know that they don't need to overpay for these services. Hopefully your employer is constantly trying to reduce the costs without reducing the quality of performance and service.

To Summarize...

- If you are eligible for a 401(k) or other pretax savings retirement plan, you should participate regardless of whether your employer offers a match or not.
- Make sure you understand the *true* performance of your retirement plan. Always calculate the cash flow of money deposited into the plan by both you and your employer.
- Do not rely on quarterly plan performance summaries as your guide to selecting investments.
- Make sure that your 401(k) allocation takes into consideration the overall asset allocation of your collective investment portfolio.

Chapter 7

Investments for the Genius

In This Chapter...

- How investment risk will impact your retirement plan
- Understanding individual stock ownership
- The risks of holding stock certificates

It doesn't take rocket science to build an investment strategy. Don't let anyone steer you otherwise. While certain investments are sophisticated and others less so, you are smart enough to build an investment portfolio.

What you need to understand is that investments come in all shapes and sizes and pose a wide array of risks. Whether you own stocks, bonds, mutual funds, certificates of deposits (CDs), or treasury bills, risks exist. In fact, I don't believe there is a single investment you can purchase that is totally risk-free. Let's take a look.

A Strategy You Could Count On—Back Then

It's likely that you grew up in the age where your mom or dad collected most of their retirement income through pensions and Social Security. Most often, they supplemented their income with high-yielding certificates of deposit (CDs) that (in the eighties) were paying in the high teens. Back then, it was the good life.

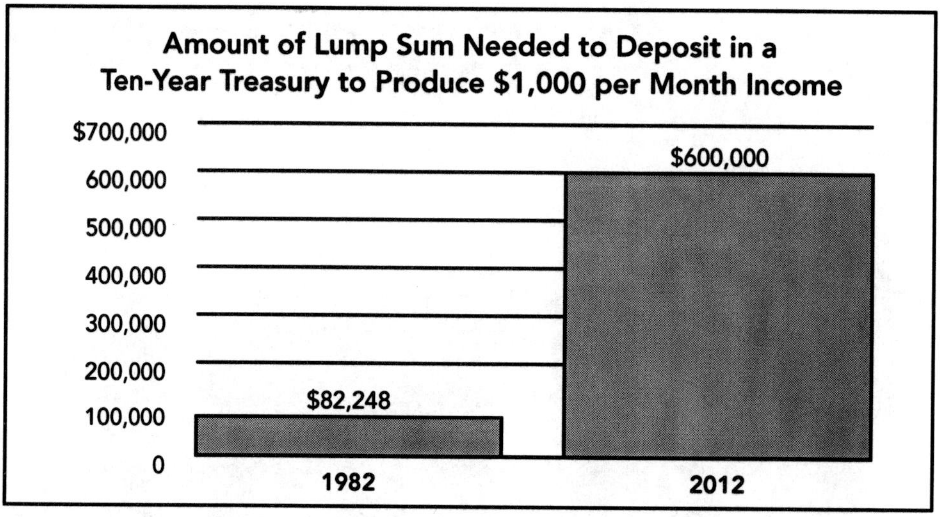

Retirement will be different from your parents' and most certainly not like that of your grandparents. You're likely to live longer, have greater responsibility for managing your money throughout retirement, and may need to use some of your money to support aging parents or adult children. Relying on bank accounts and "high-yielding" certificates of deposit as the third leg in your retirement plan won't be the solution for a successful retirement plan.

The Perfect Investment—You Gotta Have It! Don't You?

It's six o'clock. You and your family are sitting down for a nice dinner, and suddenly the phone rings. It's a fast-talking investment salesperson who wants to give you a ground-floor investment opportunity. His enthusiasm is hypnotic yet annoying at the same time. As he begins to describe the investment opportunity, you become more engaged. You forget about the kids waiting to dig in to the meal at the dinner table. You hear, "Every once in a while, an investment opportunity comes along that's such a no-brainer . . ." You excuse yourself from the table and head to the den. "Could this be the investment solution to reverse my financial mistakes?" you wonder.

> **Oh, How Times Have Changed**
>
> Did you know that in January of 1982, you could collect $1,000 per month or $12,000 per year by depositing $82,248 into a ten-year certificate of deposit paying 14.59 percent? Today, you'd need to invest close to $600,000 to get that same stream of income. Of course, inflation in those days was also double digit, where recently it has been in the very low single digits.
>
> Observation

Listening only to key sound bites, you pick up a few tempting terms:

- Risk-free
- High rate of interest
- Inflation protection
- Tax-free
- Huge potential for long-term growth

Do you buy it? It sounds *so* enticing.

Snap out of it!

Geniuses like you know that this type of investment doesn't exist. If it did, brokerage firms wouldn't need to pay cold-call salespeople to entice you into buying this last-chance opportunity. Honestly, it would never make it into the public's eye because the institutional world would scoop up every last share first.

This chapter is a precursor to several investment conversations that I'll share throughout the book. I'll focus on some of the most common investments retirees consider for their future—as well as the risks associated with them.

Every Investment Has Risks (Even the "Risk-Free" Ones)

Every investment purchase you make contains some level of risk. Whether you purchase CDs at the bank or a stock, bond, mutual fund, or real estate investment, all of them will carry some level of risk. It's up to you to decide the type and the amount of risk you want to take.

> **Are Certain Investments Too Good to Be True?**
>
> Beware of cold-call salespeople who attempt to offer once-in-a-lifetime investment opportunities. Any investment that was truly "too good to be true" would be gobbled up the large financial institutions well before they would ever be offered to people like you and me.
>
> Salespeople attempting to solicit your business with "this very special opportunity" are often looking to win a sales contest for the day. Always ask yourself, "What's in it for *them*?" More than likely, they are trying to earn a commission that serves their interests and not yours.
>
> WATCH OUT!

Investors neglect to consider *all* the risks associated with an investment. Sometimes what appears to be the safest can, in fact, hold more risk than you imagined.

Following are some common risks you encounter every day.

Market Risk

Market risk, or systemic risk, occurs when your investments have the potential to fluctuate due to changes in economic or market conditions. Stocks, bonds, exchange traded funds (ETFs), and mutual funds are typical investments that are subject to market risk. Unfortunately, too many people view market risk as the possibility of losing all their money. While this can occur in rare circumstances, investments are more likely to fluctuate than drop to a worthless value.

Inflation Risk

This is also referred to as purchasing-power risk. It's the risk that asks you to consider what would happen to your investment if the cost of goods increased. For instance, as the prices for movie tickets, postage stamps, homes, and cars increase, your money needs to have appreciated enough through earnings or growth to keep pace. A monthly fixed pension is an example of something that is subject to inflation risk. So too are bank accounts—and cash you're hiding under your mattress (or in a safe deposit box).

Interest Rate Risk

Interest rate risk is the potential that a fixed interest investment (like a bond) will decline in value if interest rates rise in the marketplace. Generally, holders of bonds, treasuries, and bond funds will see the market value of their bonds drop when interest rates increase.

In a rising-interest-rate environment, new buyers of bonds are almost assured of earning a higher interest rate on bonds they buy today rather than the bonds they previously owned. If you want to sell your bonds, you may need to accept a lower price than what you originally paid. Conversely, if you own bonds in a lowering-interest-rate environment, the value increases and your bonds/treasuries are in greater demand.

Liquidity Risk

If your investment doesn't carry a daily market value and isn't easily bought or sold on a business day, you may have liquidity risk. Your home is subject to liquidity risk. It is virtually impossible that on any given day, you and a buyer could exchange payment, move in/out, file the legal documents, complete inspections, etc., that would be necessary. In addition, you can't simply pull a window out of your house, bring it down to the bank, and exchange it for cash.

The same risk exists in the value of businesses, antiques, tangible hard assets, and more. Imagine if all the investments you owned were illiquid? What would you do if you needed to put your hands on some cash today?

Thinking about Risk

For some reason, the word *risk* has become synonymous with "loss of money." When retirees say, "I don't want risk," they are essentially saying, "I don't want to lose any money." But in order to make money, your investments need risk exposure too.

Risk doesn't always mean losing money. Risk can mean inaccessibility to money, uncertain market values, and the potential to make a lot of money—or lose a lot of money. But I think the biggest risk of all is being unable to keep up with the ever-increasing costs of life.

Pure Genius!

Other Risks

Other risks that can impact your investments include social/political risk, tax risk, estate planning risk, currency risk, call risk, and more. Always remember that no investment is completely risk-free. Being told otherwise wouldn't be just poor advice; it would be a straight-out lie.

What Is a Stock?

One of the most common types of investments that people utilize for their retirement portfolios is stocks (oftentimes referred to as "equities").

Understanding stock is not complicated. It simply means that you hold a piece of ownership in a company. When you own a stock, you are a shareholder. The complicated part of owning stocks is deciding which stocks to own, when to buy them, and when to sell them.

There are both public and private shares of stock:

- Public shares. These shares are issued by companies that trade on a stock exchange. Generally, these shares have daily liquidity. Hundreds of thousands of shares can trade hands each day through a financial adviser, brokerage firm, or online broker. Anyone can buy shares in increments as small as one share, though most elect to

Perspiration

Buying Stocks with Your Head and Your Heart

When you buy stock, you are purchasing ownership of a company. Therefore, you are entrusting the executive management of the firm to operate in a manner that will increase shareholder value (the value of the stock you own). This means that you are now part of the corporate business system. It's important to realize that sometimes business decisions can be objectionable to the public at large, employee groups, and even shareholders. These actions often have either a positive or negative effect on share prices.

As a shareholder, your continued ownership can indicate your affirmative agreement with the company's business strategy. As a shareholder, you have the right to sell your shares. In doing so, you can make a personal statement that you no longer agree with the direction/management or business model of the company. Understand, though, that your decision to sell, buy, or hold shares will go with little notice by anyone—unless you are a *very* large stockholder.

purchase shares in one-hundred-share blocks or larger. Companies like Procter & Gamble, Google, and Bank of America are examples of publicly traded stocks.

Private shares. These are shares issued by private companies and do not generally have immediate liquidity value. Small businesses fall into the private company spectrum. Usually just a few people (and sometimes only one person) own all the shares of stock.

For purposes of this book, I'll focus on *public* shares of stock.

What Is Market Cap?

When you hear the term "market cap," it generally means "the size of the company." You can calculate the market capitalization of a company by multiplying all the outstanding shares by the stock price.

Stocks generally use the following guidelines to define market caps:

- Large cap—$10 billion to $200 billion and higher
- Mid cap—$2 billion to $10 billion
- Small cap—$300 million to $2 billion

Some analysts include ultracap, microcap, and nanocap to further delineate each stock, but let's stick with the above three categories for now.

Does Size Matter?

Size should never be the sole reason to buy or sell a stock. You need to examine the fundamentals, management, debt, earnings, and so much more. If you're like most, you have little time or inclination to dive deep into a company's financial records. Instead, you're looking for macro fundamentals to help you further evaluate stocks you'd like to own. One of the first criteria is to determine whether your large-cap, mid-cap, or small-cap stock falls into the category of "value" or "growth."

Not knowing the difference between these two styles could impact the expectation you have for the stock in changing economic environments.

> **Market Cap Types**
>
> Below are some stocks you know by their market caps:
>
> - Large cap—General Electric, Google, Pfizer, Caterpillar
> - Mid cap—E-Trade, Wendy's, Tupperware
> - Small cap—Buffalo Wild Wings, Steinway Music, Nu Skin
>
> *Please note: These stocks are not recommendations, just examples.*
>
> Example

What's a Value Stock?

You can find hundreds of definitions for value stocks, but in the simplest of terms, value companies are believed to be trading for less than what their worth is (on paper). They typically have a low price-to-earnings ratio, and they generally seek to issue dividends to shareholders. Utility companies, financial institutions, and heavy equipment manufacturers might fall into that category.

What's a Growth Stock?

Growth companies have a goal of continuing to "grow" the company. They do this by allocating profits they earn into research and development so that they can continue to roll out new and improved products. Growth stocks typically do not pay dividends. Technology and computer services and consumer goods will often fall into this category.

What's the Fascination with Stocks?

For a very long time, the most popular way of investing was to work with a stockbroker who would buy and sell stocks for you. At the time, your broker would take your order over the phone, you'd send the broker a check in the mail, and then you would wait for a stock certificate to arrive. Upon receipt, you'd run your certificate down to the safe deposit box. And then, ninety days later (in most cases), you would look for the quarterly dividend check in your mailbox. That dividend check was "mad money" for some—and lifestyle income for others.

According to my mother-in-law, people didn't trust the brokerage world back in the sixties, seventies, and eighties. Holding a stock certificate in hand rather than having it listed on a brokerage statement felt more secure.

I honestly think that's the main reason so many people born between 1910 and 1939 continue to have certificates stuffed away in safe deposit boxes, personal safes, shoe boxes, and underwear drawers.

What You Need to Know About Stock Certificates

If you've purchased individual stocks lately, you probably didn't receive a stock certificate in the mail. In fact, very few companies issue stock certificates anymore. Not only is it costly to produce and mail them to you, but the likelihood of misplacing the shares is also very real. If you lose or misplace a stock certificate, replacing it costs money—sometimes up to 2 percent of the stock's value.

Yes, a Stock Certificate Might Look Pretty, But…

Owning stock certificates in a safe deposit box or underwear drawer is very dangerous. Today's brokerage accounts will safely hold, maintain, and report the value of your shares on a daily basis.

Just think. If you died, became incapacitated, got divorced, changed your name, or simply couldn't find the key to the safe deposit box, who would know that you own these shares—not to mention where they're located?

Uninspired

Today, most shares of stock are held in brokerage accounts or with transfer agents. These companies guarantee the safekeeping of your shares and can more easily accommodate registration changes to the account, stock splits, and cost-basis reporting. (Don't worry if the previous terms made your eyes glaze over. I'll explain them later on in the book.)

If you still hold stock certificates, please, please, please be smart—be a genius—and deposit them into a brokerage account (not a safe deposit box). Here are just a few reasons why:

- Death. If you were to die, who would know whether the stock certificates even existed?
- Stock splits. If your stocks split, many companies now automatically send your new shares to a transfer agent rather than to you in certificate form. Who's keeping the records?

- Cost basis. Are you maintaining record of what you paid for the stocks you own? In a brokerage account, that information can be posted to your statement for safekeeping.

- Change of registration. Let's say you want to establish a trust—or you get married or divorced. How easy will it be to change the registration printed on your certificate? How much time will it take, and at what cost? Most brokerage accounts require your signature on a form and proof of the new registration information. And guess what? They'll usually do it for free.

Buying Stocks for the Dividend

Yes, some stocks pay dividends. If that's a strategy that makes sense for your portfolio, keep them. However if you own a stock for the dividend alone and you're not worried about the fluctuation of the stock price, you may be putting your portfolio in danger.

Ownership of stock used to be a status symbol. Just think. You owned shares of a company! You had loyalty to the firm. When you went to purchase your fifteen-pound, avocado-green rotary telephone at the local five-and-dime, you could say "I own some of AT&T."

Over the past few decades, the financial services world has exploded. Technology has vastly improved, and the regulation of the securities industry is at its highest level. Most firms today insist that you hold your stocks with a brokerage firm—or at least a transfer agent, such as Computershare or BNY Mellon.

Today, you can buy and sell stocks within microseconds of one another.

What Causes Stocks to Move?

Stocks move on perceptions and beliefs of what *might* happen in the future, not so much on what has happened in the past. That's why the stock market is viewed as a forward-looking indicator and analytical measurement that attempts to explain the direction of future economic conditions.

Observation

Owning Stocks in Certificate Form versus Brokerage Account

I live in New England, and as such, we have many clients who worked for "The GE." During Jack Welch's tenure as CEO at GE, the stock price exploded. Many "average Joe" workers saw their wealth increase dramatically in their GE Savings & Security Program (the retirement plan) as well as the stock purchase program.

Upon retirement, many retirees found themselves holding 60 to 100 percent of their retirement assets in GE stock. A dangerous position, for sure, but those who worked for GE from 1965 to 2000 (a thirty-five-year-year career) watched the stock grow more than 6,000 percent in value. At its high in 2000, it sold for close to $60 per share. In 2009, it dropped to as low as $10. Around that same time, GE cut its dividend by 68 percent (from $1.24 per share to 40 cents per share), yet many people still held on. Do you know why many retirees didn't sell their shares of GE? Because despite GE's dramatic drop in value in 2009, they still had large capital gains. Many stockholders/retirees were willing to stomach the new smaller dividend from GE rather than pay the tax on the sale of the stock and reinvest their money somewhere else.

There were a number of people who did elect to sell their GE shares during the financial meltdown. Most of them held their shares in brokerage accounts or could view the value of their shares online. Every day, they were able to watch the share price move lower and lower until, finally, they couldn't sleep any longer and felt the need to sell.

But there was a large group of older individuals, longtime owners of GE, who had their shares in safe deposit boxes. They had learned to ignore price fluctuations and instead count on the dividend. Many of those people have been rewarded, as GE has worked diligently to raise its dividend again as well as increase its share price.

Small Talk

Have you ever gone to a cocktail party where attendees wanted to talk about the poor decisions they made in the stock market?

Observation

Individually, you and I can't move the direction of a stock, but when a collection of people or institutions begins to show increased or decreased interest in the management, product development, or messaging of a public company, the stock price has a tendency to move. One way public companies attempt to temper the movement of their stock prices is to utilize their public relations departments. These groups of professionals build messages about profitability, new product launches, changes in management, and overall operations in a "read between the lines" manner. It allows the media, traders, institutions, and people like you to make their own decisions on whether to buy, hold, or sell a stock.

Risks Associated with Owning Individual Stocks

The ability to buy and sell individual stocks is easier today than ever before. With access to the Internet, you can open an online brokerage account and trade stock within minutes. But is trading stock a strategy for a retirement plan? It's really a matter of how much risk you're willing to take—not to mention how much time you're willing to commit to following the stock.

It frustrates me when I see investors making buy or sell decisions on an individual stock based on "the telephone game principal," which means to place a trade after watching a sound bite that made its way to them via the news, CNBC, a blog, a website, or a newsletter. Why can't there be more geniuses like you who know that sound bites are highly edited collections of data interpretations? Later in this book, I'll share some investment principles that have been effective for retirees. I can assure you of this: Actively trading stocks will not be one of them.

When Buying Individual Stocks Can Be Russian Roulette

If you have the wherewithal to research individual stock for your own portfolio, you have unlimited resources. Here are a couple:

- The Internet. There are thousands of websites that offer commentary, charts, and outlooks for each and every stock traded on an exchange. While the tools are available to do your own research, is it really possible to know more than some individual or firm that consistently follows a stock every single day? I think not. And after all, we all know that everything you read on the Internet is true. Right? Not!

- The media. I'll pick on Jim Cramer because he's probably the most widely known and visible stock-picking aficionado in the public's eye today. I remain fascinated by Cramer's following. I can't tell you how many times I've gotten calls in my office asking about buying the "XYZ" stock that Cramer just mentioned on TV. Let's remember that Cramer's number-one job—the job of CNBC—is to be entertaining. After all, CNBC is an affiliate of General Electric (GE), a publicly traded company. GE's primary function is to increase shareholder value. One way to do that is for its NBC affiliate to be profitable. It becomes more profitable by selling more expensive ads. And if you know anything about the advertising business, you know that having more viewers leads to higher advertising revenue. That's why the Super Bowl is the home of the most expensive thirty-second commercial spot each year.

While Cramer might offer a caller on his show, *Mad Money*, a "buy, buy, buy" recommendation or a "sell, sell, sell" recommendation, he's making that decision based on what he believes is the outlook for a stock on that day. He's entitled to change his mind—and he does. Unfortunately, there are multitudes of stories about people who hear a talking head talk about a stock they like without realizing that the talking head has a right to sell a stock in his portfolio without sharing that info with everyone.

One final thought. Before venturing into buying stocks on your own, consider the amount of time you'll need to dedicate to managing your portfolio while at the same time crafting a strategy to create a retirement income stream to support your lifestyle. It's a lot of work.

The smartest way to get real information about a stock is through a real professional who, on a firsthand basis, meets directly with the management company of the stock and has boots on the ground." Honestly, you and I can't do that, and the genius in you knows that most talking heads can't either. Don't worry. In the next chapter, I will introduce you to people who can.

To Summarize...

- The term *risk* means more than just "I could lose money."
- Individual stock ownership is a very aggressive strategy for individuals.
- Beware of buying a stock solely for the dividend.
- It's time to get rid of your stock certificates and place them into brokerage accounts.

Chapter 8

Investing in Mutual Funds

In This Chapter...

- The most popular investment for retirees
- Do you know what you're paying?
- The pros and cons of mutual fund ownership
- What about ETFs?

I'm a huge proponent of mutual fund ownership, and I'm not alone. Mutual funds have become the primary investment tool for people all around the world. Whether it's saving for a grandchild's education, putting money aside for retirement, or needing to craft a strategy to draw money to support your income needs, mutual funds have become the preferred investment choice for many Americans.

Yet, despite millions of people owning mutual funds, only a small percentage of people actually understand what they own.

What Is a Mutual Fund?

Mutual funds help individual investors have many of the advantages associated with large institutional investors. A mutual fund is essentially a bucket that allows individuals, businesses, institutions, etc., to pool their money (no matter how much) and have equal access to a pile of investments that are professionally managed within a stated investment objective.

What's the Fascination with Mutual Funds?

The first mutual fund was created in 1927. Today, the mutual fund has become the most popular way for individuals to invest in the fabric of our economy. In 2013, more than 53 million households and 92.4 million individuals owned mutual funds. People like you and me control 86 percent of the $11.7 trillion in total mutual fund value, according to a report by Investment Company Institute (November 2012). More than 80 percent of people with household incomes in excess of $100,000 currently own mutual funds.

Americans continue to embrace the mutual fund story. It is far from a fleeting fad. Just look at how the number of mutual funds has skyrocketed over the past few decades. Some people would argue that there are over twenty-two thousand mutual funds—clearly a number much larger than shown in the following chart. That's because most mutual funds contain several share classes.

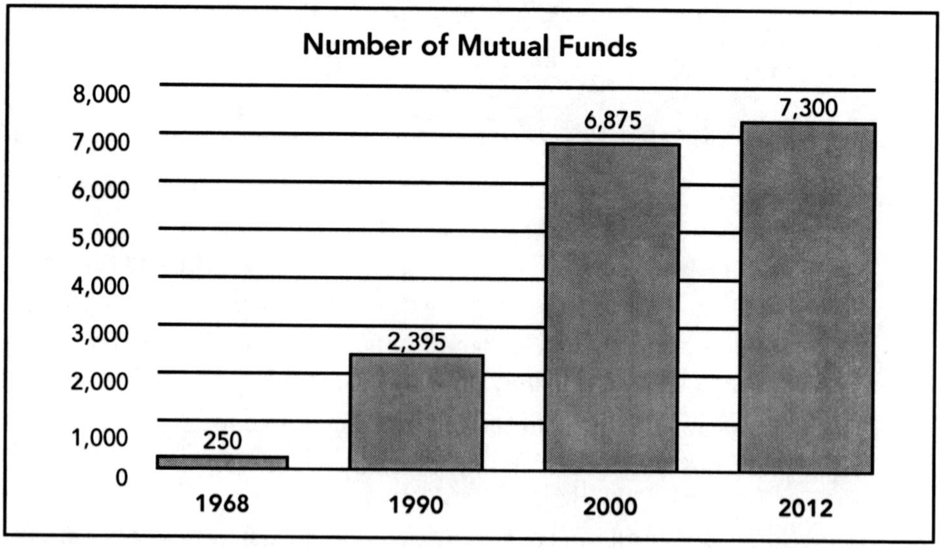

Source: morningstar.com

What Is a Share Class?

Grab one of your statements that holds a mutual fund. I don't care if it's a brokerage account, your 401(k) plan, or even a statement printed directly from a mutual fund company. Chances are, you'll see a share class letter. Yes, there are lots of different share classes—better known as mutual fund alphabet soup. Share classes help financial institutions discreetly categorize how you as the shareholder pay to own the fund.

Below are some of the most common:

- No load
- Class A shares
- Class B shares
- Class C shares
- Class I shares
- Class M shares
- Class Z shares
- Class A shares (load waived)

No-Load Fund

Individuals who elect to buy mutual funds on their own can purchase no-load funds. There are no sales charges to buy these funds. If you turn around and sell them, there are no surrender fees to get out. The only costs you incur are ones that are built into the operating costs of the fund—but those fees apply to every fund.

Many advisers also elect to use no-load funds as a means of helping clients build portfolios. Instead of you paying a sales charge, the adviser tacks on a fee that can run between 0.5 and 2 percent. (It's usually dependent on the amount of money invested.)

Pure No Load versus No Load

Many no-load funds carry a built-in extra marketing cost. It's called a 12b-1 fee. The expense is used to pay for marketing costs at the fund company level. However, there are many other funds that are considered "pure no load."

These funds do not have 12b-1 fees; however, they can build marketing costs into their operating expenses if they so choose.

The point is that every fund costs money, although costs vary among funds. It's important that you do your own due diligence when building a mutual fund portfolio.

Class A Shares

Class A shares carry up-front sales charges that can range from 1 to 5.75 percent, depending on the amount of money you invest. You don't write an extra check to cover the cost of the charge. Instead, it is automatically built in to the price of your investment on the first day you make your purchase. The cost to purchase the fund will be reflected in the market value on the day after you place the buy order.

For example, if you invest $50,000 into the XYZ mutual fund and the sales charge is 5 percent, your fund will show a value of $47,500 on the first day when you look it up online (assuming the investment performance was flat for the day). In order to recoup your cost, the fund would need to earn about 5.26 percent on the investment prior to you seeing any gain on the fund.

The more you invest in Class A shares of one fund family, the more eligible you become for a lower sales charge. Fund companies list the breakdown in their prospectuses, but be sure to note that every fund company has varying break points.

Example of Break-Point Charges for a Class A Mutual Fund

Amount of Investment	Sales Charge
Less than $25,000	5.75%
$25,000 to $49,999	5.00
$50,000 to $99,999	4.50
$100,000 to $249,999	3.50
$250,000 to $499,999	2.50
$500,000 to $749,999	2.00
$750,000 to $999,999	1.50
$1 million and above*	0.00

**A 1% fee could be imposed if liquidated within twelve months.*

(Fund) Family Benefits

Most mutual funds offer a variety of types of investment options in their family of funds. When buying Class A shares, you want to stick with one fund family and utilize the choices from the group. In doing so, you take advantage of break points (a lower sales charge).

Beware of advisers who steer you toward different fund families when purchasing Class A shares. You could be missing out on lower fees, and the adviser could be earning more money without you even knowing it.

Determining the right mutual fund mix is an individual decision. There can be benefits for owning a variety of fund families or for simply selecting one family. However, when it comes to buying Class A shares, it's important that you understand the benefits of break points.

IMPORTANT!

Class A—Load Waived

Generally these shares are purchased under two conditions:

1. The funds are purchased on behalf of a family member who works for a mutual fund company.
2. They are part of a fee-based investment program.

Generally, employees of mutual fund firms and their immediate family members have the opportunity to purchase Class A shares without having to pay the sales charge. It's no different from a perk that's offered to an employee at Macy's who receives a discount on clothing. This is referred to as load waived.

In recent years, many financial advisers have offered load-waived funds through fee-based or fee-only programs. This is when an adviser charges you an annual investment advisory fee to build a portfolio. This has become a popular option because investors gain access to popular commission-based funds (at employee pricing—load waived).

In both cases, the load waived is like buying the mutual fund at the wholesale price instead of the retail price.

Class B Shares

Class B share mutual funds are less and less prevalent today. One major reason is that they were mis-sold to the investing public. Class B share mutual funds can look and feel like no-load funds—but they are not!

When you make your investment, the value doesn't drop the next day in direct correlation to the sales charge you would have paid in a Class A fund. Instead, the Class B share fund carries a deferred sales charge.

The surrender charge is generally on a declining scale.

Year of Investment	1	2	3	4	5	6	7
Surrender fee	5%	4%	3%	3%	2%	1%	0%

Class B shares are sold by investment professionals. They earn commissions of between 4 and 5 percent when you buy the funds.

IMPORTANT!

The 12b-1 Fee

Often referred to as a marketing or servicing fee, many mutual funds, including load, no-load, and load-waived funds, carry a 12b-1 fee. The cost is located in the prospectus and in many fact sheets. It ranges anywhere from 0.25 to 1 percent. Just because you don't pay a load doesn't mean that you're not paying the 12b-1 fee.

Who keeps the 12b-1 fee? It varies. It is sometimes retained by the mutual fund company to help cover advertising costs. In other instances, it is paid to the investment adviser or the brokerage firm as a servicing fee. This fee is imposed on a quarterly basis (one-fourth of 0.25 percent) for the lifetime of your ownership. These are the costs that can add up. If you're paying them, make sure you know who gets them and how they are being used to your benefit. Hopefully if your financial planner is receiving this fee, it is because ongoing advice and service are being provided to you.

Institutional shares of mutual funds and some funds listed as "pure no load" do not generally carry 12b-1 fees.

Where does the money come from to pay the investment salesperson when there is no sales charge imposed up front? The answer? It's built into the operating costs. Typically the internal operating expense of a Class B share fund is almost 1 percent more than a Class A share fund.

Class C Shares

Class C shares are referred to as level-loaded funds. You generally pay a 1 percent up-front fee and then a continual 1 percent fee every year thereafter. I am not a fan of C share funds, unless you are going to hold them for only a short period (two years or less). Funds that are sold exclusively through investment professionals carry a 1 percent fee that you as the

Example

Declassifying Mutual Fund Share Class Expenses

Fidelity Investments is among the largest mutual fund families in the country. I've chosen one of its popular funds to display the expansiveness of share classes offered. For the most part, investors are all buying the "same fund," yet they are paying different costs.

Here's an example:

Fidelity Adviser Growth and Income	Front-End Sales Charge	Operating Expense	12b-1 Fee
FGIRX—Class A	5.75%	1.04%	0.25%
FGIRX—Class A (load waived)	0.00	1.04	0.25
FGISX—Class B	0.00	1.81	1.00
FGIUX—Class C	0.00	1.76	1.00

Source: morningstar.com, November 2013

In addition to the funds listed above, Fidelity offers many other variations of the same growth and income fund with different share classes.

investor never see on your statement. It is deducted internally; thus you may think that you're not paying any charges/fees at all.

Stockbrokers and investment salespeople who sell Class A, B, and C shares are not subject to a "fiduciary responsibility." This is an ongoing responsibility to "place the investor's interests first." Instead, they are subject only to a "suitability standard." This means that the investment salesperson needs to check only that the investments being sold to you are "suitable" based on the information you shared about your financial situation. They *do not* need to put your interests ahead of their own.

Class I Shares

These are institutional shares, and they are generally available when you have the ability to make large initial investments—typically $500,000 or more into one fund. Corporations, endowments, and very wealthy people who seek to use the services of a mutual fund manager directly generally buy Class I shares.

Good News for Retirees

More Americans are gaining access to Class I shares through registered investment advisers (RIAs) who offer fiduciary investment services for a fee to clients. As long as the firm they represent has enough money invested to meet the mutual firm's large minimum, you can access these share classes quite easily. Institutional shares do not have 12b-1 fees. Financial planners charge an investment advisory fee for access to these funds as well as additional services and benefits.

Which Share Class Is Right for You?

Choosing the right investment share class is a personal choice. If you are a do-it-yourselfer, look to purchase pure no-load funds through companies such as Schwab, Vanguard, Fidelity, or other discount brokerage firms.

If you're seeking the services and advice of a professional financial planner, consider what services you'd like to receive. If you have investable assets in excess of $250K and want to get both comprehensive financial planning advice and investment management services, I'd encourage you to work with someone who can providc Class I shares and Class A load-waived shares. Make sure, though, that the financial planner plans to offer more than just investment management services for the fee you pay.

If you're investing under $200,000 and you're just looking for investment services for a long-term investment strategy, consider Class A share funds when using a financial planner. Or, if you're a do-it-yourselfer, consider a no-load mutual fund family.

How Do Mutual Funds Make Money?

Have you ever walked into a mutual fund's headquarters? I promise you this: You're not going to find paneling on the walls, shag carpeting, and metal folding chairs. Mutual fund companies are among the most profitable business models in the country and have some of the poshest office environments in the world. Yet despite the incredibly high profit margins, investors seem to think they can buy no-load mutual funds for free. That's just not true.

Who do you think paid for the Fidelity green arrow or those hilarious ads from Invesco? You did! What about the fancy skyscrapers that carry the names of other leading investment firms? All funds make money by deducting a very small percentage every day—yes, every day—from the mutual fund you own. It's referred to as operating expenses. The problem is that it's hidden. The fee is deducted every day before the share prices are printed in the paper.

Operating expenses can pay for overhead expenses, management costs, marketing, and more. To find the operating expense of a mutual fund you own, type its symbol into any personal finance website, and you'll find out.

Great Reasons to Own a Mutual Fund

Now that I've given you all the "expensive" news about mutual funds, it's time for you to understand why I love them so much. Unlike stock investors, mutual fund investors gain the following advantages:

- Access to professional money management. Managers of mutual funds have one primary task: Make money for shareholders. That's you.
- Diversification. Mutual funds, by the guidelines of their prospectus, can have upward of hundreds of stocks or bonds in the portfolio.
- Low minimums. Usually $1,000 (or sometimes even less) can get you access into a mutual fund.
- Systematic investing and withdrawals. It's easy to add money automatically or have it sent to you (or your bank account) from the fund on a regular basis. (An important feature in retirement!)
- Thousands of flavors. The choices are abundant. If you want a basket of blue-chip stocks, small start-ups, emerging market positions, dividend-paying stocks, or a collection of stocks and bonds, they are all available for the taking.
- Daily liquidity. You can sell or buy shares on any business day.
- Your investments are separate from the assets of the mutual fund company. If a mutual fund goes out of business, you can know that your investments are held with the independent custodian and not commingled with the assets of the mutual fund firm.

Disadvantages to Owning Mutual Funds

There are also some disadvantages:

- Delayed holdings reports. Portfolio managers announce holdings on a delayed basis.
- Cost. Every mutual fund has an operating expense.
- Commissions.
- Not as advertised. Sometimes fund names don't truly reflect the composition of the portfolio.

- "Diworsification." Owning several mutual funds that all own the same stocks.
- End-of-day pricing. Mutual funds do not trade on a minute-to-minute basis. They are priced once at the end of the day.
- Capital gain distribution. Managers are not generally tax conscious when managing funds. That's because they pass all internal gains and losses on to you.

What Is a Portfolio Manager?

A portfolio manager is hired by an investment company with the sole responsibility of buying and selling stocks for an investment portfolio. These managers have a direct line to the lead management and key personnel of publicly traded companies. In a sense, they have direct access to information. They have a team of analysts who each and every day review stocks, build competitive analyses, and craft buy and sell targets for every stock in the portfolio. They also project insight into future operations, new products, management changes, and more. These analysts regularly attend conference calls so that they can hear firsthand about the future prospects of the company as well as explanations of why a company missed profitability targets during the previous quarter.

You versus the Portfolio Manager

If you're an individual investor, you may subscribe to research services or follow newsletters, websites, and more. But the truth is that the information you're receiving is left for you to decipher and assimilate. Chances are, you don't have a team of analysts helping you with your research, nor do you have the ability to monitor hundreds of stocks full time.

If you use a stockbroker or investment salesperson, don't be fooled. These people are not portfolio managers. Besides servicing your needs, they must gather new clients, serve their existing clients, manage staff, fill out paperwork, and more. They simply can't research stocks all day. It's impossible. The truth is, most financial advisers spend less than 30 percent of their day monitoring portfolios.

WATCH OUT!

Beware of "Special Distributions"

Be cautious when adding money to nonretirement mutual funds in the last quarter of each year. Toward the end of the year—often in December—portfolio managers can pay a "capital gain distribution," which can represent all of the accumulated realized gains (profits they've made in their funds) over the course of the year.

The share price of the fund includes all of these gains and must be distributed (usually at the year's end). When this distribution is made, it is taxable to all shareholders. It also causes the mutual fund to drop proportionately by the capital gain distribution, leaving investors wondering why the share price shrunk.

Here's an example of a made-up fund:

The Atomian mutual fund sold for twenty dollars per share on December 15, 2013. On December 20, it issued a two-dollar-per-share capital gain distribution to all shareholders of record as of that date. In doing so, the fund dropped to eighteen dollars per share, but all shareholders received a two-dollar-per-share distribution as cash or to reinvest. Either way, in nonretirement accounts, the distribution was taxable. From a valuation standpoint, the fund was worth about the same amount on the day of the distribution (if you reinvested the distribution). That's because you just bought more shares. If you multiplied the new number of shares by the new share price, you'd find that the account value was roughly the same.

Can you guess why I'm advising you to be a cautious investor in November and December? Imagine you just sent $50,000 to Atomian on November 20. On December 20, the day of the capital gain distribution, your account value is still the same. But surprise! You would have received a 1099 in January reflecting that 10 percent, or two dollars per share of your investment, was subject to taxes.

If you want to avoid buying into capital gain distributions, it's pretty simple. Contact the mutual fund company and ask for the date you can invest that would be after the distribution is declared (called the declaration date).

If you use a financial adviser who isn't advising you about potential capital gain distributions in your portfolio, it's time to find another adviser.

The Prospectuses

Every mutual fund comes with an owner's manual. It's called a prospectus. This legal document serves as the instruction template for, among other things, the mutual fund's investment policy guidelines. You can also find information on costs, previous holdings, past performance, risks, portfolio manager information, and more. Unfortunately, these manuals aren't written in the most user-friendly manner.

What Are Asset Classes?

One of the most commonly used terms that characterizes a mutual fund is "asset class." Asset classes help investors better understand the size, strength, and core fundamentals of a company.

When we meet with clients, we drop the names of funds and stocks that they own directly into a style box template (below). You can do the same for your own portfolio. Visit morningstar.com if you'd like to learn the asset class for each investment you own.

Stock and Stock Funds

	Value	Blend	Growth
Large Cap	Dodge & Cox Stock	Oakmark International	Marsico Growth
Mid Cap	Artisan Mid Value		Baron Asset
Small Cap	Royce Special Equity	Columbia Emerging Markets	MFS New Discovery

Bond Funds and Cash

	Short	Intermediate	Long
Large Cap	Money Market	ING GNMA	Vanguard Long-Term Treasury
Mid Cap		Loomis Sales Bond	
Small Cap	Lord Abbott Low Duration	Artio High Yield	

Note: The above is an example and not a recommendation for investment allocations.

How Are Exchange Traded Funds Different from Mutual Funds?

Unlike a mutual fund that builds its portfolio with cash that moves in and out of the portfolio from investors, an exchange traded fund (ETF) works just the opposite. An ETF is built to track an index and starts with a collection of stocks. The collection becomes a fixed portfolio and is exchanged for shares that people can buy. These shares trade on the market and move in the same direction of their corresponding index. There is a fixed number of shares available, so supply and demand can impact the value of the ETF. Thus, if there are more buyers of a particular ETF than sellers, the price of the ETF might be selling for more than its market value. This is similar to how stocks move.

In addition, ETFs trade on the open market. As such, you can buy and sell ETFs just like you can buy stocks. When buying a mutual fund, you purchase your shares at the close of the day's business.

If you're a fan of reinvesting dividends, an ETF may not be the best option for you, as all dividends pay to cash. If you want to reinvest your shares, you may

Turnover Ratio

This is a percentage number that appears in most mutual fund profile sheets. It explain how often a portfolio manager buys and sells investments. A turnover ratio of 100 percent means that the manager is a very active trader. You can expect a higher than normal expense ratio and a more aggressive investing style.

Alternatively, a manager with a turnover ratio of less than 20 percent seeks long-term value from stocks. This is typically a more conservative fund and will generally have a lower expense ratio.

An index fund has a very low turnover ratio, as stocks are bought and sold from the portfolio only when the investment has been dropped or added to the index. Index funds have low expense ratios, and they typically rely on computer modeling to maintain the funds. After all, why pay a human being to mirror an index when a computer program can be built at a much lower, more efficient cost?

Definition

be subject to trading costs. Unfortunately, while ETFs might seem like a simple investment, like mutual funds, they come in many shapes and sizes. You want to be sure you understand what they represent and how they work before investing in an ETF. Some ETFs use very sophisticated investment strategies that I don't think most people should have as a part of their portfolio.

What's an Index Fund?

An index fund is a portfolio of stocks and/or bonds that is constructed to mirror a particular index, i.e., the S&P 500. The portfolio is proportionately balanced to an index. However, as shareholders add money or take money out of the index fund, the manager needs to buy more shares of each stock. This ensures that the index fund remains true to its objective. Index funds are called "passive mutual funds."

What Is Passive versus Active Management?

When purchasing a mutual fund, you need to decide whether it makes sense to mirror indexes (passive investing) or allow a manager to pick and choose investments (active money management) in a mutual fund in an effort to outperform an index. Some active money managers make multitudes of trades each year in a fund, while others make very few. This is called turnover.

Pure Genius!

Marc's Top-Ten List for Picking Mutual Funds

1. Fund size. Avoid new funds. Select a fund with at least $750 million in assets.
2. Manager tenure. Look for a minimum five-year track record (make sure the manager has a record of investing during market downturns) and rising interest rate environments.
3. Operating expenses. They should be at or under the industry average for the asset class.
4. Morningstar stars. Ignore stars. They are based on past performance.
5. Commissions/fees. Make sure you understand all your costs.
6. Avoid "diworsification." Buy several different asset classes.
7. Keep it simple. If you don't understand the types of investments the manager is buying, stay away.
8. Fund flows. Sell any fund that is named "Fund of the Year" and appears in a major publication. History suggest that the manager can't replicate past performance because of the incredible amount of money that will soon pour in to the fund.
9. Share classes. Make sure you understand all entry, exit, and ongoing costs prior to investing.
10. Capital gain distributions. Be a cautious investor in November and December if you're adding money to a mutual fund in a nonretirement account. Make sure you know when the capital gain distributions will be paid—and invest afterward.

Does Mutual Fund Investing Require Special Skills?

Anyone can buy mutual funds. As you can see from this chapter, though, trying to select the right mutual fund at the right cost is complex and confusing. Believe it or not, mutual fund buying is not an elective in college. Nor is it a degree you can earn at a university. However, many financial institutions are working hard to deliver education on helping you make smart, informed decisions when it comes to fund selection. After all, with more than 80 percent of people relying on mutual funds to support their income needs in retirement, it's imperative that you have some basic knowledge. It's my hope that this overview of mutual funds (albeit incomplete) has given you a launching pad.

In **Chapter 9**, we'll explore some of the other ways retirees are investing their money. Trust me—there is no shortage of "other" alternatives.

To Summarize...

- Utilizing mutual funds is the most flexible way to invest.
- All mutual funds come with fees. Be sure you understand all the costs involved.
- Make sure that your mutual fund portfolio is allocated among several asset classes. Neglecting to do so could lead to "diworsification."
- Prior to embarking on mutual fund look-alikes, such as ETFs, make sure you understand all the risks.

Chapter 9

Income-Based Investments Retirees Consider

In This Chapter...

- Owning bonds and bond funds
- Do bonds carry risks?
- Real estate investment trusts
- Does gold belong in a retiree's portfolio?
- A place for annuities

The use of bonds and other income-driven investments can provide a level of security in knowing that an income check is likely to arrive in your mailbox. But that doesn't come without risk. If interest rates increase, the value of bonds decreases. If interest rates stay low, CD rates, annuity payouts, and other interest-bearing investments pay a pittance.

In this chapter, we'll explore a variety of income tools that retirees are accessing in retirement. It's far from a complete list, as new products and offerings come and go every day. I'll focus on the most popular ones.

What Is a Bond?

Think of a bond as an agreement between you and a financial entity that agrees to accept your money (a loan) in exchange for providing you with an ongoing interest payment. At maturity, assuming the entity is still in business, your initial investment (referred to as the face value) is returned to you.

> **Knowledge Pays**
>
> *An investment in knowledge pays the best interest.*
>
> Benjamin Franklin
>
> Quote

Examples of Bonds

Just like stocks, bonds come in all shapes and sizes. They also carry varying degrees of risk. Below, we'll explore just a few different types of bonds that genius investors like you might own.

Treasury Securities

Treasuries are bonds that are issued by the US government to help finance the federal government's debt. Typically, they offer the lowest risk yet also pay the lowest interest rates as compared with other types of bonds. There are three different types of treasury securities. They are designated by the length of time needed to pay back your principal investment:

- Treasury bills (T-bills). Maturity from three months to less than one year.
- Treasury notes. Maturity from one to ten years.
- Treasure bonds. Maturity from ten to thirty years (or even more).

Agency Bonds

These are bonds that are issued to help finance government-sponsored mortgage programs, such as Ginnie Mae (GNMA) and Fannie Mae (FNMA). These bonds are not issued by the US government but are backed by its full faith and credit.

Municipal Bonds

These debt instruments are issued by states, cities, towns, and other government entities. Typically they are used to build bridges, roads, schools, hospitals, and other projects that benefit the needs of the public. They may be backed by the local government itself and, thus, are called general obligation (GO) bonds. Other municipal bonds may be backed by tolls, fees, etc., and are not backed by the government itself but by the project for which the bonds were issued.

Corporate Bonds

These securities are issued by companies, such as corporations that are seeking money to help finance the company or a particular project.

Interest Rates and Bond Movement

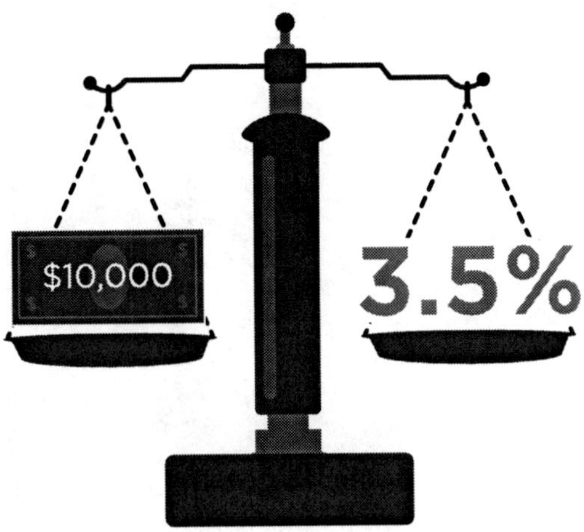

One of the best ways to illustrate how bond values change in an ever-changing interest rate environment is to imagine a scale.

Let's use the example of a $10,000 investment that pays 3.5 percent for five years. The stack of currency represents the $10,000 investment, and the percent sign is the promised payment of 3.5 percent each year. In this scenario, the scale is balanced.

Now let's imagine that six months later, another investor wants to buy a $10,000 bond that will come due in five years. Because interest rates have risen over the past six months, the investor can get 4 percent on the bond. In fact, the investor's scale looks just like yours, and it is balanced too. You begin to wonder whether you could sell your bond and buy one like the other investor's instead. Could you? Yes. But could you get $10,000 when you sold your bond to buy the better-looking one? No you couldn't. Here's why:

When you sell a bond, there needs to be a person who's willing to buy it. What buyer would give you $10,000 to take over the remaining interest payments on your 3.5 percent bond when, in the example above, a new buyer could get 4 percent on a newly issued bond today?

As such, if you wanted to sell your bond in an environment where interest rates on new bonds were higher than the ones you purchased, you'd need to accept a "discount" or reduction in face value in your bond—perhaps $8,800.

Just to be clear, the reverse happens in a falling-interest-rate environment. When current interest rates go down, the value of bonds people already own will increase.

As you can see, if you don't hold your bonds until maturity, you risk accepting more or less of the face value when you sell it. This is an example of interest rate risk.

Pure Genius!

Understanding Risk in Bonds

Let's say you invest $10,000 in a newly issued Treasury note paying 3.5 percent that matures in five years. Twice a year, you would receive an interest check for $175, because 10,000 x 3.5% = $350, and $350 ÷ 2 (times per year) = $175. At maturity, the Treasury Department would send you back your $10,000. Sounds pretty simple, right? But is it risk-free?

Treasury securities are backed by the "full faith and credit of the US government." Unless the United States goes out of business and defaults on its payments, you should feel confident that you will receive income payments and your money back at maturity.

But what if you want to sell your bonds prior to maturity? This is where the "risk" comes into play.

Bond values fluctuate daily in the open market. In reality, it is worth only its face value on its maturity date.

Default Risk on Bonds

The bigger, more painful risk to bonds is default. Just imagine if you loaned money to a company that agreed to pay you interest until maturity, but prior to maturity, the company shut its doors and went out of business. Think General Motors, Kodak, Lucent, Enron, and many more. It's very possible you'd never see the amount of money you loaned them ever again. That's a 100 percent loss of your money. Now that's painful.

Most bonds carry a "rating" that attempts to predict the claims-paying ability of the bond issuer. AAA, AA+, and A++ are all examples of high-quality bonds. If your bond carries a BB rating or less, you're likely to collect a higher interest rate, but you risk the uncertainty that the bond will be able to fulfill its full obligation of payments to you. Even the rating can sometimes be misleading. It was improper ratings in part that led to the fiscal crisis.

Managing Bond Risks

Earlier, I told you that bonds issued by the US Treasury were backed by the full faith and credit of the United States. There are lots of other entities though that offer bonds to individuals. They can be local municipalities (oftentimes referred to as muni bonds) or bonds issued by big companies, such as Coca-Cola, or small ones, such as Buffalo Wild Wings.

Let's play a game. Using the numbers 1 through 5, try ranking each of the bonds below in order of least risk to greatest risk (1 represents the least amount of risk).

Ranking	Bond
	Ten-Year Chiquita Banana Bond
	Ten-Year US Treasury
	Ten-Year Government of Greece
	Ten-Year Government of Belgium
	Ten-Year Coca-Cola

How did you do? Did you come up with 4, 1, 5, 3, 2?

Understanding Bond Price Movement

In a rising-interest-rate environment, the value of existing bonds drops in value. Conversely, in a falling-interest-rate environment, the value of existing bonds will increase.

Pure Genius!

According to ratings agencies surveyed in 2013, here's what each security earned:

- US Treasury—AAA (Moody's)
- Coca-Cola—AA (S&P)
- Belgian Government—A- (Fitch)
- Chiquita Brands—B/B1
- Government of Greece—B- (recently upgraded from CCC) (Fitch)

Picking the Bond That's Right for You

Like stocks and mutual funds, there are thousands of bonds from which to choose. One of the easiest ways to understand different types of bonds is to use a style box. This nine-block table helps illustrate bonds by using two major categories: length of maturity and risk of default. When each bond is plotted on the table, it is easier to understand why some bonds will pay higher interest rates than others.

I'll plot each of the bonds listed above into the following style box.

	Short Term (Less Than One Year)	Medium (One to Ten Years)	Long Term (Ten or More Years)
Low Default Risk		US Treasury Coca-Cola Bond	
Medium Default Risk		Belgian Government Bond	
Higher Default Risk		Chiquita Brands Bond Government of Greece Bond	

By viewing the style box above, it becomes easier to guess which bonds will pay a higher interest rate. Clearly, you'll need to get a much higher interest payment on a Greece bond than you would on a US Treasury bond.

Other Types of Investments

Stocks, bonds, and cash are commonly viewed as the trilogy of a great investment plan. Geniuses know there's more. But how much more complexity do you need in your retirement plan?"

When it comes to investing for retirement, stocks, bonds, and cash can address most of your needs. However, there are a few other alternative strategies that are worth exploration.

Alternative Investments

Investment advisers are desperate to introduce you to different breeds of investments—referred to as "alternative investments." They might include precious metals, commodities, real estate, hedging techniques, options, and more. With perhaps the exception of real estate, most individuals have no business investing in alternative investments. Typically, they have low liquidity, they aren't priced daily, they require large investment minimums, and they are simply too hard to understand—even for geniuses like you and me.

Owning Gold

I'm not a fan of owning gold—especially in retirement. Gold doesn't pay interest. It doesn't pay a dividend. Wear it around your neck, put on your wrist, or dangle it from your ears. But owning gold as a hedge against inflation is a tactical strategy that I've got a tough time endorsing.

Think back a few years ago when our television screens were smattered with gold buyers. "We'll give you *cash* for your gold," they would say. What happened to those ads? The marketing of gold, or any precious metal, for the purposes of investing is ridiculous for the average investor. I have never found a collection of retirees who could say that investing in gold was the secret to a successful retirement strategy.

Uninspired

Building a Golden Fortress

In 2007–2009, I met a man who believed that the downturn in the stock market would lead to a cataclysmic change in economic power in the world. He believed that the American currency would devalue and that the US government would become the laughingstock of the world. (He may have gotten the last part right.)

At any rate, he decided to cash in all his stocks and bonds so that he could buy gold. No, not gold mutual funds, not gold stocks, but actual bars and coins of gold.

He had a large safe built into his home where he would store the bars. We worked with him to find a company that would transport the bars in an armored vehicle directly to his home, videotape the delivery, and help him lock the safe.

His thought was that if the US dollar became worthless, he'd be "king of the mountain" with all that gold.

While the US dollar didn't devalue itself, the price of gold increased dramatically, and his net worth increased while others saw their wealth (on paper) diminish. He took his newfound wealth all in stride. That's because he believed that the worst was yet to come.

I asked him if the dollar became worthless how he believed his gold would be of value. He insisted that his gold would be the currency of choice, and if he held possession of gold, people would pay outrageous prices for it. Then I asked him how he might expect to pay for a Slurpee at 7-Eleven with his gold. Would he walk in with a diamond-plated carrot peeler and carve off a piece from his gold brick? He laughed—but only for a moment. He never considered how he would turn his gold back into a tradable currency. He also never considered that if gold was the currency of choice, our world would look dramatically different. And finally, unless he had an army of people to guard his gold, his home might get taken over and the gold could be stolen.

This humbling, but true, tale has yet to be resolved. Despite a strong pullback in the price of gold, he still has his bars and coins. Fortunately, he makes a very good living and is now accumulating cash.

Stick to the investment trilogy (stocks, bonds, and cash) as your core strategy. Buy gold when you want to treat yourself or give a gift.

Exploring a REIT

Take a moment to drive to the nearest metropolitan area. If you have someone else driving, go ahead and put a blindfold over your eyes and ask the driver to randomly drive up and down the streets. Periodically yell out the word "*stop*!" Point to the building and ask the driver to write down the address. Start the car and continue this exercise until you've identified twenty different buildings.

Now go back and visit each building with your blindfold off. Take a look at its architecture, tenants who rent here, and the neighborhood in general. Ask yourself, "In five years, will this real estate be worth more than it is today?" If you answered yes, a real estate investment trust opportunity may be worthy of your consideration.

Imagine if you had the opportunity to be a partial owner in a collection of commercial real estate buildings. They could be blue-chip high-rise buildings, first-class suburban offices, a group of golf courses, a series of shopping malls, etc. Now imagine what it would be like if tenants of your building had signed long-term leases and knew that paying their rent was a primary obligation. And what if, as an owner in this collection of real estate, you had the opportunity to get a portion of the rent each month/quarter? Intriguing, perhaps, but what if there was a recession and businesses needed to close? What if the neighborhood changed and became seedy? Would the valuations on the properties diminish? It's likely, so consider this. What if you could collect pieces of income from a series of properties, knowing that some of those properties could increase in value and others could have the potential to drop? Might that be a risk worthy of consideration? How might this investment be different from a bond or a stock?

More so, what if the stock market was going up? How might that affect the rent being paid by tenants? It probably wouldn't impact it at all. That's because, for the most part, stocks, bonds, and real estate investments are noncorrelated in price movement.

Correlation

In the world of investing, it's important to own assets that don't always move in tandem with one another. Investments that move in the same direction are referred to as "correlated." When one investment moves one way while another moves another, it's said that they are "uncorrelated." Historically, real estate investments do not correlate with stocks. When building a portfolio, it's important that your investments have a collection of noncorrelated assets.

Definition

How Is Investing in Rental Real Estate Different from REITs?

How would you like to be a landlord? If your answer is "no way," that's a quick indication that buying investment real estate may not be in your best interests. When you own real estate, you become landlord, property manager, plumber, electrician, help desk, negotiator, and guardian. Can you outsource these jobs? Certainly. But they all come at a price—and they all eat into your profit margin. However, if you are handy, can continue to hold on to great tenants, and own a piece of property that requires little upkeep, perhaps real estate ownership is for you.

Owning a REIT may make sense for you if you want to own real estate beyond your primary residence and want to collect an income check that equates to a portion of the rent collected on the property. It may also make sense if you feel more comfortable relying on professional management companies to negotiate rents, manage the property, handle the upkeep, address legal challenges, and keep your name off the title.

Annuities

One of the most popular investments offered to retirees today is annuities.

Annuities are investments offered by an insurance company. When you buy an annuity, you are given the benefit of tax deferral, regardless of the amount of money you invest. The privilege of tax deferral in an annuity comes at a cost, unlike in an individual retirement account (IRA). However, annuities can provide protection to your principal, provide guaranteed income, and more. These features come in the form of "riders," and they come at an annual cost to you. As an annuity buyer, you need to understand these costs,

Observation

Why Retirees Regret Real Estate Ownership

Owning and managing real estate property may be fun for a while, but in retirement, it can get tedious. There will come a time when wiggling under the sink to fix a leak, climbing a ladder to empty the gutters, and knocking on doors to collect the rent might begin to give hints that it's time to slow down.

Retirees tend to hold on to rental real estate for longer than they should. The necessity to meet "updating requests" from tenants will likely cause your patience to thin. Don't turn into the cranky old landlord who's living in the past.

As you age, the urgency to fix things isn't at the top of your mind. And asking for higher rents becomes "a battle not worth starting." As such, as the cost of managing the property increases and you carry the burden—rather than pass it on to a tenant.

Then without even knowing it, ten years have passed since you've put much serious money into the property. As you begin to think about its value—and how it might play into your retirement plan—you realize that in order to get what you think it's worth, you need to spend money. You grow angry. "I'm not putting another nickel into this place," you demand.

You then list the property for sale with an agent who tells you that you're asking far too much money for the property—because it needs a bunch of work. You grow stressed, and you wonder "Why did I ever decide to get into the real estate business in the first place?"

If you can relate to this scenario, perhaps it's time to put a "for sale" sign on the lawn or find someone else to manage the property. If you're thinking, "Marc has no idea what he's talking about," then you might be a great property manager and able to continue the role of landlord.

as they will impact the overall performance of your account. However, by having these riders, you are purchasing "insurance protection" that can deliver a solution you may need.

In all cases, you need to understand what annuities cost you and the impact they will have on your overall investment as compared with other investment alternatives you might consider. Remember, just because something costs more money than something else doesn't mean it's not worth it. Like with every important purchase in your life, make sure that you know what you're buying and what the costs are if you change your mind.

Annuities Come in All Shapes and Sizes

There are all kinds of annuities:

- Fixed annuity. You invest money so that you can earn a guaranteed rate of interest on a tax-deferred basis. (Rates are subject to change as listed in the annuity contract.)
- Variable annuity. You invest on a tax-deferred basis into a multitude of investment choices similar to mutual funds. These investments can fluctuate in value. They generally include a guaranteed death benefit.
- Indexed annuity. These investments are tied to an investment index (without actually investing in the index). The annuity company gives you downside protection and takes a piece of the growth when the account is up.
- Immediate annuity. You turn over an amount of money to an insurance company. In return, you are promised a guaranteed income stream for your life, for the life of your spouse and you, or for a particular number of years.

Most annuities include a surrender charge that is assessed to you if you withdraw more than 10 percent of the value of your account during the surrender period.

Annuities: the Answer to Your Woes—**Please!**

If you've ever run into an annuity salesperson, he'll be the first to tell you that the annuity is the answer to your retirement prayers. He'll tell you that it's because of annuities that retirees will never outlive their money—and that world peace is possible because of the brilliant actuaries who've developed these life-changing products. Yes, I'm exaggerating—a lot.

Annuities are a great product when sold in the right environment and with the best of your intentions in mind.

Think about it. When's the last time you went shopping for an annuity? Have you ever gone to your computer terminal and googled "how to research annuities" or "best annuities for people like me"? You probably haven't. In fact, I find that annuities become the answer to the question, "What else do you have to offer?"

Let me try this. How would you like:

- tax deferral;
- principal protection;
- a guaranteed death benefit;
- guaranteed income for life;
- the ability to invest in the stock market with protected downside risk;
- the stability of one of the world's largest insurance companies as your partner;
- the opportunity to select from among hundreds of investment choices;
- access to up to 10 percent of your money without any charges (if you're over 59½); and
- inflation protection?

Is this too good to be true? Can this really happen? If it can, why aren't they selling these babies on QVC by the millions? That's because there's more to the story—a lot more. But as the adviser starts sharing the risks and nuances of the product, you're too busy looking at the highlights of the annuity and sharp pictures of retirees enjoying life in comfort.

I'm not trying to give annuities a bad rap. In fact, I think they can make sense in a lot of people's overall retirement plans—but if sold without a full and complete understanding of your total situation, you could find yourself regretting your decision.

One of the most misunderstood features of annuities these days is the "guaranteed income benefit." After all, it sounds like a great opportunity. You get to put money aside for the future and then call upon a guaranteed income check from the annuity when it's time to start drawing money to support your needs.

Guaranteed Income Benefits in Annuities—Listen Carefully

One day I received a call into my radio show from someone singing the praises of an annuity she just bought. She said it would pay her 7 percent for the rest of her life. I asked her to tell me more about the annuity with hopes that this conversation could help educate others at the same time.

She told me that she invested $300,000 from her old 401(k) plan into an annuity at age sixty-five. Beginning at age seventy, she could take $31,500 from the account and lock that amount in forever!

"And when you die, what will be left to the kids?" I asked.

"The $300,000 plus any earnings!" she said.

Suddenly my stomach began to sour.

The listener had heard only part of what the salesperson had told her.

I probed further. "Besides the $31,500 that the annuity guarantees you, do you have access to any other money?"

"Oh yes," she answered. "I can take up to 10 percent of the account value at any time without paying a surrender charge. In fact, next year I can take $30,000 so I can buy a new car!"

This story was getting worse, not better, and the caller had no idea.

It was time to break the news to her.

I asked her to tell me the name of the product and the insurance company that issued it. Sure enough, I knew exactly the one she bought—as we had it available to our clients as well.

When I told her that if she planned to take any money from her annuity prior to beginning her guaranteed income payment, there was a strong likelihood she wouldn't be able to collect $31,500 per year at age seventy, she disagreed—initially. But after further thought, she realized that it may be true.

In addition, I told her that if she didn't touch the money until age seventy and then started the income stream as promised at $31,500, she would likely not have any money to pass on to the children. This is where she told me I was wrong—and defended the agent. She said that she bought a guaranteed death benefit rider so that she could protect her children upon her death.

I encouraged her to read the fine print. As expected, she reread the paragraph that stated that "guaranteed death benefit" was equal to the initial investment plus earnings, *less* any withdrawals. When I told her that her death benefit in all likelihood would be worth nothing by age eighty, she quickly said, "I need to call my agent back and check on this."

Before she hung up, I asked when she received her annuity in the mail. She said three days ago. I reminded her of the ten-day free-look period that's given to all annuity holders.

The following Sunday, she called the radio show again and told me that the agent didn't like me very much. He had just lost a $15,000 commission. She returned the annuity and expected to get a full refund. She then revisited her overall retirement plan before jumping into any single investment first.

Ten-Day Free Look

There's no secret. Annuities are confusing; there are all sorts of nuances. But in some cases, they can be a great solution for you. I've always found it quite rare when new annuity buyers can recite the benefits of the annuities they purchased and the rationale of why it made sense for them. It's probably the reason annuity companies have pledged to allow a ten-day free look of the policy upon issue.

This "free look" gives you the opportunity to revisit with your insurance agent, financial adviser, or other professional to ensure that the terms, restrictions, and benefits still make sense for you. If they don't, you can return the contract for a full refund, and the agent forgoes the commission. However, once the ten days pass, you must abide by the rules of annuity.

Avoid Investment Strategies Discussed on Financial News Shows

If you're looking for information on options trading, stock swaps, collateralized lending techniques or commodity plays, absolute return investing, structured products, and more, close the book. You won't find them here. That's because my experience suggests that less than 1 percent of the population is even qualified to be participants in these strategies, and only a fraction of those people understand how these esoteric products work. Just because they're talked about on CNBC doesn't mean they are suitable for your retirement plan. Stick with what you understand.

Later in this book we'll talk about integrating investment ideas into your retirement plan. We'll talk about Social Security—and perhaps why it's among the *most* misunderstood annuities out there. Believe it or not, all of those investments and income programs use stocks, bonds, and cash at their core too.

To Summarize...

- Bonds, which we once assumed to be "safe" investments, carry more risks than investors have ever imagined.
- Bond investing can be highly volatile during periods of significant interest-rate spikes.
- If you hold a bond until its maturity date, try hard to ignore its daily price.
- Retirees have no business purchasing investments they don't understand.
- The best risk-adjusted portfolios hold noncorrelating assets.
- Proceed with your eyes open when considering an annuity for your retirement income needs.

Chapter 10

Preparing to Invest Like a Genius

In This Chapter...

- The real investment return achieved by Americans
- Why tactical investing is a loser's game
- When diversification isn't what it seems
- The importance of rebalancing
- The return you want but rarely earn

The world of investments changes daily, and building a proper investment portfolio that aligns with your goals and objectives requires careful planning and ongoing monitoring.

In almost all cases, understanding your tolerance to volatility and knowing which risks you can stomach will become a primary temperature gauge for helping you select investments that work for you.

Financial Independence

Part of your heritage in this society is the opportunity to become financially independent.

Jim Rohn

Quote

Investment Principles That Geniuses (Like You) Need to Understand

Let's start with the truest truth about personal investing: *It's not rocket science.* Don't let anyone lead you to believe otherwise. As long as you have access to a calculator and can add, subtract, multiply, and divide, the basic principles around investing are relatively straightforward. What makes it complicated? This little thing called *emotion.*

As a genius, you know that it makes sense to *buy low* and *sell high.* You know that *investing for the long run* makes sense and that *past performance is not indicative of future results.* Right?

So, if we all know these basic truths, why do investors have horrible performance—especially over twenty-year time periods? The answer? Our emotions lead us to making boneheaded mistakes.

Uninspired

The Plight of the Do-It-Yourself Investor

According to a study by both Blackrock and Bloomberg, from 1992 through 2011 (twenty years), the average investor produced an annualized return of 2.1 percent. When you factor in an annualized inflation rate of 2.6 percent during the period, the average investor's net real return was –0.5 percent. Yes, you may have earned double-digit returns in certain years, but what was the average?

Retirees need to abandon many of the investment myths, old wives' tales, and lessons from the past. Neglecting to do so could lead to underperforming investments and an inability to achieve retirement success.

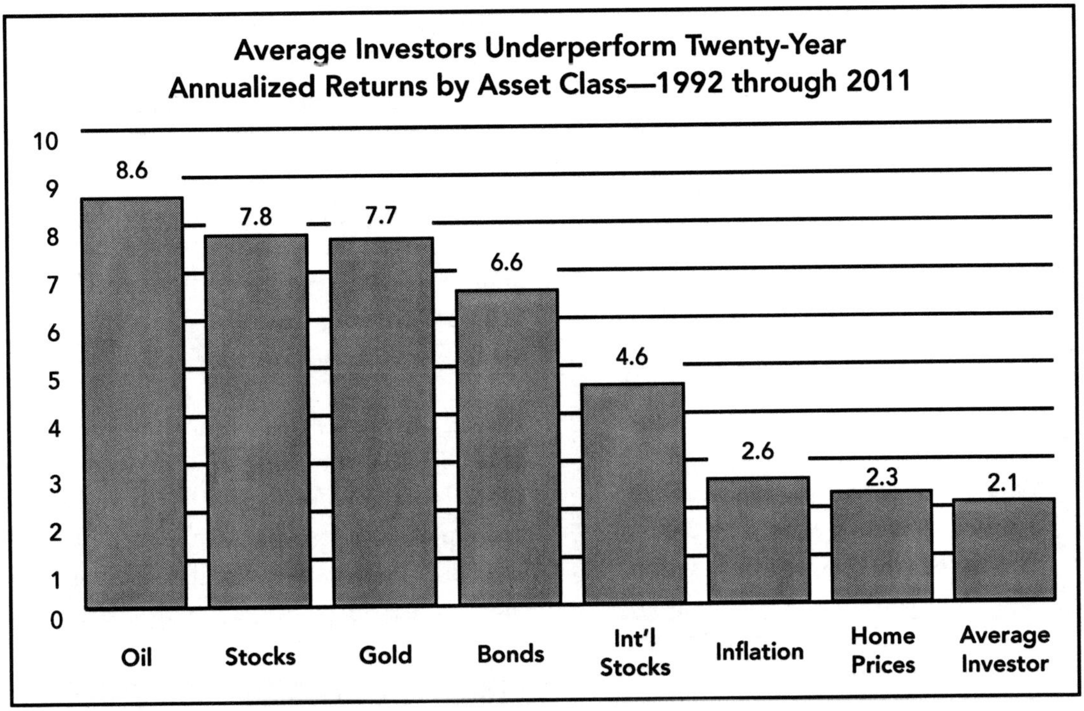

Our own emotions get us so wrapped up in trying to find the next great investment strategy that we forget the fact that investments need to serve a purpose. Achieving a solid rate of return in a given year is nice, but it's even better when consistency, patience, and goals lead the way. Chasing performance is a loser's strategy.

The secret to achieving investment success is knowing the following:

- Why you've chosen to invest
- How your investments fit into your overall financial planning strategy
- How much risk is necessary to achieve your overall goals

If you're inclined to chase the next best investment, you may be among the millions of investors with paltry returns. You can change that.

If your eyes are glued to CNBC, if your phone regularly alerts you to changes in your portfolio, and you start each day checking the futures indexes around

> **Stop Trading**
>
> Tactical investing doesn't work. Period. The only people who will attempt to convince you that it does are investment managers who are being paid to *be* tactical. Can you name any of those people on one hand? If you said Warren Buffet, you certainly named a smart investor, but he'd be the first to tell you that he's *not* tactical. Warren makes smart investment decisions and holds his investments for a very long time.
>
> So why is it that so many investors believe that they can outperform the market by making changes regularly to their portfolios? That's simple. Millions of people watch financial news channels every day. If the only advice they offered was "do nothing," you'd change the channel.
>
> Remember, CNBC, CNN, MSNBC, and Fox News are no different from ESPN, The Food Network, or TBS. They are all in the entertainment business. Trading stocks is "entertaining." Holding stocks is boring.
>
> Pure Genius!

the world, you're not ready for a peaceful retirement. Instead, you're preparing for a heart attack. Trust me. I've seen it happen.

Blaming the economic climate, our legislators, corporate America, and our country's budgetary woes for the problems with your investment portfolio is a waste of your time and energy. Focus on things you *can* control.

Investment strategies work when you take a lesson from Rip Van Winkle. Have a plan. Trust in your decisions. Go to sleep. Have pleasant dreams. Awake with no worries. Chances are, you'll have missed any bumps along the way.

When It Comes to Successful Investments, Ignore the Cocktail Party Chatter

Do you ever feel like "everyone else" is getting better returns than you? Do you dread going to a dinner party or social engagement because you can't stand all the grandstanding from people who love bragging about their big winner(s)? It's called "puffing." Investors are known for puffing up their investment returns by excluding the investments that did poorly or the money that's just sitting in cash.

I see this all the time. People walk in to my office and tell me how successful they've been at investing. What I find out, though, is that their successes are in a couple of individual stock purchases where they invested under $10,000 and doubled or tripled their money. Yes, you could call that a small victory, but it's rare when you find people who have invested the biggest portions of their portfolios in speculative investments that produced outstanding results.

Retirement planning is about getting serious with your money—and recognizing that investing for fun needs to be limited to a small fraction of your portfolio.

Avoid Investments You Don't Understand

Most people with investable assets of less than $2 million have no business investing in illiquid, misunderstood, or "bet *against* the house" types of investments out there. Speculative investing has become more and more prevalent with the recent volatility in the stock market. Yet it's rare to find that anyone would peg financial success over the past decade or more to investing in options, commodities, precious metals, absolute return investments, and structured products. If you have them in your portfolio, my guess is that you didn't put them there. They were probably recommended to you by an "investment guy." Even worse, you've likely forgotten they exist and are unaware of the risks they might contribute to your portfolio.

There is no place for these types of investments in your portfolio. Dump them, move on, and build a time-tested investment strategy.

Does Gold Belong in a Retiree's Portfolio?

If you were an owner of gold between 1992 and 2002, you were probably a frustrated investor. The price of gold fluctuated both up and down between $350 and $450 per ounce. Many people who owned gold during that time grew discouraged. They would watch television and hear reports about the greatest bull run in the history of the stock market. While everyone else (it seemed) was making money, their gold was stuck in a price rut. So they sold out and bought stocks. It seemed like an easy way to make money. Over the next ten years, the stock market was essentially flat. Its ten-year performance was close to 0 percent.

But what did gold do over the ten-year period from 2002 to 2012? It went on to touch $1,800 per ounce.

With gold prices rallying, marketers took advantage of the situation. They told stories about "how easy" it was to make money by owning gold rather than risking your money in the stock market. People of all ages would call my office asking how they could own gold stocks, gold mutual funds, and even hard pieces of gold. As the price of gold climbed from $1,300 an ounce to $1,800 an ounce, a buying frenzy ensued. People were abandoning bank accounts, stock portfolios, and even retirement plans so that they could buy gold. Investors asked their employers to include gold investment options in their 401(k) plans. But you know what happened next.

From October of 2012, the price of gold reversed its course, dropping more than 30 percent in value in less than a year. Guess what went up during the same time? That's right. The stock market.

In just a few years, we've seen a reversal in marketing. No longer is Alan Thicke of *Family Ties* fame promoting gold investments. The "we pay cash for gold" kiosks at your local shopping mall are gone. And those who decided to invest in gold in the midst of the hype are now trying to figure out their next investment strategy.

Why "Buy and Forget About It" (Hold) Works!

Did you know that the most successful investors of the past few decades were those who honored the time-tested strategy of holding tight and doing (almost) nothing? It's tough to do when a slick investment guy gets ahold of you on the phone or at a social event. It's even harder when repetitious advertisements lead you to believe that your approach is doomed to fail and that a newer approach would be better.

The Risks of Being Out of the Market

The following chart explains the unintended risks that individuals place on their portfolios when they attempt to get in and out of the market. As you can see, a passive approach—one that ignores the fluctuations of the market—historically performs better.

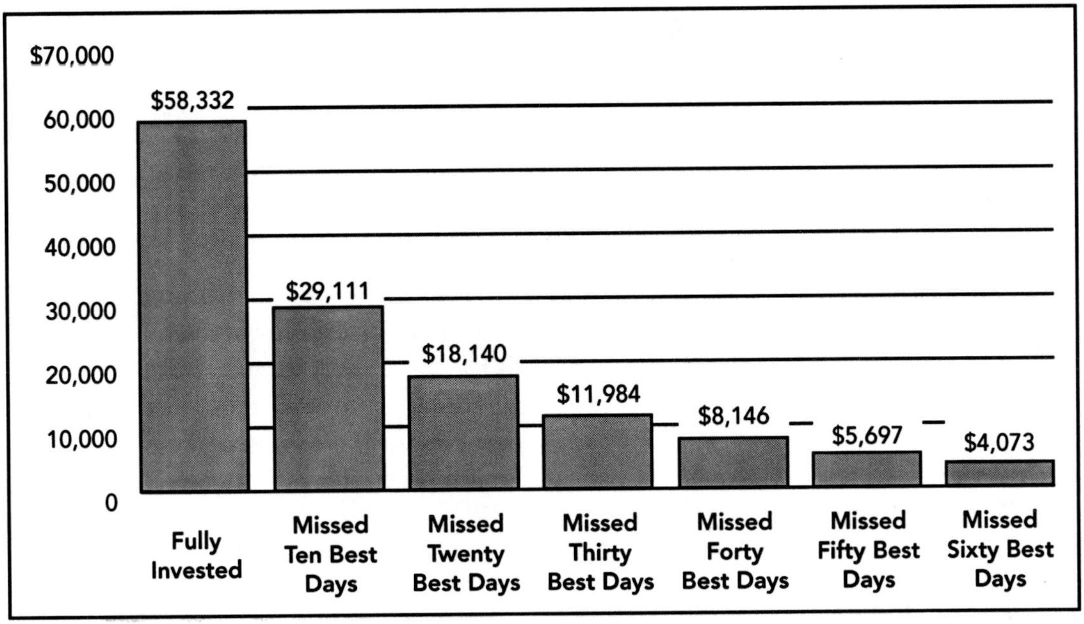

This chart is for illustrative purposes only and does not represent the performance of any investment or group of investments.

Source: Prepared by J.P. Morgan Asset Management using data from Lipper. Twenty-year annualized returns are based on the S&P 500 Total Return Index, an unmanaged, capitalization-weighted index that measures the performance of five hundred large capitalization domestic stocks representing all major industries. Past performance is not indicative of future returns. An individual cannot invest directly in an index. Data as of December 31, 2013.

My guess is that you know people—hopefully it's you—who decided to hold tight during the stock market crash of 2008–2009. Those people have smiles on their faces, don't they? They stared volatility in the eye—and let their confidence, patience, and belief in their investment strategy rule the day. Chances are, they are retiring with confidence.

Despite today's market volatility, the time-tested strategies of "buy and hold" and "asset allocation" consistently deliver solid long-term rates of return—despite what the media pundits tell you.

Geniuses know that smart investing doesn't require trading activity. Instead, investors succeed with discipline.

When economic conditions breathe fear or optimism into an investor's heart, human nature will drive irrational behavior. Whether it's investment success stories told by a colleague, an unfavorable newscast, or a Twitter post, investors tend to quickly lose sight of their long-term strategy. It seems that long term today is the 6 o'clock evening news—or, better yet, your next Twitter update.

Why Being Boring Will Serve You Well

Are You Two Times Better Than Everyone Else?

If you're interested in trading individual stocks for your investment portfolio, remember that you need to be right *twice* to achieve success. Not only do you need to know when to *buy* a stock, but you also need to know when to *sell* it to be a successful trader.

From 1997 to 2000, the day-trading companies popped up everywhere. Today, they are few and far between. If actively trading individual stocks was as easy as many believe, stockbrokers would have lines out their doors and day traders would still be gainfully employed.

Remember, the average investor scored an average 2.1 percent rate of return over the past twenty years.

Pure Genius!

I've watched people live through both very boring and very dangerous times in the stock market. Despite the gyrations in the stock market over the past couple of decades, a buy-and-hold-long-term strategy (that's attached to a solid retirement plan) has consistently been a recipe for success. It's because of that belief that calls to my office for interviews from national media outlets have dwindled.

Last year, a producer at Bloomberg News called my office for an interview, interested in getting my perspective on what was going on in Europe and where I thought the market might head. I told the producer the following:

"The news stories about Europe's troubles are just noise. In my opinion, Europe's challenges won't have any long-term negative effect in the United States. As for the direction of the market? I really don't care about where it goes this week or even this month. Long-term investors know better. Yet I remain confident that the market will be higher five years from now."

Similar to the reason you don't read headlines that say "Millions of School

Children Arrive Safely at School," the reporter quickly thanked me for my response and said, "We're looking for a more dynamic opinion than yours. Thanks for your time."

Was I insulted? Not really. But I did feel bad for viewers who later listened to two "experts" offering radically extreme sound bites.

In a split-screen interview with the Bloomberg anchor, one financial expert said that the crisis in Europe would devastate the world economy and global markets could drop up to 40 percent in the next twelve months. (That never happened.) The other prognosticator offered a forty-five-second dissertation of highly academic prose that most Harvard MBAs would have a tough time deciphering. Nevertheless, he "sounded" intelligent.

Ignore the Media for Advice

Newspapers, television, Internet, and all forms of social media are in the entertainment business. If there is no hook, no shock value, or no tug on your heartstrings, you're likely to change the station. Today's news doesn't have to be true for everyone; it just needs to reflect the story or perspective of one person. If told well, a story will sell ads and boost ratings for a network.

Should You Trust Wall Street?

Certainly after the collapse of Bear Stearns, the credit crisis, the Madoff scandal, and the subprime mortgage debacle, individuals lost faith in one of America's most regulated and profitable institutions. But avoiding investments in the stock market is a mistake—plain and simple.

The stock market is the thermometer of America's pulse. If you believe in the faith and future of this country, straying away from stock market investing may actually be—dare I say—unpatriotic.

Can you trust in the future of the economic fiber of private industry in America? Absolutely! Yet selecting individual stocks is a dangerous game—and one not necessary for retirees. Instead, rely on the 24/7 attention of mutual fund companies and their highly skilled portfolio managers. They have a much better probability of understanding the pulse of a company.

What Does "Putting All Your Eggs in One Basket" Really Mean?

We've all heard the term "don't put all your eggs in one basket." Yet, over time, some retirees have so many baskets that they lose track of what they actually own. Perhaps this sounds like you:

- Do you maintain relationships with multiple investment professionals, financial advisers, and insurance agents?
- Do you have investments spread among several different financial institutions, mutual fund companies, and insurance firms?
- Do you maintain accounts with multiple banks?
- Are investment statements scattered in different places around your home?
- Do you keep stock certificates in a safe deposit box, some in a dividend reinvestment account, and others in your underwear drawer?
- Do you hide cash around your home?

Conceptually, these all might seem like responsible strategies, but as you head into retirement, simplicity—as you'll soon see—is very important. Successful retirees achieve success by keeping their eggs in different containers while having them all organized in one big basket.

The Simplified Approach to Managing Your Money

How likely was it that your parents shared information about their personal financial situation? You may have seen the names of brokerage firms, insurance companies, banks, and more—but only for the piles of envelopes that landed in your mailbox each month. Did you ever wonder if any of these firms knew Mom or Dad's whole financial story? In reality, your parents probably didn't know what they had or how much everything was worth either.

This scattered approach creates confusion, mismanagement of investments, poorly timed distributions, and an absolute mess during retirement. It's even more complicated when someone passes away.

Keeping your personal financial information private is very important, but isn't it equally important to know where everything is and what it's all worth?

Whether you elect to work with a financial planner who will help you crystallize and illustrate your overall financial situation or choose to do it on your own, you need to believe that simpler is better. And with today's technology, you *can* simplify your financial life *and* spread your investments around without placing all your eggs in one basket.

The Unknowingly Undiversified Investor

Where I'm from, Fidelity holds a huge footprint on the investment landscape.

One afternoon, Earl P. came by our office for an initial appointment. He was fifty-nine years old and preparing for retirement in the next five years with his wife, Jean. All his life, he had done investing on his own at Fidelity. In addition, he had a 401(k) plan through work that was also managed by Fidelity. The reason for his visit was that he wanted an independent assessment on his investment portfolio. He was worried that his account wasn't doing nearly as well as he thought it should. As he put it, "I've worked hard to not have all my eggs all in one basket."

> **The Case of Diworsification**
>
> This made-up word was first spoken at a conference I attended by Burt White, chief investment officer at LPL Financial.
>
> *Diworsification*, according to Burt, is the belief that while you think you might hold a well-diversified portfolio, you actually have a collection of investments that will likely perform in similar fashion during various economic conditions. That's not diversification; it's diworsification.
>
> Definition

He had three accounts: a joint account, an IRA for himself, and another for his wife. Collectively, the portfolio totaled $750,000. They owned a collection of stocks and Fidelity mutual funds. They were as follows:

- General Electric (GE)
- AT&T (T)
- Disney (DIS)
- Exxon Mobil (XOM)

- Verizon (VZ)
- Fidelity S&P 500 Index (FUSEX)
- Fidelity Disciplined Equity (FDEQX)
- Fidelity Large Cap Stock (FLCSX)
- Fidelity Magellan (FMAGX)
- Fidelity New Millennium (FMILX)
- Fidelity Fifty
- Fidelity Growth Company (FDRGX)
- Fidelity Blue Chip (FBGRX)
- Fidelity Capital Appreciation (FDCAX)

Is this a diversified portfolio? Did Earl have the proverbial "all eggs in one basket?" Do you have a portfolio that might look like this?

Earl's portfolio *is not diversified.* It's an example of *diworsification.* In theory, and unknowingly, he had all his eggs in one basket. Here's why:

- Each fund he owns holds very similar stocks.
- The mutual funds all share similar investment objectives
- The individual stocks are already among the largest holdings in the funds he owns.
- All mutual funds and stocks are considered large cap (and will generally move in a similar pattern).

When Earl saw an "overlap analysis," a report that showed the similarities in holdings from one fund to another, he was truly surprised. He then asked a thoughtful question: "If there is so much overlap among my Fidelity funds, why does Fidelity have so many different offerings in the same investment category?"

A good question indeed.

Can You Reduce Risk by Investing Outside Your Comfort Zone?

So here's a genius-type question for you: Does having a collection of stocks and funds that all hold similar investment characteristics add risk or take risk away from a portfolio?

The answer: It *adds* risk. Think about this. Is there really a necessity to own so many similar mutual funds when they are all buying similar stocks in the portfolio?

Revisit your investment mix and make sure you're not too heavily weighted in one particular asset class.

The Benefits of Asset Allocation

There are times when certain asset classes outperform others. The intelligent bet is to have a combination of a collection of asset classes in your mix.

The Style Box—An Investor's Cheat Sheet for Investing

Morningstar Inc. is one of the largest independent evaluators of investments. One of its claims to fame (besides the "star system") was the development of the "style box." This simple illustration allows investors to visibly gauge the types of stocks or mutual funds they own.

The style box system is rather simple. There is one grid for bond funds and one grid for stocks/stock mutual funds. Each grid has nine boxes, and they illustrate various styles of investments. Style boxes also helps identify "overlap," or where an "all eggs in one basket" portfolio might exist.

In the following example, you can see that Earl P.'s money is all invested in large-cap stocks. He lacks mid-cap and small-cap exposure. The investor has no money invested in international securities. As such, when the S&P 500 goes up, the portfolio does really well. But when it goes down, the investor feels it.

In addition, many of the mutual funds already own shares of the individual stocks in their portfolios. And many of the mutual funds own the same stocks. This an example of adding risk—despite thinking that a portfolio is well diversified.

Stocks

	Value	Blend	Growth
Large Cap	General Electric (GE) AT&T (T) Exxon Mobil (XOM) Verizon (VZ) Fidelity Disciplined Equity (FDEQX) Fidelity Blue Chip (FBGRX)	Fidelity S&P 500 Index (FUSEX) Fidelity Magellan (FMAGX)	Disney (DIS) Fidelity Large Cap Stock (FLCSX) Fidelity New Millennium (FMILX) Fidelity Fifty Fidelity Growth Company (FDRGX) Fidelity Capital Appreciation (FDCAX)
Mid Cap			
Small Cap			

The Genius's Strategy to Investing

Rebalancing a portfolio is the genius's approach to strategic investing. Rather than selling out of investments and buying different ones on a regular basis, rebalancing your portfolio becomes a much more rational approach.

How to Rebalance a Portfolio

Rather than taking the tactical approach of selling one investment to buy something else, more professional financial planners agree that rebalancing your portfolio is the most prudent strategy, assuming each investment in your account is still appropriate for your portfolio.

Rebalancing aligns with the theory that asset allocation works, meaning that maintaining money in several asset classes regardless of market conditions will lead to lower risk and higher returns.

When you rebalance, you usually maintain the same investments in your portfolio but recognize that some investments have performed better than others. This would result in your initial asset allocation being a little bit out of balance. By rebalancing your portfolio, you take some of the profits from your winners and add the proceeds to those that underperformed in that period. Hint: That's called buying low and selling high!

Consider the following. Joe and Susan invested $100,000 four years ago:

- ABC Fund—$25,000 (25 percent)
- DEF Fund—$25,000 (25 percent)
- LMN Fund—$15,000 (15 percent)
- RPQ Fund—$10,000 (10 percent)
- EFG Fund—$20,000 (20 percent)
- ZLM Fund—$5,000 (5 percent)

As of today, they've seen a nice increase in their overall portfolio's value to $129,000. The style box below illustrates the current asset allocation of their portfolio.

Take a look at the following style box.

Stocks

	Value	Blend	Growth
Large Cap	ABC Fund 27%		DEF Fund 29%
Mid Cap	RPQ Fund 12%		
Small Cap	EFG Fund 17%		LMN Fund 10%

Bonds

	Short (Less Than Two Years)	Intermediate (Two to Ten Years)	Long (More Than Ten Years)
High Quality	ZLM Fund 5%		
Mid Quality			
Low Quality			

Inspiration

An Exercise for Your Portfolio

You can learn a lot about the risk to your overall financial accounts by simply dropping your investment accounts in to a style box. It's easy enough to draw one.

Grab one of your investment accounts and then head to your computer. Visit morningstar.com, finance.google.com, or another one of the popular investment programs out there.

Next, type in the symbol for your fund or stock. Look for a line that reads "asset class." You'll likely see something that says "large-cap growth" or "small-cap value." If you go to Morningstar, you'll already see the fund depicted in the style box.

Once you know the style of each investment, write the fund name in the respective box (similar to the example on the facing page). If you own a foreign fund and the style box reads "large-cap foreign," write it in the "large-cap blend" box.

In addition to writing the fund name, write in the value too.

When you're finished with an account, calculate the percentage of money each fund represents in each asset class.

If any single asset class has more than 30 percent of your money in the box, it may be worthwhile to rebalance or perhaps reallocate your portfolio.

You should do this exercise independently for each type of account you own. That means that if you have four IRAs, put all your IRA information into one style box. If you own six joint accounts, put all that information together in a separate style box.

When you're all done, you might be interested in aggregating all of your accounts together to see your overall asset allocation.

By the way, don't forget to include cash in your asset allocation. This would fall into the "short-term/high-quality" area on the "bond" style box. (See **Chapter 8**.)

	Initial Investment	Current Value	Current Allocation	Desired Allocation	Rebalance
ABC Fund	$ 25,000	$ 34,830	27%	25	$(2,580)
DEF Fund	25,000	37,410	29	25	(5,160)
LMN Fund	15,000	14,190	12	15	5,160
RPQ Fund	10,000	15,480	11	10	(2,580)
EFG Fund	20,000	21,930	17	20	3,870
ZLM Fund	5,000	5,160	4	5	1,290
Total	$100,000	$129,000	100%	100%	$ 0

To rebalance the account, based on the table above, you would need to sell a little bit from funds ABC, DEF, and RPQ and use the money to buy more shares of LMN, EFG, and ZLM.

On paper, it looks logical. Right? But emotionally, could you do it? There might even be a tax liability to selling the shares if your investment account was held in a taxable account.

Nevertheless, your first giant step into rational investing starts with believing in rebalancing regardless of how well some of your "winners" are performing.

Invest with Your Head, Not Your Heart

As certain investments perform well in your portfolio, it's not uncommon to develop an affinity for them. Others may simply hold sentimental value. And some just carry a great story. Yet when it comes to managing your own money in retirement, you need to lead with your head and not your heart. You need to stay rational, even when emotions are lighting a fire in your gut.

Four Keys to a Successful Investment Strategy

1. Dump any stockbroker or so-called financial adviser who claims to be able to "beat the market." It can't be done consistently. No one ever has done it. Well, at least no one you or I can afford.

The Rarity of 5–10 Percent Returns

You might think that earning a "market return" of 5–10 percent seems satisfactory, but would you be surprised to learn that over the past eighty-seven years, investors have seen the broad US market stock index earn between 5 and 10 percent just seven times!

That means that from 1926 through 2013, the broad US stock market scored an annual return in excess of 10 percent or less than 5 percent eighty out of eighty-seven years.

So the next time you build a stock-based portfolio with a high single-digit expected one-year annual return, be careful. You're more than likely to miss your annual target.

Pure Genius!

2. Ignore economic predictions. Economists with batting averages of .500 are among the best in the business. That means the very best ones guess wrong *at least* 50 percent of the time.

3. Don't engage in stock picking, or market timing. It's a loser's game. You need to be right twice: You need to know when to get in *and* when to get out. Not to mention, you have to do it repetitively to be successful.

4. Determine an asset allocation that works for you. Include global investments along with domestic stock and bond funds. Choose funds with reasonable fees and a turnover ratio that is in line with your tax situation.

The Truth about Investment Returns

You've probably heard that over time, the S&P 500 Index has delivered an annualized return of somewhere around 9–10 percent. So if that's true, consider this question: Over the past eighty-seven years—from 1926 through 2013—how many times has the stock market delivered a return of between 5 and 10 percent in a given year? The answer should surprise you. But maybe not if you're feeling a little genius-y!

The following histogram shared by Vanguard Investments illustrates that 7 percent of the time, the market delivered a return of 5–10 percent. Seven percent! That means that 93 percent of the time, it produced a return above or below 5–10 percent.

Calendar Year Returns: US Stocks (1926–2013)

	-35% or Worse	–34% to –30%	–29% to –25%	–24% to –20%	–19% to –15%	–14% to –10%	–9% to –5%	–4% to 0%	1% to 5%	6% to 10%	11% to 15%	16% to 20%	21% to 25%	26% to 30%	31% to 35%	36% to 40%	41% to 45%	46% to 50%	51% to 55%
15																			
												2012							
10												2010							
												2006			2003				
												1988	1999		1997				
							1990			2007	2004	1986	1998	2013	1991				
						2001	1969	1994		2005	1993	1982	1996	2009	1985				
5						2000	1962	1981	2011	1992	1971	1972	1983	1989	1980				
						1973	1946	1977	1987	1978	1968	1964	1967	1979	1955	1995			
						1966	1940	1953	1984	1956	1965	1952	1963	1976	1950	1975			
	2008			2002		1957	1932	1939	1970	1948	1959	1949	1951	1961	1938	1945	1958		1954
	1931	1937	1974	1930		1941	1929	1934	1960	1947	1926	1944	1942	1943	1936	1927	1928	1935	1933

Source: Vanguard

Note: For US stock market returns, the Standard & Poors 90 was used from 1926 through March 3, 1957; the Standard & Poors 500 Index from March 4, 1957, through 1974; The Wilshire 5000 Index from 1975 through April 22, 2005; and the MSCI US Broad Market Index thereafter.

Lessons from the Vanguard Histogram

- There have only been six years when the US stock market index (as measured by the histogram above) produced a negative return of more than 15 percent.
- Almost 50 percent of the time, the index produced an annual return in excess of 15 percent.
- Almost 50 percent of the time, the index produced returns of between -10 and 20 percent.

What other conclusions can you draw from this chart?

It's my hope that this chapter has enlightened you and, more importantly, given you the courage to take control of your portfolio.

To Summarize...

- Tactical investing is a loser's game. Buy quality and leave it alone.
- It's possible to have all your eggs in one basket while maintaining what appears to be a diversified portfolio.
- Don't let media talking heads or slick ad campaigns tempt you. Remember, they are in the entertainment business.
- Rebalancing is the key to a successfully managed portfolio in turbulent times.

Part 2

This Is *Not* Your Parents' Retirement: Advice/Instructions for Today's Retiree

Remember your parents' retirement days? Chances are, the company threw a party, Dad got a gold watch, and then Mom and Dad boarded the Lido Deck of *The Love Boat* for their celebratory cruise. Upon return, they settled into a simple lifestyle. They watched their spending, doted on the grandchildren, traveled locally, and lived in their home for as long as their health would allow.

That's probably not the retirement you imagine. You'll likely be healthier, live longer, and have more money to spend.

Chapter 11

Retiring: Could It Be the Biggest Decision of Your Life?

In This Chapter...

- Realities of retirement
- The truth about longevity
- What does it mean to retire?
- Stories of retirees

For years, you worked hard, saved money, and prepared for retirement. But with your retirement day drawing near, there's excitement, jitters, and second guessing. For some, it's reminiscent of getting married all over again. That's because retirement is the start of another phase in your life—and a major one at that. Have you prepared properly? Do you have enough money? Can you still be as generous as you've been in the past? Lots of questions—and many unanswered ones.

Retirement isn't black and white. It's okay to be nervous. It's even okay to be scared. It's normal. But fear not. You've got help.

What Does It Mean to Retire?

Let's be clear: Retirement doesn't mean cashing in everything and living off the earnings. Instead, it requires reassessing how you use money to support your lifestyle. That's because the retirement "routine" is different, especially today.

What *Is* Retirement Age?

Retirement at sixty-five is ridiculous. When I was sixty-five, I still had pimples.

George Burns

Quote

In retirement, you won't be heading off to work every day and expecting a paycheck every two weeks. Instead, *you* will be in charge. You will have control, and it will come with both risks and rewards.

To make financial matters even more daunting, relying on history to help you build a model for your retirement plan will be useless. Today's retirement is much different from when your parents and grandparents called it quits.

Retirement in the seventies and eighties was less complicated. It wasn't uncommon for retirees to approach life after work with the following mindset: "When I retire, I'll have a pension and Social Security, and I'll buy CDs (certificates of deposit) or municipal bonds that pay 5–8 percent and live off the interest."

That strategy no longer works. Managing finances in retirement today isn't that simple. Frankly, it's impossible, especially in today's low-interest-rate environment.

The Plight of the Complaining Retiree

All too often, I see sixty-year-olds approach retirement without well-designed plans—and because they don't have plans, they live in a continued world of self-inflicted misery and uncertainty. (We Jews call it *tsoris*.)

On the day the paycheck stops, survival mode commences. These retirees begin seeking the lowest-cost alternative. They hesitate before making any purchases. When they go out for dinner with friends, they suddenly want separate checks. Unknowingly, they continue reminding friends and family that they are now on fixed incomes. I feel sorry for these retirees. It's as if they suddenly need to apologize for retiring.

I've seen retirees lose friends and family simply because they spent too much time complaining and worrying about retirement.

Geniuses who read this book should view retirement as an opportunity. Embrace the free time and the independence. Welcome new adventures and lifelong learning experiences, and even splurge a little. You can do this—because you planned.

What Does Retirement Mean to You?

Despite books and magazines offering headlines that retirement can be solved "*with these three easy steps*," trust me, it doesn't work that way.

Retirement, for some, means never working again. For others, retirement is about getting out of the same old job and doing something different (with perhaps less stress and responsibility).

What's an Encore Career?

Believe it or not, a wise man by the name of Marc Freedman created the phrase "encore career" in his book *Encore: Finding Work That Matters in the Second Half of Life*.

Guess what? He's not me. I'm not even related to him. In fact, we live on two different sides of the country. He's in San Francisco, and I'm in Boston.

Mr. Freedman is CEO and founder of encore.org (formerly Civic Ventures). An encore career is defined as work performed in the "second half of life" that combines continued income, greater meaning, and social impact. These are jobs that can be paid but operate to serve the public good.

Perhaps your greatest achievement in retirement will be to find and love an encore career.

Pure Genius!

Retirement might include travel, having more time to spend with the kids, picking up a hobby, or just relaxing on the front porch. Yes, with good planning, retirement can include all the activities you want.

Living in retirement should also leave room for personal reflection. Life in retirement isn't just about the money issues. It's about staying active, making friends, doing what you love, and keeping your mind sharp. And for some, preparing for retirement can be a wake-up call. Perhaps it's time for a healthier lifestyle or serious attention to your own (possibly neglected) relationship(s) with certain family members or friends. It could even be an opportunity for an encore career.

Accepting Life in the World of Gray

Over the years, I've watched some retirees thrive in retirement and others get swallowed by it. Oftentimes, the greatest challenge is recognizing that retirement (or life, for that matter) isn't a straight path. It's not black and white. And for some, that's a tough pill to swallow.

As a retiree, you need to be exceedingly comfortable with the world of gray. If you've just left a very structured corporate environment or held a job where "exactness" was critical, settling into retirement might be tough for you.

Today's retirement is not about picking a strategy from column A, B, or C—and then forgetting about it. Retirement is a fluid process, and it requires continual assessment and review throughout your life.

Retirement planning requires integration of financial considerations *and* personal emotions. It's a mesh of facts *and* feelings. All too often, I'll see retirees make long-term decisions based on either emotion *or* logic—and then find themselves regretting the fact that they weren't more thoughtful and expressive in their thinking process.

What might seem logical and appropriate for your friends, neighbors, coworkers, and relatives may not make any sense for you. You need to be willing to accept that fact.

Avoid trying to replicate someone else's retirement plan.

Why Engineers and Scientists Struggle with Retirement Planning

If you've been working in a field where exactness and extraordinary attention to detail were at the core of your expertise, retirement may be difficult for you.

And if you're the type of person who embraces spreadsheets and analytical software programs, retirement planning may challenge your thinking.

That's because retirement in the real world is not an exact science. Retirement is filled with shades of gray (no, not *those* shades of gray), and it rarely achieves success by mapping progress on a spreadsheet.

Observation

Planning to Retire Is More Than Just Financial

It's very easy to find books on retirement planning that focus on facts, definitions, mathematical formulas, and historical perspectives. Make no mistake. These are all very important factors. But only a "dummy" or "idiot" would neglect the emotional components of retirement. A genius knows that an optimized retirement weaves facts with the real world.

That's because life happens.

If your retirement plan is built with inflexible strategies that ignore periodic large expenses, changes in health, the possibility of part-time employment, and more, your plan will be become rigid—and quite possibly costly to change.

A masterful retirement plan is built with flexibility. Just think back over the past five years. How many times did life events cause you to change your mental course and perhaps spend differently? In retirement, you're likely to face more than just a few surprises. Your retirement plan needs to be adaptive.

How you spend money and your time, and how you engage with friends and family, are things you *can* control in retirement. If the investment strategies you implement are based on long-term planning, you're going to need to trust in your strategy and let economic cycles and market conditions work through their challenges.

A Reality Check on Past Performance

> **The Secret to Success**
>
> The secret to a successful retirement is to have a personal retirement plan.
>
> Preparing for retirement is as much a financial challenge as it is a lifestyle challenge. Once retirement begins, the way you're going to think about money and life will change.
>
> **Pure Genius!**

How often have you used historical investment performance as the criteria for selecting a mutual fund? Perhaps you examine the fund's one-, three-, five-, and ten-year track records. You're not alone. Using the historical returns of an investment is a primary qualifier that investors use to pick investments. Yet, in reality, the average investor holds a mutual fund for less than 2.5 years. What's the purpose of examining the three-, five- and ten-year historical-return numbers of a fund if you don't actually hold on to your investment for a similar time period? While we all might believe that we can control our emotions, financial psychology suggests otherwise. Most investors allow emotions to overrule their rational thinking. In retirement, the paycheck is gone, and you're in change of your financial future. Are you prepared to battle the emotional hills and valleys without derailing your retirement plan?

Is Changing Your Lifestyle Necessary in Retirement?

I applaud retirees who want to continue to live life as they've grown accustomed. In fact, the transition into retirement should (financially) be a nonevent.

Emotionally? Well, that's likely to be another story.

Just think. After working for the same company for a number of years, you're about to embark on a new phase in your life where you won't see your colleagues every day. You won't be greeting the receptionist, the security guard, and the toll collector at the same time each day. Your water cooler conversation will be replaced with a morning meeting at the kitchen table (perhaps alone), and your internal alarm clock will need to be recalibrated because rush hour, the commute, and deadlines won't be pressing on your shoulders.

In reality, it's daunting. You never realize how conditioned you've become to doing the same activities every day until that's taken away from you. It's okay if you're smiling or shaking your head. You're not alone. Every retiree feels the same way.

Client Story—It's Not about the Money!

Frank was about to retire after thirty-five years as director of human resources for a large manufacturing company in Massachusetts when he and his wife, Susan, scheduled time to meet with me. He had been a do-it-yourself investor all his life. Yet now, at age sixty-three, Frank had become gun-shy. He realized that it would be up to him to replace his paycheck upon retirement—and as much as he enjoyed *giving* advice at work to others, he realized that *taking* advice from himself (especially when it had to do with living off his own money) wasn't going to be nearly as easy.

Both Frank and Susan sensed that they had ample assets to retire. They were, frankly, just looking for a second opinion. Frank had used some online software to help him see if he had enough money and resources, and we concurred that the analytical work he completed was indeed providing him a clear picture.

But something else was more bothersome. They were having a difficult time finding answers to more important questions. They were seeking answers on nonfinancial issues pertaining to retirement.

Frank feared waking up each morning without a sense of purpose. Ninety people reported to him at work and looked up to him for advice, guidance, and mentoring. Who would turn to him for advice now? Where could he be a mentor again?

A Retirement Investing Truism

In retirement, your primary responsibility is to focus on things you *can* control. The direction of the market, the political landscape, interest rates, and inflation are all out of your hands.

Pure Genius!

Susan had been a stay-at-home mom all her life. She too realized that suddenly they'd be spending a lot of time together. When I asked what they enjoyed doing together, they looked at each other and laughed. Besides eating out and watching television together, there wasn't much more that popped into their minds. They had been married for forty years, but upon reflection, Susan joked, "It's like dating all over again. I sure hope I still like him."

> **A Whole New World**
>
> Adapting to life in retirement should be about changes in schedules, new relationships, and responsibility. It shouldn't be about whether you'll be able to afford a nice evening out for dinner.
>
> Inspiration

Susan and Frank's story mirrors many of the same challenges faced in the early years of retirement. Frank and Susan's story inspired me to write *The Retirement Resource Booklet*, and I'm delighted to include it as **Chapter 25**.

How Long Will You Live in Retirement?

Close your eyes for a moment. Try to remember the family pictures on the wall that hung in your parents' home. Try to remember the faces, the clothing, and their expressions. Chances are that you are now older than they were in those photos. My guess is that you don't feel nearly as old as they did when they were your age. Medical science is allowing us to live longer and longer.

How Long Will You Live?

No one knows how long they'll live, nor does anyone know when they'll die. If they did, planning for retirement would be easy. The likelihood of living longer than you ever imagined is very possible. Many financial planners are projecting life expectancies in excess of one hundred years when presenting retirement income analyses. I can't blame them.

Over the past century, life expectancy among Americans has increased dramatically. Take a look at the following chart.

Life Expectancy			
1930	59.7	1980	73.7
1940	62.9	1990	75.4
1950	68.2	2000	77.0
1960	69.7	2010	78.7
1970	70.8	2020	?

Finding *Your* Goals and Dreams in Retirement

Years ago, a great financial planner, and even better thought leader, named George Kinder crafted a simple exercise that financial planners could use to help people understand "the meaning of money."

The objective was to assist people with exploring more than just investment allocation, performance, and income streams. Instead, it was about finding meaning between your money and your life. He knew that a successful retirement would include reflection and introspection. He knew that planning for retirement was something much bigger. His teachings taught planners like me to engage in a delicate yet energizing dialogue that illustrated how money impacts your life.

I'd like to share this exercise with you.

Over the years, I've modified his teachings slightly. I've found that when you take these questions seriously, they become powerful building blocks toward imagining life in retirement. I also think it helps you begin to better understand how retirement is so much more than "the number."

The Three Questions: Identifying Your Biggest Goals and Aspirations

Here are the rules of the exercise:

- Grab a pad of paper and pencil.
- Agree that all answers to the questions are fair game. Nothing is to be judged.

The New Deal and Social Security

Former president Franklin Roosevelt proposed his "New Deal" to America as our country emerged from the Great Depression. He launched the Social Security Administration. One segment of that program was to provide Americans working in the private sector with a government check in retirement that would be funded by private-sector employees and employers. It really was a great and innovative deal in 1935 for our country. It was sold to the public with ease. What might not have been clear at the time was the fact that life expectancy was about sixty-two years old. With many people planning to retire at sixty-five, the reality that Social Security checks would be continually paid to retirees was an easy objective to fulfill.

Unfortunately, today's Social Security program hasn't changed much, yet people are living much longer and retirees can still gain access to money as early as age sixty-two. It's no wonder that the Social Security trust fund is depleting.

Perspiration

- Agree that you will honor and respect each other's responses no matter how silly or elaborate they may seem.
- Agree with yourself and your partner (if appropriate) that all your answers will come from a place of good intent. Nothing is to be dismissed.

To make the exercise more interesting, open a bottle of wine, find a place where you won't be interrupted, and use this time to reaffirm your trust and caring with one another.

That's because this conversation may be among the most important you'll ever have.

Some advice: Capture your answers to each question on paper. Don't settle for the first gut response. Dig deeper. Say, "Tell me more about what you mean." Ask each other to describe the answers more vividly. Keep asking until you could sketch a picture or build a scenario in your mind where this could happen.

Are you ready? Here are the questions:

1. Imagine you had all the money you ever wanted. What would you do? (Remember the agreements above. Remember to keep asking until you've exhausted all the answers.)
2. Imagine you still have all the money you ever wanted, but today something happened. You visited with your

doctor. She told you that your health will remain as it is today for the next five years. However, one day in the next six to ten years, you will die without notice. How might you plan the rest of your life? (Remember the agreements above. Keep asking questions. Paint that picture in your mind.)

3. You've just returned from a visit to your doctor. You've been informed that you have less than twenty-four hours to live. What will be your regrets? (Stew on this one. Are these answers easier or harder to identify?)

Take some time to go back to the questions again. Make sure you've really exhausted what each of you wanted to share. Are you more aware of each other's true hopes and dreams?

Making Sense of the Three Questions

How did you feel after asking one another the questions? Was it easy? Was it too "touchy-feely"?

Front-Loading Your Retirement

The Nike slogan—Just Do It—isn't just for kids, you know.

The truth is that you may live in retirement for as long as you worked. However, your body won't likely be as active in the later years as it will in the first couple of decades of your retirement.

Inspiration

Without seriously exploring the three questions with your partner, or someone you trust in your life, you could regret not accomplishing many of the goals, dreams, and even unexplored possibilities that could make your retirement exceptional.

These questions can strike a nerve, touch an emotion, and ignite some unresolved issues.

If I've learned anything from retirees, it's that "doing" something in retirement *now* is always better than waiting till *later*. If you always wanted to own a Jaguar, spend more time traveling, or make sure the grandkids have money put aside for college, waiting can sometimes lead to unfulfilled wishes and outcomes.

Think about how often you look at your parents and grandparents and think their minds are still so sharp but their bodies are beginning to slow down? Don't let that be you. Embrace your retirement. Identify what's important to *you*.

Retirement, Like Life, Is Ever Changing

If you approach retirement without a plan, without a strategy, and without ongoing communication between you and (if you're fortunate) your spouse, you'll find yourself wrestling over money issues, decision making, and regret.

Having a retirement plan that allows for flexibility, fun, and safeguards will give you the opportunity to enjoy retirement to its fullest.

As you enter the beginning of this exciting phase in your life, remember that always having goals and dreams is critical. Live for what's next. I hope you will spend some quality time asking the three questions. I hope you'll share with one another your most honest and open goals. If you do, I promise that your life in retirement can become the greatest experience of your life. You'll wake up each day with a smile, and you'll finish your evening fulfilled.

To Summarize...

- A successful retirement is about more than having enough money. It's about knowing how to live.
- You're likely to live longer than you even imagine.
- Discussing and identifying your goals and dreams is a key part of a successful retirement.
- Find personal answers to the three questions, and you won't be disappointed.

Chapter 12

Retirement: Time to Get Messy

In This Chapter…

- What's the right amount to spend in retirement?
- When does retirement really start?
- Do you still need life insurance?
- Prepping your investments for retirement

Do you remember the days leading up to your first "real" job? You probably had some preconceived illusions of what life was going to be like at your new place of business. Some of it was true, but more than likely, there was so much more that you never imagined.

Retirement is just the same.

Whether its decisions you need to make regarding separating from your employer, managing your investments, having conversations with your spouse and family, or simply reimagining a new lifestyle, you're about begin a whole new journey.

How Does Your Spending Compare with Other Retirees?

If you thought the answer to that question was going to be easy, you haven't been reading this book all that carefully. ☺

Everyone is different. I have clients who earn $175,000 per year but need only $48,000 per year to spend in retirement. I have others who earn $225,000 and need every nickel they take home to cover their costs (and then some). Everyone's definition of "the right amount to spend in retirement" is different, and I can promise you this: What you think you'll need to spend early on will change over time. Both up and down.

The answer to the question, "Do I have enough money for retirement?" is very subjective. But if you don't know how much you'll need to spend each month, then how will you ever know whether you have adequate resources to support your lifestyle?

Time to Get Your Head into Retirement Mode

Everyone wants a successful retirement—even people who don't plan well. But those who succeed generally have a plan. They have a strategy. They have goals.

But it's more than that. Prior to retirement, you need to make choices. You need to simplify the financial chaos in your life so that you can focus on what you love to do.

Below are the major areas you need to address:

- Get your head in the game.
- Revisit the net worth statement.
- Reexamine your cash flow.
- Examine your insurance policies.
- Obtain cost basis and consolidate your investment accounts.
- Make decisions pertaining to your employee retirement plan.
- Address emotional issues that make your belly hurt.

Get Your Head in the Game

What does retirement *really* mean to you? Does it mean the end of work all together or just a change in employment status? Will you seek part-time work? Will you volunteer? Will you explore a contract relationship with your current employer? If your answer is *yes* or *maybe* to these questions, the next question is "for how long?" After all, when you're planning on replacing your paycheck in retirement, you'll need to know how much money will come from the following:

- New employment earnings
- Social Security
- Pensions
- Income from your investments
- Other (but it shouldn't be an inheritance)

Of course, the longer you have earned income, the longer you can allow your investments to work for you—and perhaps lead to larger income-replacement opportunities in the future.

Does Retirement Start at Sixty-Five Anymore?

No one said that work has to terminate at sixty-five years old. I have several clients who are happily working in their eighties—and it's not because they have to. They still enjoy it.

Sixty-five years old is what some people say is the new fifty. Retirees today have more options, choices, adventures, and opportunities than any generation before them. Maybe you're physically feeling pretty good right now, and perhaps you're wondering whether you need to stop working just because you're in your sixties. You don't—unless your employer is forcing you out. And even if you do choose to change places of employment, doing something you love can be very fulfilling.

Conversely, if you do plan to completely stop working in retirement, make sure that your sources of income will keep up with the pace of inflation. Just think back to what a gallon of milk, a car, and a nice dinner for two cost fifteen years ago.

Revisit Your Net Worth Statement

You should be doing this every year, but if "life has gotten in the way," it's time to get serious. Cataloging every asset and liability by ownership is a critical first step before making any retirement decisions. (Revisit **Chapter 3** if you'd like to learn how to build a net worth statement.)

Simplify Your Finances

Seek to consolidate your accounts. No one needs fourteen different bank accounts—especially in retirement. I encourage retirees to eliminate individual ownership on personal investment accounts. Instead, consider joint ownership, creating a revocable trust relationship, or simply adding a payable on death registration to the account. Individually owned accounts are the ones that can be a nuisance when you no longer can handle your own finances. Or—at worst—at death, they can be subject to probate costs and be an added burden when settling your estate.

Reexamine Your Cash Flow

Many retirees believe that to achieve retirement success, they need to accumulate enough money to replace what they earn each year. That's not necessarily true. Yet too many grow discouraged and view retirement as an insurmountable hurdle. As such, they work longer than they need to—and sometimes forgo personal dreams out of fear that they haven't saved enough. If that's how you're thinking, I hope to change that—and help you find success.

In fact, what I've learned is that for most people who have reasonably planned and lived within the constraints of their take-home pay, retirement is more achievable than they think. It just takes new thinking about money and cash flow.

Reexamine Your Life Insurance Policies

Why do you own life insurance? Why did you buy it in the first place? Chances are that you wanted to protect one or all of the following scenarios if you died:

- Provide ongoing income to your spouse and/or children
- Provide money to pay off your mortgage or other loans
- Have adequate funds to pay for your children's education costs

Pure Genius!

Gross Pay versus Net Pay

Does making a $100,000 salary mean you'll need a $100,000 income in retirement?

Probably not. Here's why.

If you're like many employed people your age, you do the following:

- Participate in your company's 401(k) plan and allocate between 10 and 20 percent of your pay
- Have money taken from your pay to buy life and disability insurance
- Pay into Social Security and Medicare
- Have federal and state taxes deducted

With all those deductions from your pay, it's possible that your take-home pay on a $100,000 salary is roughly $5,000 per month. That's $60K per year.

Think about it. Your take-home pay, not your gross pay, is responsible for paying for your mortgage, auto loans, day-to-day expenses, personal savings accounts, other life insurance policies, and more.

When you actually dig in to your spending needs, you're likely to find that the amount of money needed to support your life in retirement is far less than your *gross* pay ($100,000 in this example) and much closer to your *net* pay ($60,000).

Yes, you will need to pay taxes on some, or all, of your income. But the way you'll calculate taxes in retirement will be much different from simply relying on tax withholding from your pay stub.

I call this cash-flow versus tax-flow planning—and we'll talk about it more in **Chapter 15**.

As you approach retirement, do you still need to maintain the same level of insurance?

Insurance can play a huge role in a surviving spouse's life if adequate funds haven't been saved for retirement. It's all part of the planning process. Ignoring the insurance you own is a mistake, but so too is not knowing whether your coverage is over- or underfunded.

Uninspired

Do You Need Insurance to Bury Yourself?

I can't tell you how many people come to my office and tell me that they need insurance to bury themselves. Do you feel that way too? Unless you fear running completely out of money prior to your death, a "bury me" policy is a little unnecessary.

First of all, when you die, you're dead! The funeral home isn't inclined to wait around for your executor to fill out the life insurance claim form so it can get paid. That process can take, on the short side, four weeks to complete. Funeral homes want to get paid *now*.

Second, if you've planned well enough, someone has access to your checkbook to pay the funeral director—or, even better, you've prepaid the funeral costs.

Don't get me wrong, maintaining life insurance during your retirement years may make very good sense. But holding on to a policy just so they can bury you doesn't make sense anymore.

So why do so many people still think this way? This is an example of "old-school thinking." Remember when your grandparents lived in retirement? Their income came from Social Security and pensions. When they died, the benefits were generally reduced or—worse—terminated. There was no more money. If they didn't have much money in the bank, there wasn't any money to pay the funeral home.

Today, most people have money in the bank, personal investment accounts, retirement plans, and more. Funeral homes know this. And they're not inclined to patiently wait for your executor to collect life insurance money and then write a check to the mortuary. Just another example of how the world has changed.

Remember when reviewing your life insurance policies to seek the following sets of information:

- Type of insurance (term, whole life, universal life, variable life, etc.)
- Owner of the policy (the person who gets the bill to pay the policy)
- Insured (the person whose life the policy is written on)
- Beneficiary (the person(s) entitled to the death benefit up on the passing of the insured)
- Premium (the amount of money you pay to keep the policy in force)
- Premium schedule (the length of time you are expected to pay)
- Cash value (the amount of money you're accumulating in a policy that can be borrowed or used to reduce the premium you owe)
- Term (the length of time this policy is in force)

An In-Force Ledger

When preparing for your retirement, you should contact your insurance agent and ask for an in-force ledger on your policy. This report provides an analysis of your existing policy and how much more money is necessary to keep it in force (and for how long). Years ago, many people were sold insurance policies with proposals that featured interest rates that were unsustainable. As such, insurance owners have learned that they need to pay higher premiums, or a premium for a much longer time, just to keep the policy in force. If you own a permanent life insurance policy (whole life, universal life, or variable universal life), I implore you to request an in-force ledger.

Definition

Dangers of Not Knowing What You Paid for Investments

It's time to get serious about all your investment accounts. Take stock of everything you own and ask yourself whether your investments are still appropriate. While asset allocation and the risk in your portfolio are very important considerations, the one item that all too many retirees overlook is cost basis.

Why Is Cost Basis Important?

Throughout the course of your retirement, you'll likely be faced with making decisions on investments to sell to support your spending needs. Not to mention, what if one of the investments you own falls out of favor and you really want to sell it? If you don't know what you paid for your investment, how will you report the gain?

What Is Cost Basis?

It is the amount of money you paid to purchase an investment, plus any reinvested dividends, then adjusted to account for stock splits and spin-offs. Got all that?

Definition

Good News about Cost Basis

A few years ago, the brokerage industry was mandated by the IRS to begin logging cost-basis information on statements.

You'll now see that your investments will have one of three methods to report the gain or loss on the sale of securities:

- Average cost. When a sale is made, the average cost of all purchases is used as the cost basis.
- First in, first out (FIFO). You sell the first securities you bought regardless of gains or losses in other securities.
- Specific identification. In this option, you select particular share lots.

It's very important that you meet with your tax preparer to determine your cost-basis strategy. Once you select an option, you're stuck with it.

But beware. If you purchased shares years ago through a brokerage firm or mutual fund company—or if you hold stock certificates—be forewarned: You're going to need to recreate that information, or you could be straddled with an enormous, unsettling tax bill.

Consolidate Your Investments

Do you have multiple accounts with several different brokerage firms, mutual fund companies, and banks? Do you hold a bunch of stock certificates? If you're like the vast majority of people reading this book, you're paralyzed. You know you need to do something, but you don't know how to make the first move.

Relax. Breathe. It's really not all that hard.

Your Step-by-Step Guide to Consolidating Your Accounts

1. Sort all your accounts by ownership. If you've filled out your net worth statement appropriately, it will be pretty easy to gather that information.
    a. Put all the joint accounts together.
    b. Place your respective IRAs in separate piles (making sure that you further separate Roth IRAs from traditional IRAs).
    c. Create a pile for your trust accounts.
    d. Identify any individual accounts and determine whether they should remain separate or be placed in your trust or joint account.
2. Select a Certified Financial Planner professional or a specialist at a brokerage firm, or simply elect to do this yourself. The ultimate goal is to have you achieve the following:
    a. A consolidated statement for all your accounts
    b. Easy online access
    c. Performance reporting
    d. Cash-management services
    e. The ability to have an online dashboard view of your financial life

> **Consolidate Your Retirement Accounts**
>
> Did you know that the average retiree will have held eleven different jobs during the course of a working career? Don't lose sight of your money in retirement plans that is rightly yours!
>
> **Observation**

3. Establish new accounts with the brokerage firm.

    a. You'll want a new account number for each type of investment account, i.e., joint, trust, IRA, individual, etc.

    b. If you have accounts with individual ownership, ask for a transfer on death (TOD) form. This will allow your account to bypass probate.

    c. Complete each new account application with honest and clear answers. Include your investment objective, investment experience, net worth, tax bracket, and more.

    d. Seek help if you're getting stuck. It's very important that you fill out your paperwork correctly.

4. Sign an automated customer account transfer (ACAT) form.

    a. You will need an individual ACAT form for each account number. This means that if you have a brokerage account with GHI Company and it holds several securities, you will need only one ACAT form.

    b. If you have a statement from a mutual fund family and you have several mutual funds, you may need an ACAT for each investment.

    c. Check the box "transfer in kind." In doing so, all of your investments will transfer to your new account *as is*. That's right. They won't be sold—thus no capital gains to contend with.

    d. If you're transferring IRA accounts, you might consider whether you want to hold the securities or not. That's because there are no capital gains taxes due when investments in retirement accounts are sold. If you'd prefer to receive just the cash proceeds—or some cash and some securities—check on the appropriate box on the ACAT form.

    e. Submit the paperwork.

5. Wait and watch it work.

    a. In about ten days from the submission of your forms, the accounts will begin to transfer over.

b. Once they arrive, seek to consolidate all of your accounts onto one report so that everything arrives in one envelope. This is process called "householding."

c. You'll likely get statements from your old companies indicating that the money has transferred out.

d. For the current tax year, you will receive 1099 tax forms from the old companies and from the new one.

e. Starting in the next year, with any luck, you'll receive *one* 1099 with all your information consolidated.

Now that's genius!

Make Decisions Pertaining to Your Employee Retirement Plan

Getting your personal investments and accounts aligned is one thing. Separating from work life is another. As you approach your retirement date, you'll be asked to complete multitudes of forms, sign releases, agree to not share trade secrets, and more. The big ones may include, but won't be limited to, the following:

- Your pension
- Your 401(k), 403(b), cash balance, or other retirement plan
- Health insurance
- Continuation of other benefits, such as life insurance, disability, and/or long-term care
- Stock options
- Stock purchase plans

Making Your Personal Retirement Secret Sauce

No one's life in retirement is the same as anyone else's. Yet all too many computer modeling software systems, retirement planning websites, and financial advisers will lead you to believe that the solution is found when you select from one of the "prepackaged models." That's just not true. If the solution to retirement were simple, there wouldn't be millions of people worried about life in retirement. Nor would there be so many financial institutions vying for your business. If the answers were simple, a system would be built and the answers would be very straightforward.

You may be surprised, but once you enter into retirement, your biggest money questions will revolve around the type of car you choose to drive, the financial support you provide to adult children, the commitments you wish to make to charitable entities, and your participation in the community. Finding solutions to these questions will be what makes your secret sauce. The values you convey will play a big part in the blueprint of your retirement.

One of the Biggest Dangers Retirees Face in Retirement: The (Adult) Kids!

As parents, we do our best to raise our children with values, discipline, resourcefulness, creativity, and a sense of purpose. Though each of us has our own method, we hope that on the day they leave the nest, for college, marriage (and hopefully not prison), etc., we gave them the skills necessary to succeed.

And when our children become mature adults, we want the best for them then too.

Perhaps you'll help them with money to get started, introduce them to key contacts you know in their field of interest, and even serve as babysitters when the grandchildren come along.

But at what point does the financial support stop and the tough love begin? For many, it's the hardest conversation to have with their children. All too many people avoid the conversation, as they fear it will create a rift in the family dynamics.

Imagine for a moment if you needed to adjust your lifestyle in retirement so that your children could have everything they wanted? Would you do it? Whether you answered yes or no, you have plenty of support.

How Adult Children Are Draining Money from Their Retired Parents

Here are some real statistics about how retirees support their adult children today:

- More than half of retirees are helping with adult children's living expenses.
- Transportation costs are supported by 40 percent of retirees.
- Thirty percent of retirees continue to give adult children spending money.
- Thirteen percent currently help pay down credit card debt.
- Ten percent contributed to a down payment on a home.
- Twenty-eight percent helped with medical bills.
- Over 50 percent provide emotional support—but that's a parent's lifelong job. As we get older, the emotional support goes both ways.

Sources: Money, US News and World Report *(2011)*

Perspiration

Would You Sacrifice Your Retirement So Your Children Could Afford a Better Life?

We asked this question of a group of our own clients during a seminar. There were about one hundred people in the room. When I asked, "How many of you would sacrifice your own life in retirement so that your children could have everything they wanted?" how do you think they responded? Believe it or not, it was a dead tie. That's right, 50 percent of the hands went up. Surprisingly, many people turned to their neighbors and began very spirited discussions. They never imagined that someone about their age could have a different core opinion about such a sensitive issue.

This exercise was an example of how each one of us has our own values and beliefs—and no one is right or wrong. However, if you're not willing to consider the consequences of your actions, well then, it may be time for a "genius intervention."

Are You the Family Bank?

Years ago, we met a family who lovingly referred to themselves as The [insert your last name here] Bank and Trust Company. No, they weren't wealthy. Nor did they have any ownership in a bank or credit union. Yet when their kids needed money for anything—a spring-break trip, a car loan, or a new wardrobe—they simply went to Mom and Dad for the funds. After all, the interest rate was 0 percent and the repayment terms were on a handshake and hug.

But as their six children grew older, the need for money grew larger. Now adults, they sought funds from "the bank" for down payments for houses, Jacuzzis, home improvements, and college education funds. The Crosbys felt that they had set a precedent, so they had a hard time saying no. After all, they wanted the best for their children.

It wasn't until they started building their retirement plan that they realized the money they loaned wasn't coming back at the rate they hoped and its availability for their own income needs was going to add a crimp to their style. They uncomfortably joked that they might need to start asking for loans from their own children.

Do you feel that way sometimes?

Each one of the items above requires a decision, if applicable, on your part. In the chapters that follow, I'll delve into greater depth on helping you select choices that make sense for you. In addition, I'll revisit many of the topics discussed throughout this chapter so that we can dig a little deeper, share a few stories, and help you obtain retirement advice in a language you can understand.

Be Honest with Your Kids

Some adult children tend to think their parents are "financially well off" if they are able to transition into retirement without complaints and visible worries. Others see their parents as struggling financially because they don't seem to spend money with the same enthusiasm they do.

Don't ever be ashamed of your life. You worked hard, planned well, and now are entering the next stage in life. However, if you're wearing a mask to guard your life in retirement, be forewarned: The reflection it presents to your children can often create a message you never intended.

Remember when you taught your children to "tell the truth"? My advice to you is to be as open and honest about your financial situation with your adult, mature children. Neglecting to do so can lead to misconceptions—and unintended outcomes.

Observation

To Summarize...

- Retirement planning requires serious attention in all areas of your financial life—not just the easy ones.
- Never compare your financial situation to anyone else's. You don't know their whole story—and they don't know yours.
- Seek to find what you need to support your financial lifestyle on a monthly basis. Don't guess. Give it the attention it deserves.
- Preparing your financial assets for retirement takes time and effort, but you and your family will be thankful you did it.

Chapter 13

Social Security: It Impacts Everyone!

In This Chapter...

- The most misunderstood annuity in America
- How to apply for benefits
- Decisions, decisions, decisions
- Medicare: an introduction

Chances are that Social Security could represent somewhere between 20 and 50 percent of your collective income in retirement.

Social Security benefits are on the minds of millions of retirees. How much might you expect? When should you take your benefit? What are the chances Social Security won't be there for you?

Nervous? Don't worry. This chapter won't be nearly as painful as you're imagining.

Social Security: The Most Popular Annuity in America

Turn on your television, listen to the radio, or visit your choice of popular websites. You're likely to find advertisements and celebrity personalities telling you to stay away from annuities. They'll tell you that they are expensive and that the only people who make money are the agents who sell the product. While there may be some sliver of truth in the message, there are also many benefits that come from annuity offerings—most importantly, a guaranteed income stream.

Whether you're a fan of annuities or not, I am ambivalent. Chances are, you own (or will soon own) one without even knowing it. If you expect to receive a pension or plan to collect Social Security, you will be the proud owner of a bright and shiny annuity. How do you feel? Don't worry. You've got little to fear.

Why Your Social Security Check Is Similar to an Annuity

During your employment years, you had money automatically deducted from your pay (about 7.65 percent of earnings) on a pretax basis. It was called your FICA (Federal Insurance Contribution Act) deduction. About 85 percent of that contribution was paid into the Social Security program, with the remaining 15 percent being allocated to the Medicare trust fund. In addition, your employer was required to match your 7.65 percent contribution and send that amount to Social Security on your behalf as well.

Your contributions, along with all other employee/employer contributions, are used (in part) to pay the monthly benefits of current retirees, surviving spouses, children of deceased workers, and more. Money not used to pay benefits during a given year goes to the Social Security trust fund.

When it's your turn to collect Social Security benefits, the money you receive isn't pulled out of your personal lock box at the Social Security office. Instead, you collect money from others who pay into the system. The money you paid was spent on someone else a long, long time ago.

The same rules apply to many other annuity/pension programs. Think about it. Insurance companies collect premiums from investors. They use your money with they hopes that they can earn a higher rate than the amount they need to pay to pensioners or annuity recipients. So long as these recipients

Social Security as Part of Your Overall Investment Allocation

If you plan on receiving Social Security and/or a pension check as part of your overall retirement income stream, it's important that you view these dollars as part of the "fixed income" side of your asset allocation.

Neglecting to do so could impact your ability to meet the increased costs of goods and services as you age in retirement.

Remember, your pension is likely fixed forever, and your Social Security check probably won't keep pace with the rate of inflation.

Without your other assets outpacing the cost of living, you could find yourself unable to meet your expenses a decade or two into retirement.

Pure Genius!

collect their guaranteed income *and* the insurance company remains profitable, you probably don't care how the premiums you sent them are invested.

So let me ask you this: With today's uncertainty surrounding Social Security benefits, how willing would you be to pay a fee so that our government could manage, protect, and *guarantee* your Social Security benefits? Right now, you pay nothing. And, as such, there is a likelihood that Social Security benefit "guarantees" could change in the future.

What if insurance companies offered to *guarantee* a higher income stream, perhaps a higher rate or return, flexibility, and even some access to your principal for an investment in their annuity? Might you be willing to pay them a fee?

Perhaps now you're getting a sense as to why annuity companies may be knocking on your door.

Social Security Is a Supplement to Income—Not a Replacement

More than 22 percent of retirees rely exclusively on Social Security as their sole source of income.

Researchers estimate that Social Security will replace 56 percent of income for people who earned less than $20,000 per year, 41 percent for those who had income of about $40,000 per year, and 30 percent for those with $80,000 or more in earnings per year.

Pure Genius!

Reality Check on Social Security

Social Security is the major source of income for most of the elderly:

- Ninety percent of individuals aged sixty-five and older receive Social Security benefits.
- Social Security benefits represent about 39 percent of the income of the elderly.
- Among elderly Social Security beneficiaries, 53 percent of married couples and 74 percent of unmarried persons receive 50 percent or more of their income from Social Security.
- Among elderly Social Security beneficiaries, 23 percent of married couples and about 46 percent of unmarried persons rely on Social Security for 90 percent or more of their income.
- An estimated 161 million workers, 94 percent of all workers, are covered under Social Security.
- Fifty-one percent of the workforce has no private pension coverage.
- Thirty-four percent of the workforce has no savings set aside specifically for retirement.
- In 1940, the life expectancy of a sixty-five-year-old was almost fourteen years. Today, it is more than twenty years.
- By 2033, the number of older Americans will increase from 45.1 million today to 77.4 million.
- There are currently 2.8 workers for each Social Security beneficiary. By 2033, there will be 2.1 workers for each beneficiary.

Source: Social Security Administration

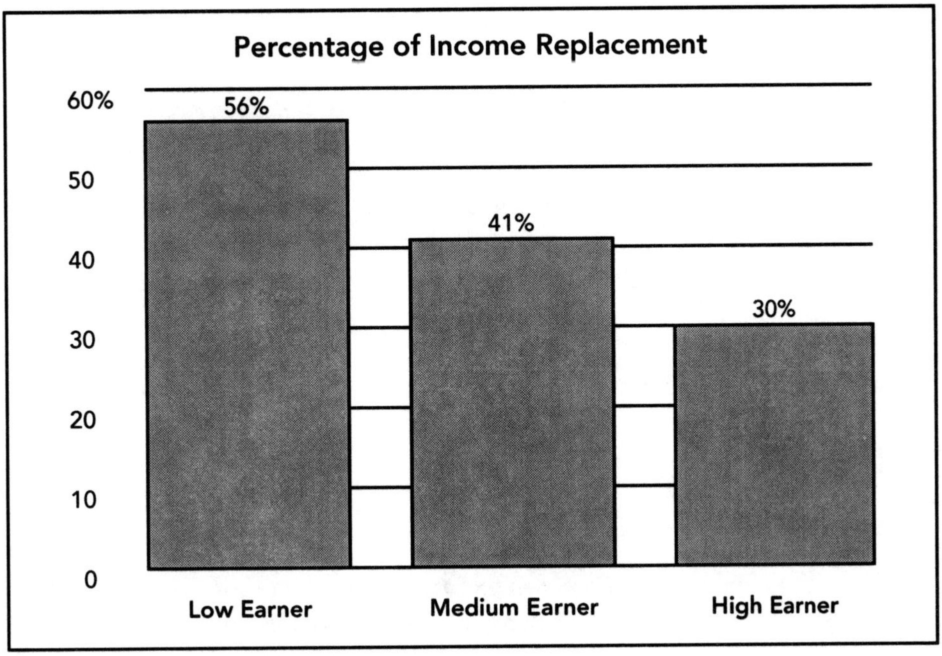

What Happened to the Annual Social Security Benefit Statement?

For decades, eligible Social Security recipients would receive benefit statements in the mail that listed earnings for previous years worked. Budget restraints caused the administration to suspend the statements. You can now easily access this information anytime you like at ssa.gov. You'll need to register one time, but you'll have personalized information and a multitude of answers to your questions.

Any information provided on Social Security is based on what the rules look like today. At any time, Congress could implement sweeping changes that could overhaul the landscape of government-funded programs for retirees. But for now, relax. You're getting a sweet deal—and one that is paying you many times more than what you put in.

Who Qualifies for Social Security?

You can qualify for Social Security benefits once you've paid into the system for ten years or forty quarters. In 2013, you will earn one credit for each $1,160 of earnings, up to a maximum of four credits each calendar year.

Applying for Social Security Benefits

All right—it's about that time to apply for benefits. Are you ready? Do you know what to do? Follow these easy steps below, and you'll be well on your way:

- Online. Use the Social Security Retirement/Medicare Benefit Application to apply for retirement, spouse's, ex-spouse's, or Medicare benefits (ssa.gov).

Perspiration

How Long Might You Live?

According to the American Academy of Actuaries:

- a sixty-five-year-old man can expect to live 18.9 more years on average and a sixty-five-year-old woman can expect to be alive another 20.9 years;
- a sixty-five-year-old man has a one in five chance of living to age ninety;
- a sixty-five-year-old woman has a one in three chance of living to age ninety;
- a sixty-five-year-old couple has a fifty-fifty chance that one of them will live until age ninety;
- a sixty-five-year-old couple has a one in three chance that one of them will live to age ninety-five; and
- a sixty-five-year-old couple has a one in ten chance that one of them will live to age one hundred.

The better you take care of yourself, the more active you'll remain in retirement. And the more nutritiously you eat, the greater the likelihood that you'll live into your nineties—or perhaps beyond.

If you had plans to die early, think again. Just because your family's history doesn't have longevity shouldn't mean that you won't be part of a new trend. It's time to start planning—for the long term.

What Is Full Retirement Age?

It's the age that you're eligible for 100 percent of your retirement benefit.

If you were born between the years 1943 and 1954, your full retirement age is sixty-six years old. That is when you can receive 100 percent of your eligible benefit.

Year of Birth	Full Retirement Age
1937	65 years
1938	65 years, 2 months
1939	65 years, 4 months
1940	65 years, 6 months
1941	65 years, 8 months
1942	65 years, 10 months
1943–1954	66
1955	66 years, 2 months
1956	66 years, 4 months
1957	66 years, 6 months
1958	66 years, 8 months
1959	66 years, 10 months
1960 and later	67

Definition

- By phone. Call 1-800-772-1213.
- In person. Visit your local Social Security office. (Call first to make an appointment.)

Reminders:

- You must be at least sixty-one years and nine months old to apply for retirement benefits.
- If you are already age sixty-two, you may be able to start your benefits in the month you apply.
- You should apply for benefits no more than four months before the date you want your benefits to start.
- Benefits are paid the month after they are due. (If your benefits start in April, you will receive your first benefit payment in May.)
- If you are not collecting Social Security and you are not ready to retire, you should still sign up for *just* Medicare benefits three months before your sixty-fifth birthday.

The Smartest People in the Room

Walk into a local coffee shop in town, and you'll hear retirees bantering about soaring health costs and the instability of the Social Security system. The rhetoric is just noise. It's something to talk about to pass the time while they sip coffee, eat oatmeal, and pick the raisins out of their muffins.

When it comes to information about Social Security, the best people to turn to are the ones you might least expect. Unlike most government agencies, Social Security employs some of the most skilled, articulate, and even entertaining experts on the subject. In fact, when I invite a guest for my radio show or to an area seminar, I know that I can fill a room when someone from the public affairs office at the Social Security Administration attends. They bring valuable information, clear answers to questions, and an element of patience I need to learn.

Make no mistake, Social Security is confusing. There are dozens of choices to consider. Trying to match someone else's Social Security strategy to yours can be a costly decision, especially if:

- you and your spouse have wide differences in age;
- you paid into both a public pension and Social Security;
- you are widowed, divorced, or remarried;
- you have young children; or
- your Social Security benefit statement doesn't include all of your employment earnings.

Like I said earlier, the folks at the Social Security office are among your best sources for answers.

When's the Right Time to Take Social Security Benefits?

If it is your intention to continue working prior to your full retirement age (FRA), it may make sense to hold off on collecting Social Security benefits. That's because if you earn more than $15,120 prior to your full retirement age *and* start collecting benefits, $1 for every $2 of Social Security benefits will be owed back to the Social Security Administration.

You can still work and receive benefits.

If You Are	You Can Make Up To	If You Make More, These Benefits Will Be Withheld
Under full retirement age	$15,120	$1 for every $2
Reaching full retirement age this year	$40,080	$1 for every $3
Full retirement age and above	No limit	No withholding

Based on 2014 Social Security guidelines.

Are You Planning to Work Between the Ages of Sixty-Two and Sixty-Six?

If it is your intent to earn more than $15,120 annually between the ages of sixty-two and sixty-six, it will generally *not* be in your best interests to begin collecting Social Security benefits.

For most people, it makes sense to wait until FRA age to collect full benefits. Collecting your benefit at age sixty-two provides you with 80 percent of your full retirement amount. If you wait until age seventy, you can access 125 percent of your full retirement amount.

Issues to Consider When Applying for Social Security Benefits

The best way to apply for Social Security is at ssa.gov.

Prior to applying, consider these factors:

- Are you still employed?
- Is there longevity in your family?
- How is your present health?
- Are you eligible for benefits on someone else's record?
- Can you support yourself if you delay taking benefits?
- Are there other family members (children) who might qualify for benefits when you apply?

Observation

Is Social Security a Finely Veiled Ponzi Scheme?

Yes, the headline is controversial, and thoughts below are "somewhat" tongue in cheek, but consider this.

Bernie Madoff became a household name after using other investors' money to provide ongoing income checks to older investors. He did so by producing his own sets of investment statements, remaining very vague about how he was investing the money, and using his minions of income recipients as marketing bait to sing his virtues. That is until one day the economics of his bait-and-switch game began to crumble beneath his feet. People began asking how they could get into an investment program that was knocking the cover off the ball. Professional money managers began getting skeptical. They wondered whether it was really possible that one person, Bernie Madoff, could outinvest thousands of professional money managers—not once, but over multiple years, and through some of the most volatile periods in our history.

Madoff's system worked for as long as the number of people and the amount of money invested with him outweighed the amount being withdrawn.

Are you sensing where I'm going?

When the Social Security system began in 1940, the likelihood of not getting back everything that you paid into the system was impossible. After all, there were 42 workers for every retiree. In 1960, there were just 4.9 workers paying in for each retiree (a 90 percent reduction over twenty years). It's widely believed that the typical family back then could have received as much as seven times what it paid into the system.

Today, there are just 2.8 workers for every retiree. And in 2035, that number is expected to drop to 1.9 workers per retiree.

At some point, either the Social Security "Ponzi scheme" will meet its maker or you'll see a dramatic shift in how the program operates. Either way, you deserve better transparency on how the system works, what it costs, and where the money is really invested.

One of the best places to gain insight into the Social Security program, and proposals on how it could be fixed, is to visit the Center for Retirement Research at Boston College at crr.bc.edu.

How Social Security Determines Your Retirement Benefit

Your retirement benefit is based on both your age and your earnings. As such, make sure that the earnings listed on your benefit statement reflect your real earnings.

The process for determining your benefit requires the following three steps:

1. Adjusting your past wages for inflation
2. Finding the average thirty highest-earnings years (not just the last)
3. Creating an average indexed monthly earnings amount (AIME)

Determining a Spouse's Benefit

A spouse becomes eligible for benefits if the following apply:

- The working spouse applies for benefits.
- The spouse is at least sixty-two, or is caring for a child age sixteen or younger, or receives Social Security disability benefits.

The maximum possible Social Security benefit equals one-half of the worker's benefit.

If a spouse is eligible based on his or her own work history, Social Security will pay the higher amount.

Passage of DOMA Gives Married Same-Sex Couples Equal Benefits

In early 2013, the Supreme Court overturned the "Defense of Marriage Act," deeming it unconstitutional. This decision gave married same-sex couples equal spousal benefits that had previously been allowed only for heterosexual married couples. This federal decision gives all married couples the opportunity to build a retirement plan together and receive survivor benefits upon the death of one of them. If a gay or lesbian couple is legally married in one state and subsequently moves to a state that does not recognize same-sex marriage, it is important to remember that Social Security and the IRS may not recognize it either—as state law usually determines one's tax status. Just be sure to check with your legal, tax, and financial adviser.

> **The Challenge of Marriage**
>
> If you changed your name due to marriage, you want to be certain that the Social Security Administration has captured all your information correctly. We've seen many people's earnings from their "maiden name" years disappear from benefits statements. It can be easily corrected by visiting the Social Security Administration office and providing your Social Security number and copies of your birth certificate and marriage license.
>
> IMPORTANT!

What Happens to Social Security Benefits When a Spouse Dies?

If a member of a married couple dies, the surviving spouse will receive a token death benefit check of $255 from the Social Security Administration. It's a slap in the face.

However, the SSA does provide the surviving spouse with the higher monthly check that was paid to either person.

For instance, assume Jack earns an SSA check of $2,300 per month and Judy received a check for $1,400. If Jack passes away, Judy will receive a one-time check of $255. She will then begin receiving a new monthly check for $2,300 per month. Her $1,400 check will no longer be sent.

Widow's Benefits

If you become widowed and don't remarry prior to age sixty, you may be eligible to receive Social Security survivor benefits as early as age sixty—or age fifty if you're disabled.

If you elect to wait until full retirement age (FRA), you will be eligible to receive full benefits.

If you remarry after age sixty, you are eligible to continue receiving survivor benefits.

Social Security and Divorce

If you were married for ten years prior to filing for divorce, you may be eligible for a Social Security benefit based on your ex's earnings. In order to qualify, you must meet the following criteria:

- Married at least 10 years
- Divorced at least two years
- At least sixty-two years old
- Not currently married
- Not eligible to an equal or higher benefit based on your own (or someone else's) work history

If your divorced spouse dies and you had been married for ten years or more, you may begin claiming survivor benefits as early as age sixty.

Even if your ex has remarried, you may still be eligible to collect Social Security benefits based on your ex's earnings.

Special Strategies When Taking Social Security

Below are answers to a few common questions asked by retirees. Remember, I'm only scratching the surface here. You'd need an entire **For the GENIUS** book to fully capture questions and answers to all the nuances relating to Social Security.

Can a Married (Nonworking) Woman Collect Benefits If She's Older Than Her Husband?

A married woman can claim Social Security benefits at age sixty-two even if her husband has yet to begin collecting. For instance, let's assume Mary is sixty-two years old and her husband is sixty. Mary is entitled to receive $690 per month at age sixty-two based on her own history of earnings. Her husband is entitled to receive $2,000 monthly when he becomes sixty-two years old.

If Mary elects to begin taking money at sixty-two, she will receive $690 a month. However, once her husband turns sixty-two and applies for his benefit of $2,000 per month, Mary's benefit will increase. She will begin receiving one-half of her husband's benefit ($1,000 a month) and no longer receive $690 per month.

What's the Break-Even Point for Determining Social Security Benefits?

The answer, if you know the date you're going to die, is really easy. Unfortunately, none of us have the ability to predict the future.

You can calculate the numbers a multitude of ways. You can factor in tax rates, or you can make assumptions on increases to Social Security benefits. But the big assumption, the granddaddy of them all, is trying to predict when you're going to die. Mathematically, if you think you'll live longer than eighty-one years, hold off drawing your Social Security benefit until age seventy—if you can afford it. However, if starting your Social Security benefit at your full retirement age (probably age sixty-six) makes sense, enjoy the cash. Travel, visit the kids, and treat yourself to something nice.

IMPORTANT!

Taxation of Social Security Benefits

Social Security checks are taxable.

The tax rate that's due on your Social Security income is subject to your adjusted gross income (AGI).

The maximum taxable amount of your Social Security income is 85 percent.

The table below illustrates the current rules as of 2013.

Adjusted Gross Income	Single	Adjusted Gross Income	Married
Under $25,000	0%	Under $32,000	0%
$25,000–$34,000	50%	$32,000–$44,000	50%
Over $34,000	85%	Over $44,000	85%

What Is File and Suspend?

File and suspend is a technique where Social Security allows one spouse to defer taking a benefit at full retirement age while allowing the spouse to collect a benefit as early as age sixty-two. Here's how it works:

Carl is sixty-six. He makes $150,000 as an engineer. His wife, Carla, aged sixty-two, worked as a travel agent for twenty-five years, earning an average salary of $45,000. Today, she is a homemaker. Carl loves to work, and he'd prefer to defer his Social Security income until age seventy, when he could collect 125 percent of his full retirement benefit of $2,500. Carla, however, wouldn't mind collecting a little "mad money" each month. If Carl files for Social Security and then "suspends" his benefits, Carla can begin collecting the benefit based on *her* earnings record of $1,050 per month. Once Carl elects to begin taking his Social Security benefit, Carla's check will bounce up to her "spousal benefit," which would be half of Carl's amount.

A Quick Peek into Medicare

By the time this book is published, the health care system in America may be turned upside down, but probably not Medicare. No members of Congress in their right minds would vote against changing anything in the Medicare system that could cost them votes from constituents. When you consider the pace at which Congress works, we're likely to see very little change—until someone sets a drop-dead deadline.

So, for now, let's view Medicare through a very wide lens.

All Americans aged sixty-five and older are eligible for Medicare. You should sign up for Medicare three months prior to reaching age sixty-five—regardless of whether you're collecting Social Security benefits or not. Neglecting to register could delay coverage for medical insurance or prescription drugs. In addition, it could result in higher medical premiums. Even if you are still working and have creditable health insurance at work, you need to sign up. Part A (hospital) is free and becomes your primary insurer for hospital stays, with your coverage from work becoming a supplement that may pick up part of what Medicare doesn't cover.

When applying for Medicare coverage today, you have two choices:

Don't Confuse Medicare with Medicaid

Medicare is the nation's health insurance program for people over the age of sixty-five and those who have long-term disabilities.

Medicaid is free or very-low-cost medical coverage provided to more than 50 million Americans who can't otherwise afford to care for themselves.

The word "Medicaid" leaves room for confusion. While there are millions of people who can't afford coverage and need Medicaid to keep them well, there are millions of others (you know who you are) who attempt to reposition (hide) assets so that they can feed off the Medicaid system and help their elderly parents become wards of the state. While I understand why people choose this route, I also believe it becomes a test of one's values and morals.

Consider this: What might happen if the "Medicaid program" was returned to its "real" name, "the welfare program"? Might people be willing to help their parents qualify for "welfare"?

Uninspired

- Medicare
- Medicare Advantage

Traditional Medicare (Part A and Part B)

The traditional Medicare program is divided into Part A (hospital insurance) and Part B (medical insurance). As a participant, you can choose from among the "Medicare approved" doctors.

Part A cost $426 in 2014, but many people get the premium at no cost if they are already receiving Social Security benefits or if they are eligible for benefits at a later time. It's also free if your spouse has Medicare-covered employment through the government. When you choose Part A coverage, you must also elect to sign up for Part B coverage. However, if you are over sixty-five and collecting benefits through your employer, this rule won't apply.

If you file a joint tax return and your adjusted gross income (AGI) was $170,000 or less, your premium for Part B coverage in 2014 is $104.90. If your income exceeds that amount, there is a slight increase in your monthly costs. You also pay a deductible of $147 per year.

Medicare Advantage Plan (Part C)

Instead of selecting the traditional Medicare program, you can elect Part C, which is called the "Medicare Advantage Plan." This program includes all the benefits of Part A and Part B, and it is offered through private insurance companies approved by Medicare. Oftentimes, HMOs and PPOs are part of this offering. With Part C coverage, you pay premiums to the insurance company. You typically need to use doctors, hospitals, etc., that are approved by your insurance company. In some cases, there is a copayment or deductible for the services.

Selecting a Prescription Drug Plan (Part D) through Medicare

If you have selected traditional Medicare, you must join a Medicare prescription drug plan. Typically, there is a monthly premium for this coverage. Private companies are approved by Medicare to offer these services.

If you are on the Medicare Advantage Plan (Part C), prescription drug coverage is typically offered. If for some reason your insurance company doesn't offer prescription coverage, you can sign on with a Medicare-approved plan.

What Is Medigap Coverage?

This protection is available only to those who subscribe to the traditional Medicare program. It is available through private insurance companies, and it serves as the "filler of the gaps." In other words, if you need to come up with out-of-pocket money to pay Medicare costs, such as deductibles, copays, and coinsurance amounts, your Medigap policy can help offset some of these costs.

Confused yet? You're not alone. And, like I said above, these rules might be different by the time you read this book. My recommendation is to visit medicare.gov or eldercare.gov to understand the most current rules and find out about the programs available.

To Summarize...

- Social Security and Medicare are critical elements of most Americans' retirement future. It is critical to examine your personal financial situation with an expert to help you make a smart choice.
- The rules surrounding Social Security have changed and will continue to change. Don't make decisions based upon "what you've heard."
- Waiting to take your Social Security benefit at your full retirement age (FRA), or even age seventy, could provide you with a significantly larger income throughout your retirement years.
- Medicare is likely to be flipped upside down in the decades to come. Make sure you remain aware of program changes, yet avoid the "chatter" of programs that are merely proposals.

Chapter 14

Pensions and the Secret Millionaire

In This Chapter...

- Understanding different pension options
- The lump sum versus the pension
- Decisions to consider when selecting a pension option
- Questions to ask yourself when considering a pension
- Why public school teachers have a better deal than they think

Traditional retirement plans used to be built using a metaphorical three-legged stool: pension, Social Security, and personal savings. But today, the stool theory might leave your retirement quite wobbly. If you're a teacher or public-sector employee, though, your pension may be the most important component of your retirement.

This is no longer your grandfather's retirement plan. The mother ship has "left the building." You are now on your own.

Can I See You in My Office?

Whether you've been with the same company for forty years or this is your last full-time job after making seven career moves, the final days of full-time employment are emotional. If you've been planning on a retirement date for years or you've been selected to consider a retirement package due to downsizing, a combination of fear, excitement, anxiety, and uncertainty will engulf your last working days.

In the weeks leading up to your retirement, your human resource department will more than likely approach you with decisions you need to make. Oftentimes, these decisions will be permanent. They'll hand you a package of paperwork that you'll need to return in short order.

The words in the package may overwhelm you, and the sums of money available may surprise you. You may be invited to a retirement planning seminar to help you understand your retirement options. Nevertheless, it's ultimately up to you to complete the documents and make some irrevocable decisions.

How well prepared will you be to answer questions that will impact your life for the next twenty-five or more years?

Your Pension: What Option Works Best?

If you're fortunate to be eligible for a pension, make sure that you understand your options. Your employer is likely to hand you a sheet of paper that calculates a guaranteed fixed monthly income amount based on your age and your years of service. Sometimes they'll include bonus factors and other features to calculate your personal retirement options. Typical pensions come with a few choices: life only, life with survivor options, period certain, and lump sum.

Life-Only Pension

The life-only option is usually the highest monthly payment available to you. For many, it's the most attractive, but often the riskiest, of all the options. It is the highest because it's based on someone guessing how long you'll live. That's right. An actuary (a highly analytical type of accountant) examines

Who Wants to Receive a Pension?

In 2010, 84 percent of union card holders and public-sector employees were entitled to a pension, yet only 21 percent of private-industry employees stood to receive a guaranteed fixed income from their employer.

Source: 2011 Bureau of Labor and Statistics

Uninspired

your age and the number of years you've been with the firm—and takes a bet, guessing how long you'll live. If you outlive the actuary's guess, you make out pretty well on your pension choice. But if you die earlier than expected, your company gets to keep the money it was supposed to pay you.

The decision to select a life-only pension should be approached with great care. Here are some of the common reasons you might elect the life-only option:

- You are single.
- Your spouse has adequate assets to support his or her lifestyle without a pension check.
- Your pension amount is very small and insignificant to your lifestyle.
- You have adequate life insurance to protect your spouse in the event of your death.

Life with Survivor Options

A popular pension selection option is one where you agree to receive a smaller monthly guaranteed fixed amount than the life-only option knowing full well that if you die, your spouse will receive a certain percentage of your pension for the rest of his or her life.

Common survivor options are as follows:

- $X to the retiree—then, at death, 100 percent of benefit to the spouse
- $X to the retiree—then, at death, 75 percent of benefit to the spouse
- $X to the retiree—then, at death, 50 percent of benefit to the spouse

Example

The Risk of Selecting the Life-Only Pension

Geff D. was a school teacher at the local high school. He won "teacher of the year" fifteen of his forty years at school. He was also the coach of the junior varsity girls basketball team and chair of the science fair. At age sixty-three, Geff was looking forward to retirement with his wife, Angie, whom he married when he was twenty. Together, they had three children and seven grandchildren. They all lived close by and enjoyed time together as a family.

Geff wasn't the type who asked others for help. His students came to him for advice all the time, and as such, he felt that he had a pretty good mind for managing his own personal financial life too. In February, Geff approached the teachers retirement board and asked for paperwork so that he could retire at the end of the school year.

He took little time to study the paperwork. After all, as a school teacher, both he and his wife would continue to receive health insurance benefits for life through the city. And his $70,000-per-year salary would pay him a $56,000 pension if he selected the life-only option, which he did.

On June 25, more than one hundred people attended a retirement party for Geff. It was a great event. Geff looked forward to an exciting future with his family.

The next morning, Geff awoke. He headed to the shower to start his first day of retirement. One hour later, when Angie realized the water was still running, she found Geff laying still on the floor of the tub. His retirement would last less than one day.

Angie would never receive a nickel of the pension because Geff selected the life-only option. When his life ended, so too did the pension.

Generally, the smaller the amount promised to the spouse, the larger the amount given to the retiree.

Period-Certain Options

This option is appearing more often in a retiree's pension option selection menu. Under this scenario, the pensioner agrees to accept a guaranteed fixed income stream for a "certain period" of years or for life, whichever is longer.

Companies will present this option as follows:

- $X per month for 120 months (ten years) or life
- $X per month for 180 months (fifteen years) or life
- $X per month for 240 months (twenty years) or life

Imagine that you selected the 180-month or life option. In year ten, you die. Your beneficiary would be entitled to receive the remainder of the fifteen years owed to you in monthly installments until the fifteen-year period was attained.

However, if you elected the 180-month option and were still alive twenty-five years later, the insurance company would be on the hook to continue paying you for the rest of your life. Of course, when you died, the monthly check would stop immediately. There would be no further pension checks to your spouse.

The Lump-Sum Option

Another popular option offered to retirees is the lump sum. This one is generally an eye-opener because in many cases, the company is offering you a very large amount of money that can be yours with a signature on the bottom of a piece of paper. More often than not, that number is six and sometimes seven figures large. It could be the largest amount of money that you've ever had access to, and it creates heart palpitations and sweaty palms. Make no mistake. It's a lot of money. But is taking the lump sum the smartest option?

If you are offered the lump-sum option, you generally have three choices on how to take the money. They are:

- Just give me my money.
- Roll the money over to an individual retirement account.
- Roll the money into an immediate annuity and begin pension payments.

Just Give Me My Money

By selecting "just give me my money," you are saying that you are willing to pay all of the taxes due, plus penalties (if applicable), so that you can have possession of your money and spend it as you see fit. More than 60 percent of people who separate from service with their employer take this option—and most of them have nothing left of their lump sum a few years later.

When you elect to take personal possession of your lump sum, you are subject to an automatic 20 percent federal tax withholding on the money. If you're under 59½, you're also subject to a 10 percent early-withdrawal penalty.

Money distributed to you as a lump sum is, in most cases, fully taxable. It's my hope if you're reading this book and planning on a long and successful retirement that you're not considering the "just give me my money" option.

Traditional and Same-Sex Married Couples Now Enjoy Equal Beneficiary Privileges

With the Supreme Court's decision to overturn the Defense of Marriage Act (DOMA), same-sex married couples are now entitled to the same rights as traditionally married couples for survivor benefits of pensions, Social Security, and more. Prior to this landmark decision, same-sex married couples were not eligible to receive survivor benefits from a spouse who was entitled to a pension. This ruling by the Supreme Court has changed the landscape on retirement planning for multitudes of same-sex married couples. It was a long, hard fight by millions of passionate Americans but one that has resulted in equal rights, equal benefits, and equal security to all married couples—no matter their sexual orientation.

Inspiration

Roll the Money Over to an IRA

This is the most popular option for retirees, as it gives them the greatest control over their retirement funds and can be done so without any tax liability.

In this instance, you instruct your employer to pay your lump sum to a financial institution to provide safekeeping of your funds until you need some, or all, of the money. The institution is referred to as a custodian. Most banks, brokerage firms, and financial institutions provide custody services so that you don't take personal possession of your retirement money. However, the money is held for your benefit and your control via the custodian.

For instance, if you were to request a rollover of your lump sum to a financial institution, you would instruct your employer to issue the check as follows:

[Name of Financial Institution/Custodian] for the Benefit of [Your Name]

Account Number __________ Social Security Number ___-__-____

Pure Genius!

What Does the Lump Sum Represent When Offered as a Replacement to a Pension?

It's important to put the lump-sum figure into context. People involved with the administration of your plan have developed a mathematical estimate of how much money (in a one-time payment) would be the equivalent risk for replacing one of your pension options. That's right. They don't care either way which option you select. The choice is yours: 100 percent access to your lump sum or your agreement to give up access to the large amount of money in exchange for a fixed monthly income check for the rest of your life (or the lives of your spouse and you). It's not an easy choice. Each decision comes with benefits and risks.

Discipline becomes the bigger, more emotional, decision when deciding to take the lump sum. If you take the money, will you manage it properly for the remainder of your life? Will you know how to draw an income stream from the money and avoid the temptation to grab periodic chunks for big purchases?

In reality, deciding which option you should select requires more than an examination of your retirement package. This is a moment when you need to look at *everything* in your financial life—before signing on the dotted line.

Putting It All Together (a Real-Life Story)

Meet Sam and Mindy Hampton. Sam had worked twenty-one years for a manufacturing company and was recently presented with a retirement package. His wife, Mindy, who raised three self-sufficient children, enjoyed volunteering her time in the community. The prospect of retirement was intimidating, especially when Sam and Mindy reviewed the pension options.

Following is a profile of their current financial life. What do you think they should consider for retirement based on the information provided?

Client Profile

Name and age: Sam (66), Mindy (64)

Location: Salem, Massachusetts

Current income (prior to retirement): Sam ($125,000), Mindy (at home)

Bank assets: $40,000

Investment assets: $135,000

Retirement assets: $275,000

Home: $350,000 (no mortgage)

Health: Sam has Type 2 diabetes and high cholesterol. Mindy is in excellent health.

Monthly Social Security income expected: Sam ($2,000), Mindy ($900)

Monthly spending goal in retirement: $6,000 per month (after tax)

Following are the actual pension numbers presented to Sam by his HR department. (Think about your situation. Which option might you select if you were faced with the same issue?)

Retirement Pension Choices	To Sam	To Mindy If She Survives Sam
Life only	$ 3,401.12	$ 0.00
50% joint and survivor	2,820.17	1,410.09
75% joint and survivor	2,695.58	2,021.69
Lump sum (one-time payment)	451,112.40	0.00

Approaching the Options

Below are key questions the Hamptons needed to consider as they selected the retirement pension choice.

- Would they need inflation protection in retirement? If so, what source would provide it?
- How important is a guaranteed income stream versus one they control?
- What's the likelihood that they would be tempted to take large amounts of money from their account if it's rolled over to an IRA?
- Do they have their eyes on short-term purchases in the first few years of retirement, such as a new car, a vacation home, etc.?

Take the Life-Only Option

If Sam elected to receive $3,4010.12 each month for the rest of his life, there would be a reasonable level of financial security in that they knew about $6,200 in gross income (including pension and Social Security) would come into the household each month. While that amount would meet their spending needs, it certainly wouldn't cover the tax liability due for the income they collected. Nor would it provide much inflation protection as the cost of goods increased each year. Finally, if Sam were to predecease Mindy, she would lose an important income stream to the household.

In order to maintain her lifestyle, she may need to sell her home and relocate to a smaller residence.

Elect a Survivor Option

By choosing the 50 percent or 75 percent survivor option, they could still collect upward of $5,000+ per month (including Social Security and pension). While Social Security might have a very small inflation amount added to the benefit each year, the pension from the company would remain flat. If Sam predeceased Mindy, there would be a continued (though smaller) pension amount. She could still draw upon other investment assets to supplement her income if needed.

Roll the Lump Sum Over to an IRA

In this case, Sam might set up an IRA account to receive the rollover proceeds from the lump sum. Sam might consider combining this lump sum with his existing IRA. For this discussion, I've elected to keep these two accounts separate. That's because Sam wanted to see if the lump sum from his employer could produce an ongoing income stream equal to somewhere between the 50 percent and 75 percent pension option.

For this example, let's assume that Sam wants a current income of $2,750 a month from his lump-sum rollover.

$2,750 x 12 Months = $33,000

A $33,000-per-year distribution from his rollover of $451,112.40 is 7.3 percent in the first year—a withdrawal percentage that's too high.

In today's investment market, could the Hamptons expect a 7.3 percent annualized long-term rate on their investments? Make no mistake. It's possible—but not without an element of risk.

Making the Choice that Works for You

From the very start of this book, I've insisted that "it depends" would be a common answer to most questions. I hope you can see how "it depends" is really the answer to the Hamptons' dilemma.

In the case of the Hamptons, there was no easy answer. They struggled with the decision. Mindy wanted to be assured that she would have enough income to support them both regardless of who died first. Sam wanted to roll the money over to an IRA and then take out $40,000 to buy a new car and another $20,000 to buy a motorcycle. They both admitted that they planned to stay in their home for no more than ten years, as all three of their children had moved to the Carolinas and Florida. In all honesty, the decision could have gone multiple ways. And they knew that each person they met to discuss the "big picture" would offer a different perspective.

Making a Decision (the Hamptons)

Here's what really happened:

- They began collectively receiving $2,800 a month from Social Security.

Pure Genius!

The Reality of *Life* in Retirement

Many retirees approach retirement with either a number or a monthly income stream in mind. Retirement is so much more than that.

Life gets in the way—and it happens way more often than you'll even plan.

Here are a few "extras" that will pop up in your retirement plan. It's important to consider how you'll pay for these items and where you'll take the money:

- A new and/or used car. It's likely that you'll buy your fair share of vehicles throughout retirement. If you can, purchase a car and hold it for five to eight years. It's likely you'll put on fewer miles each year.
- Gifts. Whether it's graduations, weddings, bar mitzvahs, or down-payment assistance to help the kids buy a home, there will always be some surprise expenses that you really want to support.
- Budget busters. Whether it's a new roof, a refurbishment to the bathroom, an updated kitchen, or an addition to the house, these costs are always greater than you expected. Should you have elderly parents, they may need financial assistance too.

- They decided to roll over the lump sum and *merge* it with Sam's existing IRA ($726,000).
- Sam decided to finance a $40,000 new car at 1.9 percent over four years. His personal investment account would make the monthly payments directly to the dealership.
- Sam paid $18,000 cash for a motorcycle using his personal investment account.
- The Hamptons started a 4.5 percent distribution from the IRA of roughly $32,670 ($2,722 a month), but they received it for only one month. (No, no one died. I already told you one horribly sad story in this chapter.)
- Sam was hired back at his company as a contractor almost immediately following his retirement date. He makes $50,000 a year working twenty-five hours a week.
- Sam and Mindy reduced their distribution from the IRA to 1.5 percent each year, and they deposit it into the personal investment account so they can build up more after-tax money.
- Mindy and Sam went on a three-week vacation and cruise of the Mediterranean.
- One year later, Mindy received an inheritance of $250,000 from her favorite aunt.
- They stopped taking money from the IRA accounts all together and agreed to wait until age 70½, when they must take distributions.

Questions to Ask While Considering a Pension Option

- Are you married or single?
- If you're married, do you want your pension to continue to your spouse if you die first?
- How is your health (yours and your spouse's)?
- Is there longevity in your family?
- Do you have adequate assets besides your pension to support your spouse and/or loved ones?
- Would you like a guaranteed income stream?
- Do you need inflation protection on your income?

Pure Genius!

If there's one thing that I've learned in my twenty-three years in this business, it's that nothing ever happens the way you imagine—and life always gets in the way.

Finding Answers in a Sea of Uncertainty

When you're faced with lifelong retirement decisions, make sure you approach them with the seriousness they deserve. Many of the decisions you'll make will be permanent; others will not. Make sure you're comfortable with the flexibility in your decision. After all, the way you view life today will be far different from your view five, ten, or twenty years down the road. Work to find the questions that you need to answer before making major decisions. Ask them honestly of yourself and those you love. Life in retirement is about living—not simply surviving.

Why Teachers Are Really Millionaires

Teachers feel like they are among the most underpaid professionals in America. To some extent, I agree with them, but when it comes to retirement, they have some of the best financial security in the country.

I find many teachers, school administrators, and other public-sector employees carry an element of jealousy when they hear that their neighbor has $500,000 in a 401(k) plan or that the Joneses across the street are millionaires.

I work really hard to teach the teachers. In actuality, they in many cases have greater financial security—financial resources—than many of their neighbors, and it's all because of their pensions.

Consider this:

Following is a chart that depicts the amount of money needed to generate the pension of a teacher who retires at age sixty-five. If you work in the private sector, are you a little jealous? If you're a teacher, do you feel a little richer?

Annual Pension	Lump Sum Needed
$48,000	$ 700,539
60,000	876,886
75,000	1,100,736

Based on a life-only payout as of September 2013.

A pension is only one part of many people's retirement plans. Making decisions on 401(k) plans, IRAs, health savings accounts, and insurance is equally pressing. In the next chapter, I'll address the many decisions retirees must make surrounding retirement accounts and insurance.

To Summarize...

- Seek objective advice when facing retirement decisions at work.
- Understand the implications of all pension options.
- Monthly pension checks do not generally increase with inflation. Make sure you have adequate assets positioned to supplement your pension.
- Select a retirement option that gives you the flexibility you need through the rest of your life.

Chapter 15

Understanding Taxes in Retirement

In This Chapter...

- Demystifying taxes
- The role of the tax preparer
- Managing taxes throughout the year
- The power of deductions
- To roll or not to roll—that is the question

Taxes remain one of the biggest certainties in life, yet it's one of America's most misunderstood topics. After all there are more than 74,000 pages of 8½ x 11 paper needed to explain the US tax code.

During employment, your taxes were typically handled through withholdings on your pay stub: federal, state, Social Security, Medicare, etc.

But now you're retired. Managing taxes is now *your* responsibility. You'll need to decide whether taxes should be withheld and from which accounts.

Demystifying Taxes for Retirees

Let's be clear. I am not an accountant, and I don't prepare tax returns. Nevertheless, one of the most important courses I took during my studies to earn the Certified Financial Planner mark was called "Tax Planning." It's not surprising that many CFP candidates find this course the hardest in the whole program.

Understanding taxes, and all the pieces and parts that go into the development of an individual tax return, may be the most overlooked item that financial advisers forget to integrate into a retiree's personal retirement plan.

It's rare when you can find a financial planner who builds side-by-side tax comparisons that help you make smart decisions on where to draw money to support your income. Many accountants offer this pro forma service to their business and corporate clients—but, for individuals, they primarily rely on information provided to them. They generally make the assumption that everything in your "tax life" is the same as it was last year. That's why it's important for *you* to understand how taxes will impact your income in retirement.

True or False: Tax Refund = Good Accountant? Taxes Owed = Bad Accountant?

I remain mystified when I meet people who say that they've got a great accountant because they get a refund each year. Accountants are not magicians. They follow a set of guidelines established by the Internal Revenue Service and, for the most part, serve as a check-and-balance service at the end of a tax year. If you're entitled to a refund, it generally means that you paid too much money to the IRS in advance. If you owe money, it means that you didn't pay enough money to the IRS prior to your tax filing.

For instance, when you started your first day on the job, you filled out a W-4 form (tax withholding) along with a bunch of other paperwork. You probably went on the advice of your employer, or your gut, and selected an allowances amount (i.e., "married, 2"). Is it possible your W-4 has remained the same throughout your working years?

Your complacency on changing tax withholdings to your pay stub may be the sole reason you pay taxes or receive a big refund each year. It has nothing to do with the accountant.

From Hero to Goat: An Accountant's Story

A few years ago, I met Paul. He had retired the previous year and at the same time chose to change accountants as well. This new preparer had done taxes for many of his friends in the neighborhood, and Paul heard about the great refunds the accountant was able to uncover. Since he was now retired and beginning to take money from investments and collect Social Security income to support his lifestyle, he thought he'd work with a tax preparer who focused on retirees.

Know Your Tax Rate

When you begin planning for your retirement, overestimating or underestimating your tax rate could dramatically disturb your ability to achieve your retirement income goal.

Perspiration

The first year, when it was time to pick up his return, he was delighted to learn that he was going to receive a $12,000 refund. The previous year, it was $800. Paul was delighted. He thanked his friends for the referral to the new accountant—and even hosted a party at his home to celebrate.

Then came the bad news.

In October of that year, Paul received a letter from the IRS saying that he owed $11,400. He was shocked and then became furious with the accountant. He called him incompetent and trashed his name throughout the neighborhood and anyone else who cared to listen.

Unfortunately, the mistake had nothing to do with the accountant—and everything to do with Paul himself. Paul didn't include the IRS Form 1099-R, a tax form, that showed he drew $36,000 from his IRA during the past year. Paul never gave it to his accountant.

When Paul retired, the investment firm that held his IRA rollover began sending him $3,000 per month from his account. The company sent paperwork for him to sign, and he diligently returned it to the firm—but he never indicated that taxes should have been withheld. As such, he received a gross check of $3,000 per month without any tax withholding. At year-end, the company sent Paul the proper tax form, but because it was one he didn't recognize, he simply tossed it in the trash.

After a heated conversation with his accountant, Paul learned that the error was his own. Paul had egg on his face. His accountant wasn't a hero or a rat. He was doing his job based on the information that was provided. The accountant had no idea that Paul neglected to provide him a form—because it was the first year Paul began taking money from his IRA.

Fortunately, Paul had money in his account to pay the taxes due.

To the accountant's credit, he reminded Paul that since he was continuing to receive $3,000 per month this year and it was already October, taxes were once again going to be due in April. The accountant helped him set up an estimated tax payment plan and then had him change his tax withholdings on his IRA distributions for future years.

In the end, Paul owed his new accountant a big apology. Though it was a tough lesson, Paul realized that a big refund or tax due is simply a function of over- or under-withholding taxes during the year. He appreciated his new accountant for the proactive advice for the upcoming tax year and was delighted to learn that he could have taxes withheld from his IRA on future distributions so that he wouldn't need to pay estimated taxes.

Using In-State Bank Accounts versus Out-of-State or Online Banks

Did you know that many states offer favorable tax treatment for interest earned on bank accounts that you hold in your state of residence? In the state of Massachusetts, for instance, you are subject to paying only a maximum 12 percent tax rate on interest if it comes from an in-state bank.

With interest rates so low these days, the tax rate may not be all that meaningful. However, as rates increase, you might look at the tax savings of having an in-house bank account rather than one that's online or out of state.

Pure Genius!

What Might Cause You to Owe More Taxes Than the Previous Year?

There are many reasons you may owe more or less in taxes each year. Here are some of the most likely reasons why you could owe money at year-end.

Need More Income? Stop Reinvesting Dividends

Betty visited our office with hopes of uncovering a couple hundred dollars, or more, per month, to help with increased expenses. A former telephone company worker, she had AT&T, Verizon, and other shares that were all held in book-entry accounts. When I looked at Betty's tax return, I noticed that she paid tax on almost $3,000 per year in dividends, yet she was reinvesting to buy more shares. She was surprised to learn that reinvested dividends were taxable. She thought that taxes were due only if you took the dividend check.

With a few clicks on the transfer agent's website, we were able to have her dividends sent to her on a quarterly basis. She felt relieved that she wouldn't need to sell any of her investments to create the excess cash flow.

Pure Genius!

Interest Payments

As interest rates on certificates of deposit and savings accounts have dwindled, so too has the interest that is subject to tax. Regardless of whether you take your interest each month or reinvest it, you are still responsible for paying tax.

Dividends

Similar to interest from banks, dividends are subject to taxes whether you have them paid in cash or reinvested. Many stocks that issue dividends are subject to a maximum tax rate of 15 percent if you fall into the 25, 28, 33, or 35 percent tax bracket. If you are in the 10 and/or 15 percent tax bracket, you will have a 0 percent tax rate on dividends and capital gains. However, if your taxable income is $400,000 ($450K for married couples), you will be subject to a 20 percent tax on dividends and capital gains.

You generally can't have taxes withheld from dividend payments.

Capital Gains

When you buy or sell an investment, it has the potential of being subject to capital gain taxes. These taxes are due even if you choose to reinvest the proceeds from the sale into another investment. For instance, if you bought one hundred shares of Coca-Cola at $20 ($2,000) and then sold it two years later at $40 a share ($4,000), you would be subject to a long-term capital gains tax on the amount of money you made ($2,000). That federal tax could be as much as 20 percent, or $400. (If you're a high earner, you may pay a surcharge because of the Obamacare tax. To learn more about Obamacare, check out *Obamacare for the GENIUS.*)

Capital Gains Distributions from Mutual Funds

This is typically a special distribution paid to shareholders toward the end of each calendar year. It represents a distribution of the net gains that a mutual fund manager earned while trading stock in the portfolio over the course of the year. By prospectus, the manager needs to pay out the "net realized gains" to shareholders. In years of positive market performance or high volatility, mutual fund companies have been known to make distributions of upward of 15 to 20 percent of the value of the account. This can be a surprise taxable dividend to shareholders and one that should be reviewed as part of a tax plan each year.

Liquidation of EE Savings Bonds

Many retirees find themselves with stacks of EE savings bonds that they've accumulated over their lifetimes. These bonds accrue interest each year and aren't subject to tax until they're redeemed. In most cases, the accrued interest is taxable at your ordinary income tax rate. Since taxes are not withheld when savings bonds are redeemed, you could find yourself having to come up with some money at tax time.

Sale of a Business or Property

The sale of a business or an investment property often results in a tax liability. Generally, an accountant will give you a sense of the taxes due on a transaction like this, and you can determine whether making estimated payments make sense. Typically, this transaction is a one-time event. Make sure that your future tax planning doesn't incorporate this transaction occurring each year.

The Dangers of Ignoring Perks from Your Business

Business ownership comes with perks. If you ran an office, you likely took advantage of office supplies, a printer here, and a computer there. Perhaps you wrote off "travel," "business meals," "auto perks," and more. Once your business is gone, so too are the perks. Make sure that you've accounted for your

Pure Genius!

EE Bonds Double in Seven or Eight Years, Right?

Bonds issued over the past ten or more years will take twenty years to double in value. Bonds purchased in the 1990s and 2000s will take between eighteen and twenty years. So if you thought EE savings bonds would double in seven or eight years, *think again.*

We all know that a hundred-dollar EE savings bond costs fifty dollars. Over time, it's supposed to double in value, right? What it does is accrue interest, and these days, interest rates on savings are pitiful.

What do you think a hundred-dollar EE savings bond that you purchased for fifty dollars years ago was worth in October of 2013? Take a look at these examples:

Series	Face Value	Issue Date	Next Accrual	Final Maturity	Issue Price	Interest	Interest Rate	Value
EE	$100	1/2011	10/2013	1/2041	$50	$ 0.76	0.60%	$ 50.76
EE	100	1/2001	10/2013	1/2031	50	22.20	0.68	72.20
EE	100	1/1991	1/2014	1/2021	50	104.08	4.00	154.08
EE	100	1/1981	n/a	1/2011	50	256.88	n/a	306.88

It's important to note that after thirty years, EE bonds stop paying interest.

The US Treasury Department has an online calculator to help you view the value of your bonds and the interest that has accrued.

Here's the link: treasurydirect.gov/indiv/tools/tools_savingsbondcalc.htm.

true expense needs prior to placing a value on your business. Remember, you worked hard to build your business. Make sure you're rewarded for your sweat.

Social Security Income

Generally, individuals do not have taxes withheld from their Social Security checks. The maximum amount paid to someone collecting at their full retirement age in 2013 is $30,396. If you're married and your partner receives a spousal benefit of half that amount, it's possible to have income of close to $45,000 (without any taxes withheld). In a worst-case scenario, 85 percent of your social security income will be subject to tax. We'll discuss this further in **Chapter 16**.

Larger-Than-Expected Withdrawals from Retirement Plans or Annuities

Typically, money that is taken from retirement plans is taxable on the very first dollar. This means that if you need $30,000 to purchase a car and you draw that money from your IRA, you are likely to owe tax on all $30,000 you received. Without proper planning, this is an unwelcome surprise during tax time.

When distributions are made from an annuity, they follow the "last-in, first-out" principal. Let's say you invested $50,000 in a nonqualified annuity ten years ago, and today it is worth $100,000. If you request $30,000, all money is recognized as "taxable"; thus it would be subject to ordinary income tax rates. However, if you requested $60,000 from the account, you would need to pay taxes on only $50,000—$10,000 of the $60,000 would be considered a return of your own money.

Reasons You May Find Yourself with a Tax Refund

More often than not, your accountant didn't do anything different. As much as you might like to thank him or her for the nice refund check, you were the cause of your own refund. Here are a few reasons why:

Overestimating Your Tax Payments

A couple of years ago, your accountant may have advised you to increase your estimated tax payments due to a year when your income was higher than normal. Perhaps it was for some of the reasons stated above, but now your income is lower, and there's no need to keep up with such large estimated payments.

Reduction in Interest Rates

Interest rates on CDs, savings accounts, and bonds have never been higher than they were in the early 1980s. Over time, these rates have dropped, causing you to earn less and less interest each year. Less interest translates to less taxes due, and if you've been making estimated payments based on old interest estimates, your refund has likely increased quite a bit.

Pure Genius!

A Planning Tip for Annuities Held Since 1981

If you own a nonqualified annuity that was originally purchased prior to August 14, 1981, then you may qualify for first-in, first-out treatment on distributions. That's right. If you invested $50,000 on January 10, 1981, and the annuity account was now worth $200,000, for example, the first $50,000 you removed from the annuity would be tax-free to you (as it reflects a return of your initial investment).

Many people own annuities today that have been transferred a few times from previous annuity companies via a 1035 tax-free exchange program. Did you know that each company sends the original purchase price to the receiving annuity company? Consider this example:

Let's say you invested $50,000 with Annuity Company A in February of 1981, and by 1994 it grew to $80,000.

In 1994, you transferred the $80,000 from Company A to Annuity Company B, and it grew to $150,000.

In 2000, you transferred the $150,000 from Company B to Annuity Company C, where it is now worth $250,000.

Assuming the paperwork was completed properly, your original cost of $50,000 should been carried from company to company. And because you purchased the original annuity in 1981, you may be eligible to remove the first $50,000 for free.

> **Choices and More Choices**
>
> Many retirees rely on a variety of income sources to support their spending needs. Social Security, pensions, and part-time employment may each impact your tax liability differently. Now try supplementing your spending needs from places such as the bank, retirement accounts, personal investments, and more. All these sources could have an impact on how other pieces of your retirement income streams are taxed. Ignoring this important fact could cost you more tax money than you need to pay.
>
> Perspiration

Tax Withholdings Are Too High

It's possible that you've elected to have too much tax withheld from IRA distributions. An IRA or annuity distribution form requires you to elect tax withholdings. Make sure you don't overestimate.

All too often, I see retirees simply selecting 28 percent federal tax withholding on their IRA and annuity distributions because they think that they are in the 28 percent tax bracket. That's a flawed assumption, and it can often lead to a larger-than-expected refund at year-end.

Taking Less from IRAs and More from Personal Investments

Remember, in most cases, when you take money from your IRA, it's all taxable. When you take money from a personal account at the bank, there are no taxes due. In addition, if you sell investments in your personal account and use those proceeds to support your income, only a portion of that money may be taxable. Coordinating the right mix of where to take money is not only a "genius trait" but could also be the reason your refund is higher (or lower) than you expected.

Positioning Accounts for Retirement

Many retirees work so diligently to put money aside in their retirement accounts that they neglect to save money in personal investment accounts. All too often, I see retirees with 98 percent of their investment assets in retirement plans and 2 percent in a joint investment accounts. This imbalance between retirement and nonretirement accounts can lead to a rapid decline in your net worth if you need additional sums of money that exceed your retirement income needs.

Let say, for instance, you want to buy a car or pay for a daughter's wedding, and the bulk of your money is held in IRA accounts. If that cost is $35,000, you could find yourself having to take $50,000 (or more) from your IRA so that you net $35,000. If you had ample dollars in a personal investment account, you could draw on that money with (potentially) little to no taxes due.

New Deductions Are Available

When you're working, your taxable income is often higher than when you're retired. That doesn't mean you will have less income in retirement. You just have a variety of places to access money, and some of those sources may not be as taxable as others. With that in mind, you now may be eligible for deductions on Schedule A of your tax return that had otherwise been out of your reach. Here are a few examples below:

Medical Deductions

In 2013, if your medical costs exceeded 10 percent (it used to be 7.5 percent) of your adjusted gross income, the overage may have been eligible as a deduction. When you're working, your employer might be covering some or all of your medical costs. In retirement, you may be footing more of the bill. In addition, long-term-care insurance, day-to-day medical expenses, and prescription drug costs can add up. Keep track of these receipts. They could mean more money in your pocket. Also, if you are in a long-term-care facility for medically needed services, these costs will generally be deductible as well.

Finding Your Balance

Seek to find a balance between your personal investment accounts and your retirement accounts.

Perspiration

Unreimbursed Expenses

Are you aware that if the costs for tax preparation, legal fees, and investment advisory fees exceed 2 percent of your adjusted gross income, they may be eligible as a deduction? Let's say your adjusted gross income is $100,000. If you paid $500 for tax preparation, $1,500 for preparation of estate documents, and $3,500 in investment advisory fees (totaling $5,500), then $3,500 of those expenses could be eligible for deductibility on Schedule A. That's because $100,000 x 2 percent = $2,000. $5,500 – $2,000 = $3,500.

Charitable Contributions

In years when you've been more generous than others to charitable organizations, your tax return will reflect changes to the taxes you owe. I see individuals becoming more charitably inclined with both cash and "in kind" items, such as investments, cars, fixtures, and more. This generosity can lead to larger tax deductions and greater tax refunds.

Accountants Add Value

An accountant's job is to prepare your tax return in the most accurate manner possible. However, the accountant can't read your mind. During tax season, accountants can prepare hundreds if not thousands of personal

WATCH OUT!

A Note about Taking a Tax Deduction for Investment Costs

Commissions you pay to brokers and insurance agents are *not* eligible as deductible items on Schedule A. However, investment advisory fees paid to financial advisers for professional services, financial planning, and investment advice may be eligible for deductibility. Make sure you know the difference.

Most registered investment advisory firms provide a listing of the fees you paid them at the end of the calendar year. Check with your tax preparer to see if you're eligible for a deduction.

Also, if you pay investment advisory fees for retirement accounts, I would strongly encourage you to pay them from a nonretirement account or ask your adviser to send you a bill for the fees. If you pay your fees by having money deducted directly from your IRA account, you may not be eligible for a deduction. Many tax preparers consider fees withdrawn directly from an IRA to be a "distribution" and ineligible for a tax deduction.

income tax returns during a ninety-day period of time. When it's time to prepare *your* return, the accountant is going to rely on the documentation you've provided. Accountants are not clairvoyant, and they most certainly won't guess about streams of income, charitable contributions you've made, or fees you've paid to other professionals. You need to tell your accountant about all those things.

Preparing Taxes on Your Own

Most people have the ability to prepare taxes on their own or at a low cost. There are several very good tax-preparation programs available for individuals. If you're computer savvy and willing to make a few judgment calls on your own, I have no problem with you doing taxes independently.

Yet, with the tax laws changing regularly, paying a tax preparer may be worth a few hundred dollars each year. After all, retirement is a time to relax—not stress yourself.

When you retire, you'll begin receiving some new tax forms in addition to the ones you're familiar with. They could include the following:

- SSA-1099. This form reports Social Security benefits paid to you.
- 1099-R. This form is for distributions from pensions, annuities, IRAs, retirement plans, and more.
- 1099-MISC. This form is for other sources of income such as contract work, lottery winnings, and self-employed income.

Each of these forms contains important information that needs to be reported appropriately to the IRS.

Despite all the new forms, most retirees don't need to pay $1,000 or more to a CPA for tax preparation. The H&R Blocks or Jackson Hewitts of the world can quickly, and efficiently, put your mind at ease at a very reasonable cost.

What's Better: Owing Money or Getting a Refund at Tax Time?

In retirement, and even in your working years, you should work hard to coordinate your tax withholdings such that the refund or payment due at tax time is negligible. Planning for a huge refund in April not only gives the IRS free use of your money, but it also serves as a spending temptation when the check arrives. If you build a big refund into your planning and don't get one in a particular year, you may be both disappointed and unable to meet your budgeted expenditures.

The 401(k) Dilemma: Take the Cash or Let It Roll?

Your retirement assets are likely to play a significant role in your income strategy at retirement. Yet more than 50 percent of people who leave their jobs elect to cash in their 401(k) plans to pay off expenses or simply reinvest the money with expectation that they can do better than the tax-deferred benefits of an IRA rollover. As a genius, you know that putting money aside for your future is critically important, yet the temptation of having money now can feel exhilarating. Below is a chart that will show the impact of cashing out your 401(k) and investing it on your own versus rolling it into an IRA rollover account for use in the future.

	Take the Money Now	Roll the Money Over to an IRA
Distribution amount	$ 50,000	$ 50,000
20% tax withholding	(10,000)	0
10% early-withdrawal penalty (if under 59½)	(5,000)	0
Available for reinvestment	35,000	50,000
Value in 10 years	63,778	90,698
Value in 20 years	115,857	165,520
Value in 30 years	210,790	301,129

Based on a 6 percent annualized growth rate. For illustrative purposes only.

But You Still Need to Pay Taxes on Your IRA Eventually, Right?

Yes, taxes (at ordinary income tax rates) will be due on distributions from your IRA. But unlike cashing out your account, most retirees take small distributions from their accounts each year as a supplement to their income needs. As such, only the distribution that they take is subject to tax. The remainder continues to grow tax deferred.

Also, if you elect to take money from the account where you had already paid tax, you should know that all earnings are subject to capital gains tax rates. That's right, you'll still owe taxes on the earnings. It's up to your tax preparer to assist with the right tax-reporting method.

To Summarize...

- Your previous year's tax return can be a great tool for helping you plan the following year.
- The definition of a great accountant shouldn't be whether you get a refund or not.
- Plan accordingly to have the appropriate taxes withheld each year.
- Paying a tax preparer during retirement can remove a huge time suck from your life.

Chapter 16

Maximizing Your Money in Retirement

In This Chapter...

- Why some people pay more taxes than others
- Dispelling the myths of tax brackets
- A tutorial on calculating income taxes
- Making wise distribution decisions

Chances are, you were never given an instruction booklet on how to spend money in retirement. Making smart decisions on where to draw money to support your retirement needs could be the single most important lesson in achieving success.

Will you be in a higher or lower tax bracket in retirement? The decisions you make on where to draw money to meet your spending needs will likely hold the answers.

Let's make sure you make some smart choices.

Tax Bracket and Tax Rates: What's the Difference?

Our current tax system is considered progressive. No, not progressive in the sense that it's forward thinking. It's progressive because your taxable income is taxed differently as you show more reportable income.

Marginal Tax Bracket

The term "marginal tax bracket" represents the tax rate you'll pay on your "last" dollar of taxable income—not all your taxable income.

Definition

Consider the Martins and the Nelsons. Both couples file joint tax returns. This year, the Martins reported "taxable income" of $50,000 and the Nelsons reported "taxable income" of $100,000.

- How much do you think each of these couples will owe in taxes based on their "taxable income?"
- Can you calculate the "marginal tax rate" for the Martins and for the Nelsons?
- What rate of tax do you think they paid on their "taxable income"?

Enter your guesses in the chart below.

Married Filing Joint	Taxable Income	Federal Tax Due	Marginal Tax Rate	Tax Rate/ Taxable Income
The Martins	$ 50,000			
The Nelsons	100,000			

If you're like many Americans, you're stuck already. You have no idea what I'm talking about. Don't worry. You'll understand this by the end of the chapter. If you've got a head for "genius conversation" (and you do), you know that this exercise is not going to be as easy as it seems. But in the end, you'll know more about tax planning than you ever did before.

Think back. Did I say that the Martins had a *total income* of $50,000 or *taxable income* of $50,000? There's a big difference. Did you know that?

Tax Terms

Tax rate. Tax rates are percentages. In 2013, the federal tax rates were 0, 10, 15, 25, 28, 33, 35, and 39.6 percent.

Marginal tax bracket. This is the tax rate you pay on your last dollar of earnings.

Total income. This amount is the total taxable income listed on your IRS Form 1040 prior to any deductions or adjustments.

Adjustable gross income. This is defined as total income less certain deductions. The amount is found on the bottom of page 1 on your 1040 federal tax form and at the top of page 2 of the same form.

Taxable income. This amount is derived after taking all deductions, exemptions, and credits from your adjusted gross income. Your taxable income is the amount to which you apply the taxes that are owed.

Effective tax rate. This the percentage of federal taxes you pay on your taxable income.

Definition

Gross Income

Your *gross* income is located on the front page of IRS Form 1040 of your tax return. It's the number that tallies all the taxable amounts of income you are reporting.

Adjustments to Gross Income

The first deduction opportunities appear near the bottom of your 1040. They are located in a section called "Adjustments to Income." If eligible, this is where you can take deductions for IRA contributions, moving expenses, self-employed health insurance costs, alimony, and more. After these amounts are reduced from your gross income, you are left with your adjustable gross income (AGI). This amount is the last number that appears on page 1 of your 1040. It is also the first number you'll see atop page 2.

On page 2, you have the opportunity to make further reductions to your AGI.

Standard Deduction

The standard deduction is a predetermined dollar amount that nonitemizers use to reduce their AGI. This amount is subject to change each year. If you are over the age of sixty-five or are blind, you are entitled to an increase to your standard deduction.

Standard Deductions for 2014

Filing Status	Standard	Over Age Sixty-Five or Blind
Single or married filing separately	$6,200	$1,550
Married filing jointly or qualified widow(er) with dependent children	1,200	1,200 per spouse
Head of household	9,100	1,550

Itemized Deduction

If you file a Schedule A, you itemize your deductions. Your eligible itemized deduction is determined by tallying deductible items, such as mortgage interest, health care costs, charitable deductions, property tax, and more. There may also be some adjustments to your itemized deductions depending on your AGI.

You are allowed to select the larger of your itemized deductions or your standard deduction.

Personal Exemption

This is a fixed amount indexed annually for inflation ($3,950 in 2014). As a taxpayer, you can multiply the number of dependents in your household by the personal exemption amount and record it as your personal exemption. Thus, if you're married and have two dependent children, your personal exemption in 2013 would have been $15,200. Once again, certain restrictions may apply due to a large adjusted gross income.

See where I'm going here? Your taxable income is much different from the income you think you earned.

Believe it or not, there are even more deductions available to some taxpayers that I haven't even mentioned here.

A Tax Fact

Your gross income may or may not be larger than your adjusted gross income (AGI), but your AGI will *always* be larger than your taxable income—unless both numbers are zero. Remember, your federal income tax is calculated on your *taxable income*, not your adjusted gross income.

Pure Genius!

About Tax Advice in This Book

The tax-planning advice provided in this book is general in nature. Consult with a tax professional about your individual tax circumstances.

Your personal tax situation requires individual attention. You never want to compare your tax liability with someone else's unless you have all the facts first. Not to mention, it's probably in poor taste to ask others about how much tax they owe to the government.

IMPORTANT!

How to Calculate the Taxes You Owe

I'll admit, calculating your personal taxes can be more easily determined by using tax-preparation software or hiring a tax preparer. However, for the benefit of those geniuses who enjoy working with numbers, I'll show you a quick and dirty method for calculating the taxes you owe on your own.

Below, you'll find the tax brackets as of 2013. You'll note that there are seven brackets in the federal tax code for individual returns. They are referred to as marginal tax brackets because each section of your taxable income is subject to a different tax amount. The highest bracket from which you pay tax is referred to as your marginal tax bracket.

Rate	Single Filers	Married Joint Filers	Head of Household Filers
10.0%	$0 to $8,925	$0 to $17,850	$0 to $12,750
15.0%	$8,925 to $36,250	$17,850 to $72,500	$12,750 to $48,600
25.0%	$36,250 to $87,850	$72,500 to $146,400	$48,600 to $125,450
28.0%	$87,850 to $183,250	$146,400 to $223,050	$125,450 to $203,150
33.0%	$183,250 to $398,350	$223,050 to $398,350	$203,150 to $398,350
35.0%	$398,350 to $400,000	$398,350 to $450,000	$398,350 to $425,000
39.6%	$400,000 and up	$450,000 and up	$425,000 and up

Revisiting the Martins and the Nelsons

Let's revisit how you answered the tax questions regarding the Martins and the Nelsons. I have provided the answers using the tax chart above. Take a guess, and write your answers on the next page.

Married Filing Joint	Taxable Income	Federal Tax		Marginal Rate		Tax Rate/ Taxable Income	
		Guess	Actual	Guess	Actual	Guess	Actual
The Martins	$ 50,000		$ 6,604		15%		13.21%
The Nelsons	100,000		16,876		25		16.88

How did you do? Were you close? Were you surprised by the answers? And remember, the "taxable income" is the amount of money subject to taxes *after* deductions. So in reality, both the Martins and Nelsons pay an even smaller tax rate when compared with their gross income or their adjusted gross income. How is this possible? Check out how to calculate the "effective tax yield."

Your Effective Tax Yield

Let's use the example of the Martins and the Nelsons again. We said that they respectfully had taxable income of $50,000 and $100,000. Would you be surprised to learn that their *gross* incomes were a lot closer? The Martins had a gross income of $101,000, and the Nelsons had a gross income of $119,000. If you simply looked at the taxable income number, you might have made different assumptions about their incomes—and their overall financial life.

In order to determine taxable income, you need to do the following:

	Martins	Nelsons
Gross income	$101,000	$119,600
Adjustments	(8,000)	(0)
Adjusted gross income	$ 93,000	$119,600
Standard or itemized deductions	(28,000)	(12,000)
Personal exemptions	(15,200)	(7,600)
Taxable income	$ 50,000	$100,000
Federal taxes due	$ 6,604	$ 16,876
Marginal rate	15.00%	25.00%
Effective tax rate	13.21%	16.88%

The percentage of tax you pay on your adjusted gross income is referred to as your effective tax yield. It is one of the most important numbers to become familiar with while you're in retirement. It serves as a baseline guide in helping you plan tax withholding amounts in the future.

Calculating Your *Real* Tax Rate

Your effective tax rate is a very important number to know—especially in retirement. It can serve as an important factor when determining how much money you'd like to have withheld from the money you'll be drawing from your accounts in retirement.

Pull out your last year's tax return. Go ahead. Fill in the numbers in the chart below. You might be surprised with your own results.

Your Tax Info	
Gross income	$
Adjustments	
Adjusted gross income	$
Standard or itemized deductions	
Personal exemptions	
Taxable income	$
Federal taxes due	$
Marginal rate	%
Effective tax rate	%

Taxes and the Rich

In early 2012, President Barack Obama said that anyone who made over $250,000 was considered rich? What did he mean by that statement? Was he talking to individuals, or was he talking to households? Was he taking about gross income, adjusted gross income, or taxable income? No one ever got a straight answer to that question, and it left many people wondering whether changes in the tax code would impact their lives.

Our politicians are "masters of spin."

A Neighborhood Reality

Meet the Alberts, the Boyds, and the Cooks. They all live on the same street in Gary, Indiana. They have been friends for years and enjoy similar things in life. None of them have any children at home. They are all married and range in age from sixty-six to sixty-nine. In 2013, none of them itemized their deductions. Each couple took a standard deduction of $11,900, plus $2,300 (because they are all over sixty-five), and a personal exemption of $7,800 in 2013.

Each of them reported $80,000 in gross income during the year, yet each of them collected money from different sources and none of them had any taxes withheld.

Before peeking at the end of this chapter to find the answers, I'd encourage you to stick with me, as I think you'll figure it out as you work through the following scenarios.

Inspiration

What Is Rich?

The amount of taxes you pay, or income you make each year, should never be a threshold for determining who is rich and who isn't. As I mentioned earlier, it is a rarity to find anyone who would proclaim themselves as rich—though you and I know that we could point to people we know (forget about celebrities and sports figures) who we would describe as being rich.

When you hear a politician discuss the rich, or even the poor, I would encourage you to turn a deaf ear. That's because their definition is not likely to be all that clear. The words rich, poor, middle class, and affluent are buzzwords designed to allow you to formulate an opinion with little framework to support it.

If your mind is active, you have a loving family, and you can wake up each morning with a smile, richness has already found its way into your life. No amount of money will ever take that away from you.

	The Alberts	The Boyds	The Cooks
Pension income	$ 0	$45,000	$15,000
Social Security income	35,000	10,000	20,000
Annuity distribution	0	15,000	0
Money drawn from joint bank account	10,000	5,000	0
Distributions from IRA	35,000	5,000	45,000
Total collected income	80,000	80,000	80,000
Approximate taxes due			

Who do you think owed the largest amount in taxes?

- ❑ The Alberts
- ❑ The Boyds
- ❑ The Cooks
- ❑ They all paid roughly the same amount.

Taxation on Pension Income

In most cases, monthly pension checks received from an employer are fully taxable. That's because the contributions that both you and your employer made into the plan were done so on a pretax basis. As such, it only makes sense that any money received would be subject to tax.

Taxation on Social Security Income

At most, only 85 percent of your Social Security income can be subject to federal tax. However, if your gross income falls within certain guidelines, less and less of the Social Security income you receive could be subject to tax.

Percentage of Social Security Income Subject to Tax	Individual Filer Income	Joint Filer Income
0%	Under $25,000	Under $32,000
50%	$25,000–$34,000	$32,000–$44,000
85%	Over $34,000	Over $44,000

Exceptions apply. Always consult with a tax professional to determine taxes due in your personal situation.

Taxation on Annuity Income

If you receive income from an annuity, make sure you understand whether your income is part of an "annuitized income stream" or if it's just a withdrawal from your annuity account:

- Annuitized income. When you annuitize your income, you have agreed to receive an ongoing income stream where part of your check reflects a return of your own money and the other part reflects earnings. If your annuity is a nonretirement account annuity, only a portion of your monthly income will be taxable. We discussed this briefly in the previous chapter. That's because it's subject to an "exclusion ratio."
- A payout from your annuity. Unless you hold a nonretirement annuity that was purchased prior to August 14, 1981, chances are you will be subject to a "last-in, first-out" tax treatment on your annuity. This means that if you invested $100,000 in your annuity and today it was worth $200,000, the first $100K that you withdraw from the account would be subject to ordinary income tax. Once you've exhausted all of the earnings, then withdrawals would be tax-free to you, as they would be a return of your own money.

Exclusion Ratio

Generally discussed when one annuitizes an annuity, the exclusion ratio identifies which portion of an income check is subject to tax and which portion isn't.

As an example, Jim invested $100,000 into a nonretirement annuity in 2003. Today, the annuity is worth $200,000. Jim would like to annuitize his payment and receive a check each month for the rest of his life. It is possible since half of Jim's annuity represents his initial investment that half of his annuitized check could represent a return of his own money. Thus, if he were begin an income of $500 a month, only $250 would be subject to tax.

Definition

Taxation on Money in the Bank

When you walk up to the local ATM and request one hundred dollars, how much of that money is subject to tax? None. The money held in personal (not retirement) accounts at a bank represents (in most cases) "after-tax money." Since you pay taxes on the interest earned on your accounts each year (whether you use the interest or not), all the money in the bank is yours to use without having to pay taxes.

Taxation on Retirement Account Distributions

Generally, any money that you pull from an IRA/retirement account is fully taxable to you. Yes, there are a few exceptions—most significantly, if you take money from a Roth IRA. Money drawn from a Roth IRA is generally tax-free.

How Tax-Free Income Could Make Your Social Security Check More Taxable

One income source that generally isn't included when calculating your adjusted gross income is "tax-free income." However, when calculating whether your Social Security income should be taxable, tax-free income *is* included. It's called your "provisional income."

Earlier in the book, we mentioned that a married couple with a modified adjusted gross income (MAGI) of under $32,000 would be free of paying tax on their Social Security income. Well, consider this. Mary and Bruce have the following sources of income in retirement:

Source	Amount
Part-time employment	$18,000
Distribution from IRA	10,000
Interest and dividend income	1,000
Tax-free income	4,000
Total MAGI	29,000 (tax-free income not included)
Total provisional income	33,000 (includes tax-free income)
Social Security income	15,000

Based on the chart above, Mary and Bruce have provisional income of $33,000. According to the chart above, if your MAGI is more than $32,000 but under $44,000, as a married couple, 50 percent of Social Security income could be subject to tax. Just think, if Bruce and Mary better selected where they took money from their accounts, they might be able to avoid having to pay tax on any of their Social Security income.

Based on the above information, let's revisit the income situations of the Alberts, the Boyds, and the Cooks.

Revisiting the Alberts

Source	Amount
Pension income	$ 0
Social Security income	35,000
Annuity distribution	0
Money drawn from joint bank account	10,000
Distributions from IRA	35,000
Total collected income	$80,000

In the case of the Alberts, only 50 percent of their Social Security income will be subject to tax. That's because their provisional income is only $35,000. The money in the bank is not subject to tax, as it's a return of their own money. Only the distribution from the IRA is fully taxable.

Income Subject to Tax in 2013	
Social Security income (only 50% is subject to tax)	$17,500.00
Distributions from IRA	35,000.00
Adjusted gross income	52,500.00
Less standard deduction	(14,200.00)
Less personal exemption	(7,800.00)
Taxable income	$30,500.00
Taxes due	$ 3,682.50
Net income less taxes ($80,000 less taxes due)	$76,317.50

Revisiting the Boyds

In the case of the Boyds, 100 percent of their Social Security income will be subject to tax. That's because their provisional income is $65,000. While the money in the bank is not subject to tax, as it's a return of their own money, the pension, annuity, and retirement distributions *are* fully taxable.

Source	Amount
Pension income	$45,000
Social Security income	10,000
Annuity distribution	15,000
Money drawn from joint bank account	5,000
Distributions from IRA	5,000
Total collected income	$80,000

Income Subject to Tax in 2013	
Pension income	$45,000.00
Annuity distribution	15,000.00
IRA distributions	5,000.00
Social Security income (85% taxable)	8,500.00
Adjusted gross income	$73,500.00
Less standard deduction	(14,200.00)
Less personal exemption	(7,800.00)
Taxable income	$51,500.00
Taxes due	$ 6,832.50
Net income less taxes ($80,000 less taxes due)	$73,167.50

Revisiting the Cooks

So, we've already seen that despite the Alberts and the Boyds taking the same gross income to meet their spending needs, the Boyds pay quite a bit more in taxes simply because of which sources of income provided them with the money they needed.

In the case of the Cooks, it's clear that all of their income will be fully taxable. They have elected not to take any money from their bank—and instead relied exclusively on fully taxable accounts to provide them with their income needs.

Source	Amount
Pension income	$15,000
Social Security income	20,000
Annuity distribution	0
Joint owned money in the bank	0
Distributions from IRA	45,000
Total collected income	$80,000

Income Subject to Tax in 2013	
Pension income	$15,000.00
IRA distributions	45,000.00
Social Security income (85% taxable)	17,000.00
Adjusted gross income	77,000.00
Less standard deduction	(14,200.00)
Less personal exemption	(7,800.00)
Taxable income	$55,000.00
Taxes due	$ 7,357.50
Net income less taxes ($80,000 less taxes due)	$72,642.50

Drawing Conclusions from the Alberts, the Boyds, and the Cooks

So how did you do? Who did you think would be paying the most taxes?

If you guessed the Cooks, you were right. The Alberts paid the least amount in taxes despite having the same gross income as the Boyds and Cooks.

	Alberts	Boyds	Cooks
Gross income	$80,000.00	$80,000.00	$80,000.00
Adjusted gross income	52,500.00	73,500.00	77,000.00
Taxable income	$30,500.00	$51,500.00	$55,000.00
Taxes due on income	$ 3,682.50	$ 6,832.50	$ 7,373.50
Marginal tax bracket	15.00%	15.00%	15.00%
Effective tax rate	12.07%	13.26%	13.40%
In pocket—after tax	$76,317.50	$73,167.50	$72,642.50

A Key to Crafting a Smart Retirement Income

It's my hope that the above example illustrates the importance of knowing how to select the proper places in which to draw money to support your retirement income needs.

The more choices you have from which to draw money, the greater flexibility you will have when needing to make tax-informed decisions. If you have accumulated the bulk of your money in retirement accounts, you may want to consider strategies that could reduce your retirement holding and increase your personal investment holdings. Yes, it might mean that you have to pay taxes on some of the money now, but having access to both retirement *and* nonretirement money is a key card to play when you need more money.

The Smart Retiree

Over the years, I've learned that the happiest retirees are ones who realized that it's critically important to regularly assess where you draw money each year so that you minimize taxes and allow the money you don't use to have the potential to grow in the future.

Pure Genius!

Remember, each individual's situation is different. Despite believing that your income, assets, and spending lifestyle are similar to people you know, the "types" of investments everyone owns can be different. Do your best to ignore "what everyone else is doing" and focus on your needs, your lifestyle, your spending, and your assets. If you can't do it on your own, or you find it all too overwhelming, seek the advice of a Certified Financial Planner professional. It's likely that you'll spend 25 to 30 percent of your life in retirement. I'm sure you want to make wise decisions when it comes to making your money last as long as you can.

To Summarize...

- The tax liability on your sources of income can vary. Know how each source of income will impact your overall tax burden.
- Make sure you truly understand what tax rate you pay against the income you collect.
- When you make smart decisions concerning the places from which you take money to support your retirement income needs, you increase your ability to extend the longevity of your financial resources.
- Social Security is taxable at different amounts—based on your provisional income. If possible, manage your sources of income to reduce the amount of your Social Security benefit that's taxable.

Chapter 17

Ideas on Drawing Income to Meet Your Spending Needs

In This Chapter...

- Finding a retirement income strategy that works for you
- How should you draw income when rates are so low?
- Does the infamous 4 percent retirement withdrawal rate work?
- How much do you need to take from your IRA?
- Should you convert your IRA to a Roth?

Make no mistake, the business of selling "effective" retirement income strategies is a billion-dollar industry. Every insurance company, mutual fund firm, annuity representative, and financial adviser has a collection of strategies they believe makes sense for you. If you attempt to do it yourself, there are websites, apps, books, and mail-order systems. Most programs come with good intentions, but in all honesty, they work only in certain circumstances. As a genius, it's up to you to separate the nonsense from the logic.

How Will You Know Which Retirement Income Strategy Is Best for You?

Everyone has an opinion on the subject of retirement income strategies. Some financial firms and advisers will present strategies that come with "guarantees," and others will present concepts that offer income flexibility. Only you know what will make you sleep well at night.

Retirement Age or Retirement Income?

The question isn't at what age I want to retire, it's at what income.

George Foreman

Quote

Before we jump into explaining some of the most common approaches, let me ask you a few questions:

- Are you willing to sacrifice access to your principal investment if a guaranteed income stream could be delivered?
- Do you imagine needing chunks of money on a periodic basis from your investments that are over and above your month-to-month spending needs?
- Are you willing to assume risks associated with market volatility in hopes of increasing your investable assets and potentially increasing your income stream?
- To what extent do you believe your other sources of income (pensions, Social Security, etc.) will be able to keep pace with inflation?
- Are you concerned about inflation risk?
- Are you fundamentally opposed to any financial strategies because you've heard how they didn't work for someone else?
- Do you believe that you need to restructure your spending lifestyle because interest rates are so low?

- How much of an influence does your parents' approach to living in retirement have on your personal retirement plans?
- Do you and your spouse (partner) share similar values and philosophies when it comes to spending, saving, and investing money?
- Are you more comfortable building a simple retirement income strategy or one that is highly diversified with several moving parts?

Those are only a few of the important questions that retirees need to consider when it's time to structure an income strategy to support their needs.

There's No Crystal-Ball Solution

In the pages that follow, I hope to share answers to common questions people ask when having to draw income to support their retirement income. None of them are the crystal-ball answer. Sorry. It's up to you to examine your overall financial net worth and your cash flow.

The financial services community knows you're confused, overwhelmed—and, in many cases, misinformed. They have spent millions of advertising and marketing dollars on your vulnerability. It's their hope that they can sell you a system, or a template, that will lead you to achieving retirement income bliss. I've walked through hundreds of exhibit halls where well-intentioned financial firms truly want to ease your anxiety. Yet, the truth is that your retirement income plan can't be confined to a box. It needs fluidity and flexibility.

The Truth of the Matter

In providing answers to common questions, please note that my musings are not the end-all. With more than two decades of experience in this business, I continue to learn and develop new ideas each day. My recommendations are just a smattering of the possibilities available to you. It's up to you to draw conclusions from the information provided. You need to be confident in the decisions you make.

Many approaches that work for your friends, neighbors, and relatives apply specifically to their personal situations. While they may also work for you, make sure that you've asked all the right questions and explored all the opportunities. Frankly, it's the primary reason that you really need to understand your own personal financial situation prior to making any major retirement decisions.

Remember, what might make sense for the neighbors could be a huge mistake for you.

What Is the Right Withdrawal Rate in Retirement?

Unfortunately, the best answer to the question "What is the right withdrawal rate in retirement?" is "It depends." Yes, I know, that nugget of foresight won't sell newspapers or get my face on CNBC. If there was truly one answer to that question, life would be simple. But you know (because you're a genius) that life is complicated. It's far from easy.

A Common Strategy for Retirement Income Planning

Below is one strategy that many retirees choose to consider. I'll say right up front: It doesn't work for everyone. However, it is one prudent approach toward building a retirement income plan that has the potential to offer sustainability.

Corey and Olivia F., both aged seventy-two, want a gross income of $8,000 a month in retirement. (That's $96,000 per year.) Their fixed income sources are as follows:

Sources of Income	Monthly Amount
Corey's Social Security	$2,500
Olivia's Social Security	1,250
Pension	500
Required minimum distribution (IRAs)	1,900
Total fixed expected income	$6,150
Total needed income	$8,000
Monthly income needed from investments	$1,850

Here is a simplified version of their net worth statement.

Assets and Liabilities	
Assets	
Bank account	$ 15,000
Investment assets	400,000
Retirement assets	600,000
Primary residence	500,000
Liabilities	
Mortgage	$ 0

Since they both are over the age of 70½, Corey and Olivia are subject to a required minimum distribution (RMD). It doesn't matter how their IRA account is invested (all cash, all stock, or a combination of several asset classes).

Since they will need an additional $1,850 per month, or $22,200 per year, to meet their monthly gross expenses, where is the best place to draw the money to obtain the income they need?

The most logical approach would be to establish a monthly systematic payout of $1,850 per month from the investment assets. This would send a fixed amount of money every month to a bank account, where they would then use the funds to meet expenses.

A $1,850-per-month payout would equate to a 5.56 percent distribution. But what if the account wasn't earning 5.56 percent in interest and dividends? What if Olivia and Corey needed to draw upon some of the profits from their investment—or even some of the losses—to keep the distributions alive? Could this strategy be sustainable?

While this approach may sound risky, it's the one most financial advisers (even the very best ones) use to help clients achieve retirement success. And it can work.

The Risk of Managing Your Own Retirement Income Plan

Unfortunately, when individuals attempt to do it on their own, they have trouble sustaining the strategy. Why? Because emotions get in the way.

During market turbulence, it's only natural to get far too emotional about your investment accounts. All too often, people abandon the strategy and attempt to seek alternative investment ideas. Over time, the initial strategy, and investment portfolio, look far different from the one that was initially constructed.

One Significant Reason to Use a Financial Planner

Financial planners earn their salt more so during turbulent times than when markets are heading in a positive direction. No, it's not that they are able to identify new snazzy investment opportunities that might not be familiar to the general public. It's because they remind you how important a long-term view is on your retirement plan and your investment account during the most uncertain of times.

More often than not, the best move is no move at all. A financial planner can be that leader, guide, and rational sounding board when your emotions are pulling your heart in another direction.

If you don't have that kind of a relationship with your financial planner, it might be time to shop around.

Inspiration

Without a careful eye and a rational approach to rebalancing the portfolio, the sustainability of this distribution strategy may run into danger—especially if the markets endure a significant downturn in the early years of retirement.

A Story from the Crypt

Make no mistake, 2008–2009 was the most emotionally draining period of time in my career.

It seemed that clients would call our office every day wondering when we were finally going to take them out of the market and place all their money into cash.

At the time, about 65 percent of our clients were in retirement. (That's still the case today.) As news about the financial markets grew more frantic, so too did the calls from clients.

"How much more does the market have to drop before you get me out of it?" people would ask.

As much as Marion (my business partner) and I wanted to succumb to our clients' requests, we knew in our heads, *and* in our hearts, that the worst approach was to sell out.

"But this time is different. It's a new normal!" people would exclaim. Their panic and high anxiety were being fueled by the media, the Internet, and a continued thirst to want moment-to-moment news breaks.

While Marion and I worried about whether we were making the right moves for our clients by holding on to their positions and maintaining the commitment to each client's rebalance strategy, we wondered how our clients would react if we continued to make maneuvers each time the markets bobbed and weaved.

In the end, our decision to hang tight, stick with the strategy, remain rational, and not let our emotions drive our choices galvanized the trust we sought to build with our clients.

Lessons Learned

The period of rockiness in 2008–2009 taught us some valuable lessons. The most important one was that people needed to continually dip into their investment accounts to meet their monthly distributions. Their emergency funds had been depleted and never replenished. Over time, they started dipping into their investment accounts to meet spending needs at a very ill-timed period in the markets. Perhaps you found yourself in a similar situation.

As we began crawling out of the doldrums of stock market misery, we crafted a strategy that I'd like to share with you. It was developed so that retirees would never have to feel so vulnerable again. We called it the safe harbor retirement income strategy.

A Fresh Approach to Retirement Income Planning: The Safe Harbor Strategy

How would you react if just as you started your retirement income plan, a financial crisis in both the stock and bond markets occurred and your portfolio dropped almost 30 percent in a matter of months? What would you do? Would you still be comfortable taking a monthly income check from your investment portfolio? Or would you sell out of everything and preserve what was left of your portfolio?

Would you panic?

Finding Your Secret Sauce

Your sources of income (Social Security, pension, etc.) contribute heavily toward determining the proper asset allocation of your investable assets.

When you can find the proper allocation of your assets between cash, stocks, bonds, real estate, and more, you will begin to enjoy retirement with a greater sense of calmness. It's even more comforting to build a strategy that would require only tweaking, rather than a massive overhaul, during turbulent market conditions. After all, it's the patient investor who enjoys retirement the most.

Pure Genius!

We all had those emotions during the financial market meltdown in 2008–2009. I promised myself and my retired clients that we wouldn't allow that "I need to throw up" feeling to ever happen again.

So we employed a plan that kept clients invested while giving them access to money that wouldn't be impacted by another market roller coaster.

Here's what we did:

We identified how much money they expected to draw from their investment accounts over the next three years and immediately moved it to their local bank accounts. It didn't matter the least bit whether the bank account paid interest or not. We wanted the money to be safe and away from market volatility.

The remaining funds stayed fully invested. This gave their investments time to travel through the market cycle. At the end of each year, we would consider replenishing the bank account with money from the investments equal to the amount that had been spent from the bank. However, if the markets hadn't started a positive trajectory, we could wait another year to replace the cash.

Putting the Safe Harbor Retirement Income Strategy to Use

Still confused? I refer you to the original example I shared earlier in the chapter.

Corey and Olivia needed to take $1,850 per month (or $22,800 per year) to supplement their income. Imagine if they took roughly $75,000 (or three years' needed income) from their personal investment account and placed it in the bank. (Yes, the personal investment account would drop to $325,000.)

Each month, Corey and Olivia would draw out $1,850 from the bank account to meet their income needs. Although the money would deplete from the bank, the dollars in the investment account would have the potential to rebound from a market decline.

At a time of their choosing (typically once each year), they would pull another $22,800 from the investment account and replenish the cash position.

Is there a risk? Of course. This strategy would be in danger if the portfolio went through a prolonged three- to six-year period of continual negative returns. I would suggest implementing this strategy only when working with a professional. After all, it's hard to stay rational in emotional times.

The Total-Return Approach

Another common strategy is the "total return" retirement income strategy.

How does it work? Essentially, you build an investment portfolio that leaves roughly 5 to 8 percent of your investable assets in cash. Once a month, you have a check for a predetermined amount electronically withdrawn from the cash account and deposited into your checking account. As the cash portion of your investment portfolio depletes to 3 to 5 percent of the value, you simply rebalance the overall investment portfolio and replenish the cash account. This forces you to take some profits from investments doing well and replenish investments that have underperformed (or have depleted, such as your cash account).

Here's an example:

	Value	Current Allocation	Desired Allocation	For Perfect Balance		New Allocation
MRF Fund	$ 100,000	15%	15%	$ 0	No change	$100,000
IHF Fund	160,000	16	15	(10,000)	Sell	150,000
JKF Fund	310,000	31	25	(60,000)	Sell	250,000
NJF Fund	200,000	20	17	(30,000)	Sell	170,000
CAF Fund	150,000	15	20	50,000	Buy	200,000
Cash	80,000	3	8	50,000	Buy	130,000
Totals	$1,000,000	100%	100%	$ 0		$1,000,000

While it may seem counterintuitive to sell from your winners and add to your losers, this strategic process is called rebalancing (which we discussed in **Chapter 8**), and when it's incorporated with a retirement distribution strategy, it's called a total-return approach.

One way to continually replenish the cash account is to have all dividends and interest paid to the cash account (rather than reinvested) so that rebalancing doesn't have to happen as frequently. In all honesty, a strategy that employs a distribution plan of between 3 and 5.5 percent of the account requires little rebalancing. The secret to success is to ignore the waves of the market, tune out the disruptive jibber-jabber you hear on TV, and settle into a retirement rhythm that meets your needs.

I happen to believe that if you don't take more than 5.5 to 6 percent of the value of your accounts and your portfolio has at least a 50 percent allocation to equities, you have the potential to sustain a comfortable retirement income.

The Bucket Strategy

Here's another modification of the above-mentioned strategies.

Try to remember back to when your parents had "pin money." There were envelopes designated for each bill for the month. The utility bill, the mortgage, the milk delivery, the newspaper, etc. Each expense had its own envelope, and each month it would be replenished. The idea of utilizing a bucket strategy for retirement follows the same theory.

Imagine having four buckets.

The first bucket holds three years' worth of cash (similar to the "safe harbor strategy"). You would draw on that money each month to pick up the difference in expense money you needed after receiving Social Security or pension money.

After three years, that bucket would be relatively depleted. You would refill that bucket with money from a second bucket. This bucket would have been holding funds that were coming due in three years (such as a three-year CD). They might earn a small rate of interest, but you would be certain that the money would be there for your needs.

Once you emptied the second bucket into the first bucket, you'd reach into the third bucket. This bucket would have been holding about 50 percent of your total investable assets. The bucket would invest money roughly fifty-fifty in a combination of stocks and bond funds.

Think about it. You wouldn't be touching this money until the end of year three. This means that before ever having to touch the money, there would be "hope" that the account would grow in value such that you could pull out enough money to replace the money in bucket two. This money would then be used to purchase an investment coming due in three years (probably a CD). The remainder of money in bucket three would stay invested.

Finally, what ever money you took from bucket three and placed in bucket two would be replenished with money from a fourth bucket. Any profits earned in this 100 percent equity-based investment account would be removed and added to bucket three. The remainder of money in bucket four would stay fully invested.

This process would continue every three years—or every year if you wanted to manage the money annually.

The illustration below depicts, in the simplest terms, the strategy:

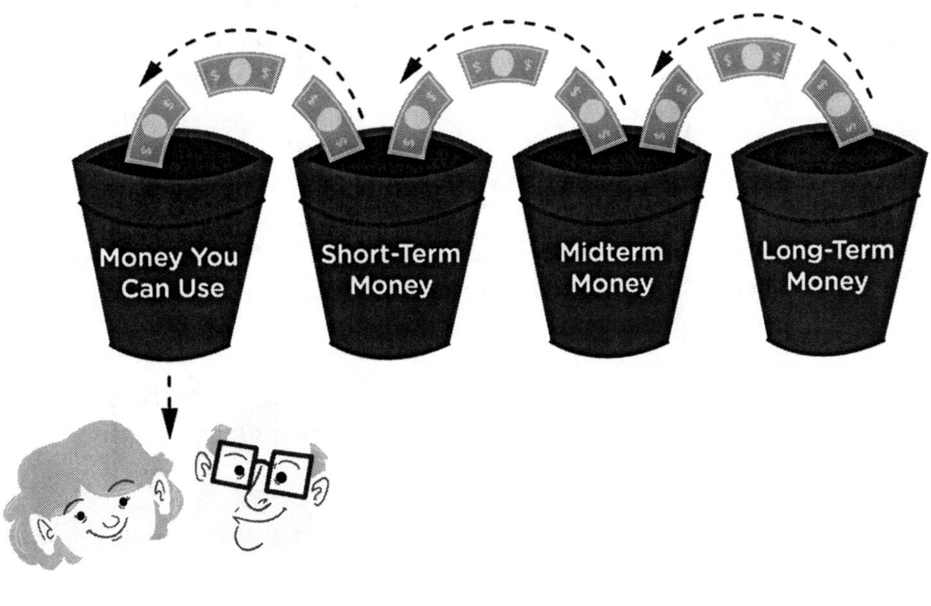

I'm not a huge fan of the bucket approach for the following reasons:

- I don't think people ever like to watch an account deplete to $0. That would be the case with bucket one every three years.
- While there appears to be a methodical process for managing the cash flow of funds, my experience tells me that programs like this sound good on paper but never work in reality. Your mood and emotions around your money are likely to be influenced by market conditions, lifestyle needs, events happening in the family, and more.
- There is a huge assumption that you can achieve competitive rates of return within each bucket to meet your spending needs.

How Should You Draw Income When Rates Are So Low?

Mr. Moore was a seventy-year-old retiree who recently complained that he couldn't retire even though he had $1 million in investable assets. He told a Boston news reporter that he would need to find part-time work at Walmart or Target to meet his day-to-day expenses.

Mr. Moore was widowed about seven years ago. He was collecting around $2,000 per month from Social Security. He owned his home worth $400,000 outright, and he had $1 million scattered around five different banks in certificates of deposit, each of which paid 1 percent per year (approximately $800 in total each month). Because he needed $4,000 per month to meet his spending needs, he felt that he needed to find employment that would give him an additional $1,200 per month, or $400 per week.

Do you sometimes feel like Mr. Moore? Do you still reminisce over the days when CDs paid 12 to 18 percent? Do you wish CDs would just pay 5 to 6 percent now so you could get the income you need?

As you know, times have changed. High-interest-bearing certificate deposits and high-yield securities have gone the way of the encyclopedia, the record player, and the seat-belt-less car.

As such, the days of living off your interest and dividends are virtually impossible for most retirees.

Can You Just Live Off Your Dividends and Interest in Retirement?

Unlike the aforementioned Mr. Moore who refused to move his $1 million from the banks that paid him 1 percent each year, many investors have constructed portfolios that consist of dividend-paying stocks, bonds, real estate investment trusts, preferred stocks, closed-end funds, and more.

Trying to live exclusively off interest and dividend income can be a quiet killer. That's because many investors get so comfortable knowing that their monthly or quarterly dividends are coming in the mail that they forget to see how the underlying investments are actually doing.

It's usually not until the dividend drops, a bond comes due, or the stock they own appears in the headlines that many retirees check in on the long-term likelihood of their income needs continuing. This especially happens to retirees who leave their stock certificates in safe deposit boxes or with transfer agents.

Loyal to a Fault: the GE Employee

Jody K. was an eighty-year-old woman who thought she owned $800,000 in General Electric (GE) stock. One day, she read that her dividend was about to be cut. She had no idea that her stock had dropped 50 percent in value. You see, all she cared about was that the dividend hit her bank account each quarter. Now her stock was worth $400,000 and she was about to be dealt a cut to her dividend that would impact her ability to meet her future spending needs.

Jody's GE stock certificates had sat in a safe deposit box for more than twenty years. She assumed that the dividend would continue and that the stock would just increase (or perhaps even split). After all, it had "always done that in the past," according to her.

Maybe you know someone like her.

Does the 4 Percent Rule Work?

The 4 percent withdrawal discussion began with William Bengen, a well-respected academic and successful financial planner, who wrote the white paper *Safe Withdrawal Rates*. The basis of his theory was that if you structured a well-balanced investment portfolio and simply took 4 percent of the value from the account each year (adjusted for inflation), running out of money would be practically impossible. Let me try to explain how this strategy would work.

Imagine you had an investment account worth $500,000 that was invested 50 percent in stocks and 50 percent in bonds and cash. Using Bengen's statistical modeling program, you would run historical performance iterations of fifty-fifty stock-to-bond models going back as far as 1926. He concluded that the 4 percent distribution number appeared to be the most logical number to call the "safe withdrawal rate."

I've said many times that any financial planning strategy based on an academic model and "virtual" projections neglects to integrate the elements of "life." Thus, in my humble opinion, academic models in the world of financial planning are deeply flawed. Long-term academic-based financial projections simply can't incorporate your unique financial needs. Yet the reality is that most investors want a guideline. They want a rule of thumb, or some expert, to offer a long-term "proven" strategy. Unfortunately, investors tend to take research as gospel and neglect to revisit and review how the strategy integrates into their own financial plans.

Putting the 4 Percent Rule to the Test

Many research models and white papers make for great reading in academic journals. In fact, it can be a resource for a researcher to make quite a bit of money on the speaking circuit and become the "go-to" expert when media needs a source.

Last year, William Bengen retired. What he learned was that while the 4 percent rule worked in theory, it didn't work in real life. How did he find this out? He tried implementing the strategy (finally) on his own personal retirement plan. He concluded that in today's low-interest-rate market, relying exclusively on his 4 percent safe withdrawal rate would lead to problems down the road.

Mr. Bengen's conclusions do not surprise me, as any retirement income plan requires ongoing change, flexibility, and review. Submitting to a handcuffing strategy may work for some—but is dangerous for others.

The other area where I struggle with Bengen's new findings is that he's been retired for only a couple of years. His strategy was designed to work over a twenty-five- to thirty-year period of time. Just because today's interest rate environment is lousy doesn't mean that will be the case in five or ten years. Not to mention, the stock market could exceed market expectations and offset the potential shortcomings from the interest-rate environment.

Closing Thoughts on Retirement Income Strategies

In this chapter, we've explored only a few income strategies retirees consider for their portfolios. Other approaches include purchasing immediate annuities or buying a guaranteed lifetime income strategy from an annuity company. While I'm not completely opposed to these approaches, I find them to be among the most limiting and expensive options around, especially if you're part of the mass affluent baby boomer community. That's not to say that retirement income streams delivered from annuity companies won't work. They can. It's just that there are so many different "bells and whistles," and an ever-changing array of payout options and qualifying factors, that it's virtually impossible to write about the available annuity income options when, in reality, they will look far different by the time this book is published and in your hands. In addition, the mass affluent have limited resources. A significant guaranteed income stream from an annuity requires one to give up access to a large portion of investable assets. This can be dangerous if you intend to access additional chunks of money later in life.

In my office, we pay out more than $900,000 each month to retirees. Some collect $200 per month from their investment accounts, and others $10,000. Each person holds a unique set of variables that need to be factored in to a retirement income plan. Whether it's income from a business, rental income, part-time income, Social Security, or pensions—or just drawing money from the investment account—each piece of the puzzle holds its own complexity in the life of a retiree.

To Summarize...

- Each retiree needs to build a unique retirement income strategy.
- The "4 percent safe withdrawal rate" theory has flaws.
- Consider a "safe harbor retirement income" approach.
- Understand how each piece of your financial life impacts your decisions to draw upon funds.
- Look to build a retirement income plan that is flexible, fluid, and reasonably priced.

Chapter 18

IRA Distributions: Yours and Those You Inherit

In This Chapter...

- How much do you really need to take from your IRA?
- Should you convert your IRA to a Roth?
- Challenges surrounding inherited IRAs
- What is a stretch IRA?

How and when to take money from an IRA is one of the most common questions I get asked on my radio show every week. There are multiple misconceptions regarding IRAs, especially the rules regarding distributions. Since it's likely that you own an IRA, and possibly several, you want to be certain that you're aware of requirements, options, and implications when it comes to taking money from these accounts.

In this chapter, we will help clear up the mysteries. Let's try to set the record straight.

A Few IRA Distribution Basics

IRAs are investments that allow for earnings to grow tax deferred. In most cases, withdrawals from IRAs are fully taxable at ordinary income tax rates.

Withdrawals taken from an IRA prior to age 59½ can be subject to an IRS 10 percent early-withdrawal penalty, but not always.

At age 70½, you will be required to take a minimum distribution from your IRA account. It will be taxable to you.

IRAs can be held in a variety of investment vehicles, including bank accounts, certificates of deposit, stocks, mutual funds, bonds, annuities, and real estate.

But, like everything else with investing, there are always exceptions to the rules. Below are just a couple of them:

- The nondeductible IRA. If your IRA was funded with after-tax dollars, only the earnings of the account will be taxable at the time of distribution. That's because when you withdraw your contributions, it's a return of your own money. Hopefully you filed IRS Form 8606, "Nondeductible IRAs," and have records of the total amount of money you placed into these IRA accounts. This will allow you to substantiate why the distribution from your IRA isn't fully taxable. When you withdraw money from a nondeductible IRA, the withdrawal comes out on a pro rata basis. In other words, if 35 percent of the value of the nondeductible IRA is your contributions and 65 percent represents your earning, then only 65 percent will be taxable. Your tax preparer is best suited to help you document a "partially taxable distribution" from your IRA.
- Distributions from a Roth IRA. When you take money from a Roth IRA, all earnings are tax-free if the Roth IRA is five years or older and you are over age 59½. Contributions may be drawn tax-free.

There is no requirement to take any money from your Roth IRA—even after age 70½. This asset can be passed along without ever having to take a distribution. When your beneficiaries receive a Roth IRA, they can remove money from the account (regardless of their age) without owing any taxes on the distribution. They can also take the money using the required minimum-distribution rules based on life expectancy, which can extend the life of your Roth IRA for a very long time.

Thoughts on Taking Distributions from IRAs

When you elect to take a distribution from a traditional IRA account, it will generally be taxable to you. You will receive documentation of the distribution on IRS Form 1099-R from the financial institution that serves as the custodian of your IRA account (typically a bank, brokerage house, or mutual fund company). Remember, an IRA is held by a financial institution for your benefit. The moment you take personal possession of your IRA money, it becomes taxable as ordinary income to you unless it is rolled over within sixty days to a new IRA.

Converting Your 401(k) Accounts to IRAs

Upon departure from employment, you are usually given the opportunity to roll your existing 401(k) account over to an IRA. I strongly recommend this option, unless you are over age fifty-five and separated from service. In that event, if needed, you may withdraw money from your 401(k) without penalty. But, of course, you still have to pay income taxes.

If you have 401(k)-type plans residing with former employers, roll them over to an IRA account. Under current rules, it's advisable to combine all of your 401(k) rollover IRAs with any existing IRAs you already own, especially if you are over 59½ years of age.

One Important Exception: Don't Mix Nondeductible IRAs with Deductible IRAs

Never commingle IRAs you funded with posttax dollars with retirement accounts that were funded with pretax dollars. You could find yourself paying more tax than necessary at distribution time. That's because every dollar you distribute from a pretax IRA is subject to tax. (After all, you never paid income tax on the contributions or the earnings.) When you remove money from a post-tax-funded IRA account, a portion of your distribution should be free of tax and counted as a return of your own money. That's because a portion of your nondeductible IRA contains money that you invested on an after-tax basis. For instance, if you invested $5,000 into a nondeductible IRA and it's worth $10,000 today, when you take a distribution from the account (after age 59½), only $5,000 (the earnings) of the $10,000 should be subject to tax.

Taking a Distribution from Your IRA Prior to Age 59½

It is generally unadvisable to take money out of your IRA for anything other than supporting your retirement lifestyle. However, the government does allow a few exceptions. While I strongly encourage you to find alternative means of accessing money prior to retirement, below are a few ways you can access funds without having to pay the IRS 10 percent tax penalty:

- Die or become disabled.
- Use the funds for qualified higher-education expenses, such as tuition for you or your dependents.
- Make a first-time home purchase (up to $10,000).
- Pay medical insurance premiums (if you're unemployed).
- Pay an IRS levy on the IRA.
- Take a distribution in a series of substantially equal payments for five years or until age 59½, whichever comes later.
- Pay an investment adviser for managing your money.
- Borrow the funds (as long as you return the money within sixty days).

> **Drawing Your Required Minimum Distribution**
>
> It is generally financially sound to begin taking distributions from your IRA in the year you turn 70½. Choosing to delay your distribution until April 1 of the year following the date you turn 70½ can result in having to take two distributions in the same tax year.
>
> Pure Genius!

Taking Distributions from Your IRA If You Are Over 59½

Once you reach the magical age of 59½, you have the opportunity to access your IRA funds without having to pay a 10 percent income tax penalty. However, it's likely that any money you draw from your IRA will be fully taxable when you take possession of the funds.

Pure Genius!

Will You Check the Right Box on Your Retirement Distribution Paperwork?

Don C., age fifty-eight, was notified that a former company where he worked was shutting its doors. Don still had $100,000 in the old 401(k) plan and was told he needed to move it elsewhere. In reality, the company had been sending correspondence for more than six months. Don ignored the letters thinking they were junk mail.

One day, the human resources department called Don on the phone insisting that they needed instructions on what to do with the money. His choices included rolling the money to his current employer's 401(k) plan, rolling the money into an IRA, or taking the money outright.

Don completed the forms and elected to take the money. He figured that he'd add the funds to his existing IRA account when the check arrived. A week later, Don called our office. He was furious with his former employer. He had just received a check for $80,000 and insisted that his company kept $20,000.

We explained that it wasn't the case at all. The reason for the smaller check was how he completed his paperwork. It was Don's fault.

He wasn't aware that by requesting a check made payable to him rather than a financial institution, 20 percent of the account value would be withheld for federal taxes. In addition, by selecting this option, Don would have had $100,000 added to his adjusted gross income. Don sought answers to fix the problem.

There was a solution. Don had sixty days to roll the money over and place it in his IRA, but he had only $80,000. So Don decided to withdraw $20,000 from his bank account and add it to his IRA as a rollover contribution.

At tax time, Don reported that $100,000 was rolled from his former employer into his IRA. And because he completed the rollover within the sixty-day time limit, he recouped the $20,000 from the IRS in the form of a refund at tax time.

How Much Money Do I Need to Take at 70½?

You do *not* need to take all of the money out of your IRA when you reach age 70½. The required minimum distribution (RMD) is the minimum you must withdraw each year after turning age 70½ and is based on your life expectancy. However, the IRS allows you to delay taking your first distribution. Confusing? Let me help you clear things up.

Assume you turned 70½ this year. You could delay taking your first distribution until no later than April 1 of the following year. By delaying, you would also need to take a distribution during the year you turn 71. As such, you could end up having to take two distributions during that year. The opportunity to delay that payment until the "next" April isn't allowed after the first year.

The required minimum distribution from your IRA is based on an IRS chart called the "Uniform Lifetime Table." This chart illustrates the percentage of money you need to take from your IRA, based on its value at the beginning of each calendar year.

Required minimum distributions for IRAs:

Age of Retiree	Distribution Period (in Years)	Age of Retiree	Distribution Period (in Years)	Age of Retiree	Distribution Period (in Years)	Age of Retiree	Distribution Period (in Years)
70	27.4	82	17.1	94	9.1	105	4.5
71	26.5	83	16.3	95	8.6	106	4.2
72	25.6	84	15.5	96	8.1	107	3.9
73	24.7	85	14.8	97	7.6	108	3.7
74	23.8	86	14.1	98	7.1	109	3.4
75	22.9	87	13.4	99	6.7	110	3.1
76	22.0	88	12.7	100	6.3	111	2.9
77	21.2	89	12.0	101	5.9	112	2.6
78	20.3	90	11.4	102	5.5	113	2.4
79	19.5	91	10.8	103	5.2	114	2.1
80	18.7	92	10.2	104	4.9	115 or older	1.9
81	17.9	93	9.6				

Here's how to read the table. Assume you are turning 70½ this year and the value of your IRA was worth $450,000 on December 31 of the previous year. You would simply divide $450,000 by 27.4. That would result in a required distribution for this year of $16,423.36 (3.65 percent of the account). The remaining dollars in your IRA could stay intact—and grow tax deferred.

By examining the chart, you can see that each year, you have to take a slightly larger percentage of your IRA, but even at age ninety, you're still "required" to take only 8.77 percent (divide the value of your account on December 31 by 11.4 [the factor at age ninety]). So, in reality, you never have to fully liquidate your IRA account.

Calculating Your RMD on Multiple IRA Accounts

Many people have IRA accounts spread all over the place. It is critical that you gather the previous year-end value on all of your IRAs when calculating your minimum distribution. While you can take the entire distribution from one of your IRAs and leave the others alone, the amount you take must meet the minimum amount for the collective value of the IRAs.

Failing to take the full amount of your RMD could result in an IRS penalty equal to 50 percent of the uncollected amount and you will owe income tax, plus interest.

Calculating Your Required Minimum Distribution

The formula to determine your minimum distribution can be calculated as follows:

> End-of-Year Account Value ÷ Uniform Lifetime Table Factor = Required Minimum Distribution

Example

If I Convert My IRA to a Roth, Won't My Income Be Tax-free?

Yes, but it's not that simple.

By now, you know that when you take money from a traditional IRA, it is generally fully taxable. When you take money from a Roth IRA, it is tax-free. So wouldn't it make sense to convert your IRA to a Roth IRA so that you could take the money out tax-free? It's a question I field from people all the time.

Here's the kicker that halts that theory.

If you elect to convert your IRA to a Roth, you must pay taxes in the year of the conversion on the entire amount of money you are converting from your IRA prior to placing it in the Roth. That's right, in order to make your taxable IRA into a tax-free Roth IRA, you need to have the convertible amount of your IRA included as part of your gross income for the year. And what's even worse, it's likely that you'll need to come up with the money to pay the taxes from somewhere else. That's because you're likely going to want to have the full amount of your IRA converted to a Roth.

Here's how it works:

Jenni G. is sixty-four and has a $100,000 IRA that she'd like to convert to a Roth. At the time of the conversion, Jenni needs to report the $100,000 as additional income on her tax return—thus resulting in additional tax liability when she files her taxes. In this example, it could result in Jenni owing $25,000 in additional taxes. Where will she find the money?

Her best option would be to take money from a personal investment account or bank account to pay the taxes. If she drew money from another IRA to pay the tax, that would further increase her tax liability. If she put less money into the Roth (i.e., $75,000 instead of $100,000) so that she could use $25,000 to pay the taxes, that may be imprudent too. Remember, had she not converted the IRA to a Roth, all of her $100,000 could have grown tax deferred rather than $75,000 growing tax-free in a Roth.

Converting IRAs to Roths prior to retirement, or even in retirement, needs to be explored very carefully.

Do I Have to Spend My IRA Distributions?

No, but you must take the distribution. Many retirees find that they do not need their required minimum distributions to fund their spending needs. In some cases, it's like newfound money. The choice is yours. Spend it. Save it. Invest it (in a personal investment account). Gift it. Donate it.

These are all choices that are yours. However, remember that IRA distributions are taxable, so you'll want to have the requisite taxes withheld, or tucked away, so that it's not a surprise to you come tax time.

Distributions from Inherited IRAs

As you age, it's likely that you will become the beneficiary of a parent's or loved one's assets. In some cases, you may be named as the beneficiary of an IRA. Depending on your relationship to the deceased, you will have some options on how to receive the money.

No distribution is required at the death of an IRA owner, unless the deceased was age 70½ or older and had not yet taken the minimum distribution in the year of the death. This distribution is taxable to the deceased's estate and must be made prior to the IRA being inherited by the beneficiary.

Inheriting a Spouse's IRA

If you are the spouse of an IRA owner, you generally have four options from which to choose:

- Roll the assets over into a new or existing IRA in your own name.

  This is an option that no other beneficiary of an IRA has: You can roll inherited IRA assets over into your own IRA and treat these assets as if they were your own. This may be a good choice if you don't have an immediate need for your spouse's IRA assets and you are looking to keep the money in a tax-advantaged account for as long as possible. If you have not reached age 70½ but your spouse has, this option enables you to delay taking distributions until you reach age 70½ rather than continue your spouse's RMDs.

  If you are under age 59½ and you *do* need to access some or all of the assets you inherit from a traditional IRA, you will be subject to a 10 percent early-withdrawal penalty if you roll those assets into your own IRA and then take a distribution prior to age 59½.

- Transfer the assets to an inherited IRA.

  Transferring assets to an inherited IRA may make the most sense if you are under age 59½ and need to access some or all of your spouse's IRA assets now or before you attain the age of 59½. Why? Because you won't be subject to a 10 percent penalty when you take withdrawals from an inherited IRA prior to age 59½, as you would be if you were withdrawing assets from a noninherited IRA you may own.

The timing of your first RMD will be based on the age your spouse attained, not your age. If your spouse was older than 70½, you must begin RMDs by December 31 of the year following your spouse's death. The RMD amounts will be based on the IRS's "Single Life Expectancy" table (appendix C in IRS publication 590), based on your age. Taking the RMD each year does not limit you from taking more money if you want it.

If your spouse was under age 70½, you can delay commencing RMDs until the year your spouse would have turned 70½, even if you are older than 70½.

Another option is to invoke the five-year rule. As long as your spouse was under age 70½ at the time of death, you have five years during which you can withdraw inherited assets from an inherited IRA at any time, in any amount, as long as all the assets are withdrawn by December 31 of the fifth year following your spouse's death. However, keep in mind that these larger distributions could push you into a higher tax bracket.

Roll the IRA assets over into a new or existing IRA and convert the assets to a Roth IRA.

If you don't anticipate needing to rely on RMDs from your spouse's IRA to pay your living expenses, you may want to consider rolling the assets over into an IRA in your name (option 1 above) and then converting the assets into a Roth IRA. This assumes that the IRA you inherited is a traditional IRA and not already a Roth IRA.

With a Roth IRA, contributions are not tax deductible, and you pay no tax when you withdraw assets, provided certain conditions are met. However, you will have to pay taxes on the amount of money you convert from your traditional IRA into a Roth IRA. Therefore, converting to a Roth IRA may make sense for people who anticipate being in a higher tax bracket in the future and who have assets in a nonretirement account to pay the income tax associated with the amount converted to a Roth IRA.

The Required Beginning Date

The required beginning date is no later than April 1 following turning 70½.

Rules pertaining to death distributions are predicated first by answering one simple question: Did the deceased die prior to the required beginning date or not? A "yes" answer will create one set of outcomes; a "no" answer, a different set of variables.

Definition

- Disclaim (decline to inherit) all or part of the assets.

If you choose this option, the IRA assets will pass to your spouse's contingent beneficiaries. This could be your children, another relative, a trust, or a charity.

When assets pass directly to the IRA owner's children or grandchildren, the potential for tax-deferred (or tax-free) growth will be stretched out over a much longer period. Though the children or grandchildren will need to begin taking RMDs in the year after the IRA owner's death, RMD calculations will be based on the longer life expectancies of these younger inheritors.

Death Distribution to a Nonspouse

Let's say you are the daughter, son, grandchild, friend, or coworker of an IRA owner who has named you as the beneficiary. It's critical that you—and the owner of the IRA—understand the rules that govern IRA inheritances.

When you don't understand the rules regarding distributions of IRAs to nonspouse beneficiaries, it can result in paying higher taxes, losing out on tax-advantaged growth—and, most importantly, consequences the deceased had never imagined.

Two Important Ages if You're a Nonspouse Beneficiary: 70½ and 59½

The IRS requires IRA owners to start taking required minimum distributions (RMDs) no later than April 1 following the year in which they turn 70½. These rules also apply to whoever inherits an IRA. In addition, distributions taken prior to age 59½ (either by the IRA owner or the inheritor) could be subject to a 10 percent early-withdrawal penalty, depending on the type of IRA.

Options for Nonspouse Beneficiaries

If you are the beneficiary of an IRA, you should consider your age, the age of the IRA owner, your income needs, and the type of IRA you inherit. Unlike a spouse, if you're a nonspouse beneficiary, you don't have the option of rolling the assets into your own IRA. You generally have a few options:

- Transfer the assets to an inherited IRA beneficiary distribution account.

  When you transfer assets from a traditional IRA into an IRA beneficiary distribution account (inherited IRA), the RMD rules still apply. You must withdraw a certain amount of money from your inherited IRA each year, based on your age and life expectancy. In the case of a nonspouse inheritor, though, RMDs will need to begin before the inheritor reaches age 70½. These distributions may be taxed as ordinary income. However, if the original IRA was a Roth IRA and the assets were in the account for five years or more, distributions may be tax-free. It's my recommendation to consult a tax adviser if you feel you've inherited a Roth IRA that wasn't opened for five years before the original owner passed away.

  If the original IRA owner dies before reaching age 70½ (before RMDs would be required), you also have the option to distribute your inherited IRA under the five-year rule. This allows you to take distributions however you'd like without penalty, as long as all assets are completely distributed from your inherited IRA by December 31 of the fifth year following the IRA owner's death.

  If the original IRA owner died after reaching age 70½, then you must continue to take annual RMDs from your inherited IRA. You may elect to calculate those RMDs by using your own age (see discussion above) or by using the deceased IRA owner's age in the year of death.

- Take the money and run.

  As the beneficiary, you can elect to have your share paid directly to you. You will need to pay tax on the distribution as ordinary income in the year you receive the funds. While not generally advisable, if your share of the IRA is a small amount and won't impact your tax liability

What If You Are One of Several Beneficiaries of an IRA?

If you are listed as a nonspouse beneficiary along with one or more other beneficiaries, it's important to separate your shares of the deceased's IRA in your name and then complete your first RMD by December 31 of the year following the original IRA owner's death. If you don't meet this deadline, your RMD calculation will be based on the oldest beneficiary's life expectancy. If that person is older than you are, you will need to take larger RMDs, which will deplete your tax-advantaged assets more quickly.

When you establish an inherited IRA, be sure your IRA custodian registers the account properly. The account registration should include the name of the person who died, an indication that the account is an IRA beneficiary distribution account, and the inheritor's name.

IMPORTANT!

too significantly, you may be best served by taking the money and not be bothered by an additional account to manage.

- Don't accept the IRA by disclaiming it.

  As a beneficiary, you have the opportunity to disclaim or decline to inherit all or some of the assets. If you choose this election, the money will pass to the other eligible beneficiaries. If no other beneficiaries exist, the assets will pass to the original IRA owner's spouse and then to the estate. Be careful. A decision to disclaim IRA assets must be made within nine months of the original IRA owner's death and before you take possession of the assets. This is an irrevocable decision. No do-overs on this one.

Other Important Items Concerning Inheriting IRAs and Distributions

- There is no option for a sixty-day rollover when inheriting IRA assets. If you receive a check, the money will be taxed as ordinary income and is ineligible to be deposited into an inherited IRA you may own at another firm or back into the inherited IRA that it was withdrawn from to begin with.
- Commingling of IRAs is not permitted. If you inherit different types of IRAs (Roth, traditional, SEP, etc.) from other IRA owners, you cannot combine them into a single inherited IRA. Distribution rules will vary for entities such as trusts, estates, or charities.

- Review your beneficiary designations. Life events such as marriage, divorce, deaths, new children, etc., have been known to be forgotten triggers on IRA designation paperwork, especially when there are retirement accounts still lingering with old employers. Don't create an unnecessary surprise for the family—unless, of course, you want to.
- Remember that IRA beneficiary designations supersede a will. As do beneficiary designations on life insurance, annuities, trusts, and more.

The decisions surrounding IRA distributions, whether they are your own or from an IRA you inherit, can have implications on your overall retirement plan. In many cases, retirement assets represent more than 50 to 70 percent of a retiree's retirement planning assets. It is critical that you understand the implications of your decisions.

Perspiration

Stretching an Inherited IRA: The Real Story

An IRA can last for several generations if only small amounts are withdrawn from a beneficiary IRA. That's because upon your receipt of this asset, you too need to name a beneficiary. Just think how powerful it could be to leave a legacy for generation to generation. By withdrawing just the RMD, the remaining money could blossom, and build wealth, for others.

Do you sense a "but wait" coming? There is:

If you watch PBS, you can find IRA "gurus" who profess the value of stretching an IRA—an opportunity to build a lifelong legacy to the family. You can defer taxes for decades and reap income benefits that could supplement your income.

But here's the truth. It doesn't happen that way in real life. More often than not, people of modest means, and even those with assets under $2 million, find opportunity, fortune, and "free money" when they inherit assets. Believe me, most beneficiaries will spend the money at a rate faster than those computer-generated stretch IRA spreadsheets suggest. It's human nature. Inherited assets mean the opportunity to pay off debts, upgrade purchases, and become more charitable without thinking twice about the taxes due. That's because it's viewed as free money.

To Summarize...

- You don't need to cash in your entire IRA account at age 70½. All you need to do is take the required minimum distribution.
- Surviving spouses have a larger number of options than nonspouses when inheriting IRAs.
- IRA distributions are generally a significant part of a retiree's income. You need to know your options and recognize the implications of each decision.
- If only take you the required minimum distribution from your IRA, it is highly likely that you will never deplete your IRA account.
- The "stretch IRA" concept works in theory but has some stumbling blocks in real life.

Part 3

The Elephant in the Room: Issues Retirees Can No Longer Ignore

Living longer brings new challenges and opportunities, but it also holds its share of aches and pains. Retirees are faced with complex questions as they age. From long-term-care needs to determining whether your current living environment is manageable, there are tough issues to confront. Will you make rational decisions, or will your emotions overrule? Will you be open and educated enough to address the elephants in the room?

Chapter 19

Where Will You Live in Retirement?

In This Chapter...

- Should you buy a retirement home?
- Do you need to downsize?
- A you considering a relocation to another state?
- Are you sacrificing your comfort?

Emotions can leave you in a state of retirement paralysis. Without answers to pressing questions, you can feel stuck—and sometimes alone.

In the early stages of retirement, I see all too many people making expensive mistakes. And many times it's because they *over*analyze a situation. While you may have good intentions, the impact and outcome may have different consequences than what initially looked rosy.

Mostly it's because it's easy to forget about that pesky little thing called *life*.

Can We Afford a Second Property?

It's not uncommon for retirees to explore the prospect of spending weeks to months in a different location in retirement.

> **Keep Laughing**
>
> *You don't stop laughing when you grow old; you grow old when you stop laughing.*
>
> George Bernard Shaw
>
> Quote

If you already live in a warm climate, spending your winters up north is probably not in your plans. But if you're like many folks who have lived through annual snowstorms, slushy roads, black ice, and blistery wind chills, the prospect of living by the beach or pool for the winter is a welcome respite.

To Rent or Buy? That Is the Question

Just because you think you have enough money to purchase a "winter/summer place" doesn't mean you should just lay out the cash and buy it. Remember, real estate values don't move in just one direction. And the costs associated with a second property can be a real eye-opener—especially when you consider how much money you'll lay out when you're *not* there.

I'll use the state of Florida as my example for this discussion, but it could apply to Texas, Arizona, and other popular Southern retirement hot spots.

What once was a giant swampland, Florida has turned into a dynamic state filled with communities of all age groups, all ethnicities, and an array of lifestyles that ranges from trailer parks to gated golf communities with multi-million-dollar homes. If Florida is a potential retirement destination, the first thing you'll need to decide is the type of retirement lifestyle you would like to enjoy. Are you a golfer? Do you enjoy fishing? Are you a shopper, boater, billiards player, or gardener? Would you like to be surrounded by great restaurants, or would you prefer to be in a community where potluck dinners are the norm?

There are so many choices in Florida that unless you have your eye on a particular community and feel that it's the only place you could see yourself living, avoid buying and rent instead. Remember, you're likely to spend 25 to 30 percent of your life in retirement.

Are You Throwing Money down the Toilet If You Rent?

When I encourage people to rent versus buy property in Florida (or any other retirement destination), I'm oftentimes looked at as if I'm wearing a Yankees cap. (If you're a Red Sox fan, you'll understand the reference.)

Renting is not a bad thing. Yes, it's true that you don't build equity in your property, but neither do you have the responsibility that comes with true home ownership, such as mowing the lawn, performing household repairs, paying property taxes, and so much more. Sometimes I think that it's the term "rent" that makes people turn up their noses. It's no wonder that the

Observation

The Villages

One of the most popular locations where the mass affluent baby boomer chooses to rent and/or buy is The Villages. It's a community located about one hour north of Orlando, and it has a population in excess of one hundred thousand—most aged sixty-five or more. It is truly a city in itself. Most people get around town on their "pimped out" golf carts. The community has its own hotels so the kids can visit—but keep their distance too. There are restaurants, shopping malls, parks, golf courses, tennis clubs, concert venues, and more. However, if you're looking for the beach—you're out of luck. Don't worry. There are lots of pools.

Many people find that their expenses drop dramatically by staying at a place like The Villages. Instead of going out to fancy restaurants each night, people host cooking parties, cocktail events, card games, and movie nights. It's like reliving your childhood with house parties every night. The only difference is that you don't have to ask your parents if you're allowed to go.

More of these communities will pop up all throughout the South. So do your homework, rely on the Internet, and ask around. Your dream retirement location may be more of a reality than you have ever imagined.

auto industry chooses to *lease* cars rather than *rent* them to you on a long-term basis. (Psst! It's the same thing!)

Yes, the monthly cost to rent a property, especially during the prime season, is expensive. But think about this: What would it cost you to maintain a property that you owned and visited for only a couple of months a year? In some cases, I've shown people that they could rent a room at the Ritz Carlton for the month rather than pay for a property they plan to visit only one to two months each year.

Searching for the Right Location

Many retirees rely on the advice of friends and family to determine where to live in the winter. It's really up to you to "kick the tires" and see what you like.

Costs You Might Forget about If You Own a Second Property (in the South)

While many people love to visit the South in the winter months, the summer months can be really, really quiet. That's because the weather is a lot more tolerable up north, and the humidity isn't as bad (usually). However, if you own a property in Florida, you will still need to run your air conditioner. If you don't, mold will build up in your house—and that's not an expense you'd like to address when it's time to visit next winter. In addition, the costs of watering your lawn, mowing the grass, tending to the pool, and more are expenses that require attention in your absence. These are added costs that extend beyond any mortgage, property tax, and insurance cost that you need to pay.

So here are a few questions to ask yourself if you're planning on exploring the purchase, or rental, of a property down South.

- What will my personal budget allow for when considering a second property?
- What are the total "real" expenses to rent a property?
- What are the total "real" expenses to own a property (even when I'm not there)?
- How many months do I intend on living in the property?
- How many times do I intend on traveling back up north?

- What costs and upkeep are necessary to maintain my primary home when I'm not there?
- How far away is the nearest doctor, hospital, bank, grocery story, pharmacy, etc.?
- Will I be paying the costs for kids and grandkids to visit?
- Do I want to explore living in different communities, or can I be happy with one location?
- As I age, will I want to spend more time up north, or will I still continue to head south in the winter?
- How easy will it be to sell the place if I become disabled and can't travel there anymore?

It's up to you to decide whether it's affordable, but it's even more important to examine the costs prior to making a long-term (and possibly illiquid) decision.

Does it Make Sense to Downsize?

For many retirees, the house they live in today is the house they've been living in for decades. In fact, I wouldn't be surprised if you paid more for your last car than you did for your first house. One of the giant wild cards that retirees hold in their financial deck of cards is the equity in their homes. In fact, it's not all that peculiar to see retirees trying to eke out a retirement living on their Social Security, investments, and retirement accounts while neglecting to take advantage of the equity in their own homes. I've seen all too many retirees shortchange their own retirement lifestyles because they neglected to utilize the equity in their homes.

Instead, your children end up inheriting the house (and your remaining assets) and find themselves more financially well off than they ever imagined while you spent *your* retirement worrying each day about whether you might outlive your money.

Now before you start thinking that I'm suggesting you explore reverse mortgages—relax. I'm not about to do that. Reverse mortgages are appealing under certain circumstances. If accessing the equity in your home is the last and final opportunity to provide yourself with financial resources to support your retirement income needs, then contact a qualified lender to discuss this strategy. In addition, if it is not your intent to pass along an inheritance to others, gaining access to the equity in your home to enhance your retirement may be an option to consider. The US Department of Housing and Urban Development's website (hud.gov) is a great unbiased resource.

The Agony of Downsizing

Let's say you purchased your home thirty-five years ago for $150,000 and today its estimated value is $525,000.

You have such great memories in your house: Thanksgiving dinners, first days of school, prom pictures, anniversary parties, family game nights, and more. But with memories comes a lot of stuff. Yup, stuff. And the thought of having to go through it all and clean it out is a task you want to avoid at all costs. Frankly, it's usually the primary reason people live in their houses too long.

As much as you might enjoy being the maternal home where everyone visits, as you age, maintaining both the inside and the outside of the house becomes more difficult. If your finances allow for the added expenses of upkeep, maintenance, and contract services, that's wonderful. But at some point, many retirees tell me that their houses just get too large. They begin by heating only parts of the house. Portions of the home go completely unused. The stairs become more challenging to climb, especially if the laundry facilities are in the basement.

And for others, after living in a home for forty years or more, the cost of maintaining the house—though perhaps affordable—is an amount larger than you really want (or need) to spend.

Client Story: Lucy's Windows

Lucy, at age seventy-four, was finding it chillier in the house. The windows were drafty, especially in the wintertime.

One year she came to our office for her annual financial planning review, and she said she felt it was time to change the windows. She wanted to know if she had enough money.

Lucy, a widow with no children, had more than enough money. In fact, her investable assets were more than $800,000, and her home was worth another $350,000. She needed less than $40,000 per year to support her lifestyle, and half of her retirement income was covered through Social Security and a small pension check from the town.

Inspiration

When I Was a Kid

Think back to when your grandparents passed away. What did your parents inherit? Chances are that it wasn't much. That's because all Grandma and Grandpa had was a pension (which terminated at death), Social Security (also terminated at death), and a few thousand dollars in a bank account. The other asset was the house. While it may have been fully paid for, it was worth all of $20,000 to $40,000. That was it. And it got split equally among the siblings. In the end, the inheritance might have provided a token financial legacy that certainly didn't financially change your parents' lives.

Fast forward to today. When we die, we are likely to leave our children an enormous sum of money—an amount that *will* change their lives financially.

Many retirees elect to live off distributions from their investment accounts. That's because most retirees today don't have pension incomes. In doing so, they will leave a large lump sum of money to pass along. In addition, there is typically a very large amount of equity in the house. That money will also get passed to the kids. And for the most part, it will be free from taxes.

The legacy you leave to your children is likely to be significantly larger than the one you inherited. In today's retirement environment, many people are faced with a choice—and it's one that might be truly unfathomable to grasp. You have the opportunity to enhance your life in retirement but, in doing so, leave a reduced legacy to the kids. The choice is yours. Do you want to maximize your retirement life to its fullest or leave a giant legacy to the next generation? In most cases, retirees would love to do a little of each. Yet if you don't understand the "big picture" associated with your overall financial life, you may struggle with realizing the spectrum of choices available to you.

We encouraged Lucy to gather quotes from contractors and hire someone to replace the windows in her home, since she surely had enough money to cover the costs.

The following year, Lucy visited our office. We asked about her new windows. She told us that she was so happy that her bedroom was nice and warm. When asked about the rest of the house, she told us that she thought that the cost of windows was very expensive and that she couldn't imagine writing such a large check to one company in any given year. The total cost of the project was going to be $35,000, yet she didn't feel comfortable writing a check larger than $5,000. This year, she said, she would replace the windows in her kitchen and family room.

As you age, the connection between today's cost of goods and your memory of what things used to cost can be a paralyzing issue. In Lucy's case, she was shell shocked by the cost of comfort, and she neglected herself the energy-saving value of new windows despite having more than enough money to foot the whole bill.

To Summarize...

- If you're considering a second property in retirement, seriously explore the value of renting first so that you're sure where you'd like to reside.
- If you're feeling house rich and cash poor, explore the value of downsizing.
- Be careful about aligning yourself with rules of thumb. Many of those strategies work better in theory than in reality.
- Ensure that your retirement income is sufficient prior to being overly generous to the kids.

Chapter 20

What Keeps You Up at Night?

In This Chapter...

- Can I still help the kids out during retirement?
- Can you come to terms with today's cost of living?
- Will medical costs sabotage your retirement?
- Do you need long-term-care insurance?

There are so many issues that stir fear, surprise, and uncertainty in the lives of retirees. From health care costs to lifestyle changes, retirees worry about it all. Perhaps that's the reason seniors are up with the roosters and have dinner at four thirty.

Yet family-related issues remain the largest impediment preventing retirees from achieving financial peace of mind.

If you want success, you'll need to identify the "elephants" and initiate some tough conversations.

How Much Can I Afford to Give to the Kids?

My two younger brothers and I never needed to significantly rely on our parents for ongoing financial support after we got married and had kids. No, we were far from "rich" growing up. We wore Toughskins jeans and learned about the value of a dollar. We walked to school, shoveled the driveway, and cut the lawn. My parents, to their credit, did their best to instill the values of hard work and responsibility. They insisted that we become active in our community at a very young age, find part-time employment as soon as we were eligible, and seek out leadership opportunities in volunteer capacities as often as we could. This guidance allowed us to become independent, confident in our abilities to achieve goals, resourceful, and level headed. Unfortunately, there are many families whose children, through no real fault of the parents, missed the messages their parents tried to instill. Today, the kids can't seem to dig themselves out of holes.

As parents, you want to do the best you can for your children—but at what point does it pose a financial liability to your retirement lifestyle?

Economic Outpatient Support

Years ago, Thomas J. Stanley and William D. Danko authored a best-selling book, *The Millionaire Next Door*. The thesis of the book explained that there are millionaires living all around us, and most can't be identified based on the clothes they wear, the cars they drive, or the homes they reside in. As interesting as I found most of the research, I was even more compelled by a particular chapter that talked about the fragility of children of millionaires and their inability to find financial independence.

The term "economic outpatient support" is an expression that needs more play in our day-to-day society. The concept is that all too many adult children rely on financial support from parents and grandparents as part of their day-to-day lifestyles. These children have become so used to Mom or Dad paying part of the mortgage, auto insurance bills, day care costs, and family vacations—or settling up credit card debt each year. And because Mom and/or Dad are providing these funds, the children are spending money on other "luxuries": designer clothing, granite countertops, hot tubs, fancy cars, landscapers, snow plow service, to name just a few—items Mom or Dad could never afford when they were kids.

Then Mom and Dad decide to retire. They realize that retirement is expensive and they can't continue to be as financially generous and supportive to their children as they've been in the past.

Yet a new dilemma can arise. If you've been the source of financial support to your children, it's possible that you've given them an indication that you are financially secure and that your ability to help them out isn't of any financial impact to you at all. In fact, having to tell them otherwise might be among the most difficult conversations you've ever had with your children.

At some point, you realize you're going to need to reassess how much financial support you're willing to provide to your adult children. No, I'm not talking about Christmas gifts, graduation presents, and birthday gifts. I'm talking about severing the way you support your children who are capable (or have the potential of being capable) of providing an income for themselves and their families on their own.

The Millionaire in You

If you are fortunate enough to be a millionaire, chances are that you don't "feel" like one. Yet, on paper, when you actually list everything you own (bank accounts, investments, real estate, retirement plans, and the present value of pensions and Social Security) and subtract everything you owe (mortgages, credit card debt, auto loans, etc.), you'll be surprised that your net worth actually exceeds $1 million. In fact, personal experience has shown that no matter what your net worth is, you don't feel that "rich," do you? It is sometimes hard to grasp.

Inspiration

One of Your Toughest Conversations

So, when is it time to close the checkbook, shut down the "Bank of You," and reallocate resources that enable you to live your retirement to its fullest? Good question. But, then again, it's likely that 50 percent of readers will disagree with this approach and continue to sacrifice their retirement lifestyles for their kids. While it may be uncomfortable to say no to the kids, living life to its fullest is something you deserve.

Have You Been Held Hostage?

This is a sad story. The Griffins began retirement on September 1, 2007. The next eighteen months were among the most tumultuous times in the financial markets.

Unfortunately, like most everyone, their investment accounts dropped significantly in the eighteen months that followed. Mrs. Griffin would call our office crying, wishing her husband would find new employment so they wouldn't need to take money from their accounts. Their daily fights over money and the markets were leading to a destructive relationship. She would yell and Mr. Griffin would yell back.

No, I'm not a psychologist by trade, and I'm most certainly not licensed in that field. However, many clients feel very comfortable sharing their emotional and financial woes with financial planners because we've shown the ability to listen rationally to both sides of the conversation.

After listening to both sides, I assured them that despite the drop in their portfolio value, we remained confident that they could achieve their financial goals. Yet if they could be a bit more careful about spending over their budget that year, they'd likely position themselves better.

That's when Mrs. Griffin started to cry.

Revealing the Elephant in the Room

She explained that she had been giving her daughter $400 each week to cover the cost of day care for their four-year-old granddaughter—something they had never shared with us before.

According to Mrs. Griffin, her daughter expressed disappointment in being unable to find a job. Yet most days, she could be found at the shopping mall, at the gym, or out to lunch with friends.

While you might think the daughter was appreciative of the mother doling out $1,600 per month, she accepted this money, in Mrs. Griffin's words, "as payment for getting to see her grandchild."

It turns out that her daughter had no intentions of finding work, especially if she could count on her mother paying for day care costs. Mrs. Griffin had always given her daughter money every month—even prior to the children—but increased it to help her out when the baby came. It turns out that the daughter simply expected this money to be part of her income.

"I don't want to stop seeing my granddaughter," she yelled. "I'm a prisoner to my own grandchild. I have to keep giving her the money."

Mr. Griffin sat silent. He knew this practice had been ongoing yet never raised the issue, as he felt it could lead to another fight.

We offered to host a meeting between the Griffins and their only daughter to begin a dialogue. They were interested. The daughter refused.

Will You Rock the Boat?

To this day, the Griffins still send their daughter $1,600 per month. She no longer needs it for day care, as the granddaughter is in public school. Fortunately, they get to see her whenever they want. The financial markets have improved and the Griffins are less concerned about their ability to fulfill their retirement goals. But they still have yet to converse with their daughter about the emotional and mental drain they felt and continue to feel.

Have you ever found yourself held financially hostage by your children? Do you have the courage to have this important conversation?

Everything Is So Expensive These Days

I'll bet that you can remember when gas was under a dollar a gallon, maybe even under fifty cents. You can still recall the days when penny candy really cost "pennies" and when life could be lived simply and inexpensively. With any luck, you can still hear your mom telling you to "save for a rainy day" and your father reminding you that his growing up in the "depression era" made him tougher and more appreciative of life.

All these lessons and memories are part of your DNA, and in most cases, they remain part of your personal financial fabric. Yet this frugality mindset often interrupts a retiree's ability to live a bigger life. Make no mistake, life today is far different from *Happy Days, Leave It to Beaver, The Brady Bunch*, and *The Courtship of Eddie's Father*. Life is faster. The world has changed.

That's the Way I've Always Done It!

It's been proven over and over that as we age, we are less willing to adapt to change (especially when it comes to our money). If you are one who always bought CDs at the bank, the prospect of moving your money into the stock market is worse than imagining a ride on Disney's Tower of Terror. Yet despite CDs paying around 1 percent and your retirement spending needs requiring you to earn 4 to 5 percent on your money, you're still reluctant to make a change. That's because it might mean spending money and taking a chance.

How Do You Plan for Periodic Large Expenses in Retirement?

One of the biggest surprises that impacts a retiree's financial plan is the fact that periodic large expenses are a part of life—and not normally built in to a financial plan. It's important to change that strategy. What are some of the likely big purchases in store for you over the next ten to twenty years? An automobile is usually one of those forgotten major expenses. Ask yourself "how often do I typically buy a car?" Are you someone who runs your cars into the ground, or do you prefer a new vehicle every three or four years? In retirement, do you imagine owning one or two cars? My experience suggests that limiting your life to one car (if you're married) can be burdensome. Either way, you need to build these expenses into your plan.

Here are few others.

Helping Pay Your Grandchildren's College Costs

In spite of your personal financial requirements in retirement, you may want to help with your grandchildren's college education. It is a wonderful lifetime gift, and if it makes you feel good, you may want to do it—even if it means a sacrifice to you. I get it. But do you have a plan?

Will you have a segregated account set aside for each grandchild? Might you write a personal check to the school your grandchild plans to attend? Have you discussed how much you'd like to contribute—let alone how much you can afford? I strongly recommend having this conversation well before you build your retirement plan. This is part of the "goals" conversation, and one that can't be overlooked.

Major Vacations

Have you ever given thought to taking the whole family away for a vacation? Do you know how much it would cost? Are you prepared to plan for it? If it's your intent to schedule an excursion for the entire family, begin planning at least two years in advance. All the adult children need to coordinate work schedules so that everyone is available at the same time. Begin visiting with travel agents to have them coordinate an itinerary that will fulfill your overall objectives. Whatever the cost, add 20 percent. There will always be additional expenses. Money allocated for a major vacation should be built in to an overall plan.

Helping the Adult Kids

Do you anticipate helping your children with down payments on homes or businesses? How much do you feel comfortable contributing? Have this conversation prior to being faced with a knee-jerk reaction when your daughter comes knocking on the door. This too has to be built in to your retirement plan.

Health Care

How do you imagine health care will impact your financial plan? Some research suggests that medical costs, especially for retirees, will increase at 6 to 8 percent each year. Are you factoring this statistic into your plan?

Should You Fear Medical Costs in Retirement?

As you age, your need for prescription drugs, medical devices, and professional health care will become more prevalent. Fortunately, with today's advances in health science, retirees are comfortably living well beyond ninety years old. There's even a greater chance that you will live longer than that.

A few years ago, Fidelity Investments commissioned a study on the average aggregate medical costs that retirees will spend after age sixty-five. It would run more than $250,000. Does that mean you'll need to have a quarter of a million dollars set aside exclusively for health care costs in retirement? Absolutely not. But you do need to consider it as part of your plans in retirement.

Let's do just a little math. Imagine you live until age ninety. That's twenty-five years from the age of sixty-five. So go ahead, divide $250,000 by twenty-five years. That equals $10,000 per year, or $800 per month. Yes, it's a large amount of money, but my guess is that it's not going to relegate you to living on the streets and eating dog food. (And if it does, the government has programs to consider.)

The reality is that more than half of those costs will be spent during the last one to two years of your life.

Medical costs will be expensive as you age, but probably not as drastically as you imagine. There is an option, however, that you should consider. It's called long-term-care insurance, and it's a wealth-preserving strategy that is surprisingly affordable if purchased correctly.

Is Long-Term-Care Insurance Right for You?

The underlying belief about long-term-care insurance by many preretirees is "it costs too much money." My personal opinion is that if you first examine your financial situation and then review your current medical condition, you may be surprised by how affordable it can be. That's because the best way to buy long-term care insurance is by "programming the costs" into your financial life by planning for this potential outcome.

How Is Long-Term-Care Insurance Sold?

Long-term-care insurance is generally sold with the following parameters:

- Daily benefit. The amount of money that the insurance company will pay toward the daily cost of care.
- Period of years. The number of years the policy will continue to provide benefits.
- Deductible (elimination period). How long you will need to pay out of pocket before the insurance company pays benefits.
- Inflation factor (simple, compound, etc.). An opportunity to increase your daily benefit over time.

There are many other "bells and whistles" that can be added to a policy, including return of premium, spousal benefits, waiver of premium, etc. But for now, let's stick with the basics.

> **STOP**
>
> **The Coverage You Need**
>
> Beware of unscrupulous salespeople who ask what you can afford each month for a long-term-care policy. The coverage you purchase should be built around what your financial situation requires—not just what you can afford to pay. Build the amount of coverage you need into your personal financial plan, and develop a strategy that allows you to pay for the coverage you need.
>
> **WATCH OUT!**

Considerations for Long-Term-Care Parameters That Work for You

If you've ever needed to care for, or assist in, the payment of long-term-care costs, you know that it's a burden, both financially and emotionally, on the well spouse and/or family. But if you've been fortunate never to have needed to care for an elderly parent in a long-term care or home or health facility, it's often hard to imagine the real emotional drain it can take on a family.

One of the reasons that people neglect purchasing long-term-care insurance is they believe that the cost is much too high. In reality, LTC insurance is among the most reasonably priced investments in your future (if purchased correctly).

What Does Long-Term-Care Insurance Cover?

Most long-term-care policies will provide for home, health, or nursing home care. Unlike life insurance where a medical exam is needed to determine the likelihood of you living for a long time, a long-term-care application process is designed to determine the likelihood of you becoming so disabled that you are unable to care for yourself.

LTC insurance is typically sold in daily benefit amounts—for instance, $150 or $200 per day. The cost of long-term-care facilities varies from state to state and region to region and depends on the level of care required.

According to Genworth Financial, one of the largest providers of LTC coverage, the average costs for care is as follows:

Long-Term Care Average Costs	
Nursing home (private room)	$230/day
Nursing home (semiprivate room)	$207/day
Assisted living (one bedroom)	$115/day
Home health aide (licensed)	$19/hour

So try to figure out how much of your household income you could forgo if your spouse was no longer living at home and instead in a nursing home facility. Imagine allocating your spouse's Social Security check and any pension income to the nursing home. Could you maintain your lifestyle on your income, assets, and resources? If the answer is yes, then consider purchasing a daily benefit that's equal to the difference between the money allocated to the home and the current monthly costs of the facility. In other words, you don't need to purchase 100 percent of the daily cost (although the insurance salesperson will likely try to convince you otherwise), because some of the costs at home will be included in the cost of the long-term care. In addition, there unfortunately will not be dinners out, vacations, trips to see the kids and grandchildren, etc.

Once you've determined your daily benefit, you'll want to choose your benefit period and elimination period. I generally advise clients to select a four- or five-year benefit period.

The elimination period is a bit trickier. Depending on your age and your personal financial resources, selecting a longer elimination period can significantly reduce the cost of insurance. If you're young (under age fifty-five), the difference in elimination-period cost is negligible. However, if you are over sixty-four, the variance in costs can be significant.

Finally, decide if you want inflation protection. I strongly encourage people to purchase the coverage—but to focus on the "simple interest" option and not the "compound interest" option. The difference in costs is dramatic.

What Triggers the Issuance of Long-Term-Care Benefits?

There are multitudes of different policies, but the vast majority require you to be unable to perform a certain number of "activities of daily living." They may include the following:

- Bathing and showering
- Toileting
- Dressing
- Eating
- Functional mobility
- Feeding
- Personal hygiene
- Bowel and bladder management

In addition, many policies will issue benefits if you show signs of cognitive impairment—such as Alzheimer's or Parkinson's disease.

When's the Ideal Time to Buy Long-Term-Care Insurance?

Programming Your Daily Benefit for Long-Term-Care Insurance

Let's imagine that the daily cost of a private room in a nursing home in your community is $230 a day. Your spouse has Social Security income of $1,000 month and $650 a month in a small pension—a total of $1,650 a month, or $55 per day. Deduct that amount from the average cost of the nursing home ($230 a day), and the result is $175. Consider applying for a policy with a $175-a-day daily benefit.

Example

Consider LTC insurance between fifty-nine and sixty-four years old. During this window, you can typically purchase a long-term-care policy for both you and your spouse for somewhere between $300 and $400 a month. Purchasing LTC coverage earlier than that may be counterproductive. That's because the world of LTC insurance is changing every day. You want to be certain that the product you buy today is the product you will still own when and/or if you need the coverage.

Remember that the LTC insurance company expects to collect premiums from you for a long time. Chances are, you won't need to request benefits for at least twenty to thirty years from the time of your initial purchase. While it's true that your health conditions may/will change between now and when you need benefits, I don't believe that buying coverage pre-fifty-nine is worth the extra cost. After all, to qualify for LTC benefits, you need to be unable to perform certain activities of daily living. Unlike applying for life insurance, having a heart attack, high cholesterol, and/or diabetes is not always a deal breaker when obtaining LTC insurance.

How Long Do People Generally Stay in a Nursing Home?

A nursing home is typically the last place (besides hospice) someone will live. It's a rarity when someone returns home after spending any meaningful time in a nursing facility. But what many people don't realize is the actual length of time someone spends in a nursing home facility. According to a geriatric and palliative care resource, the average length of stay is shorter than you may imagine:

- Median length of stay in a nursing home before death was five months. This means that 50 percent stay a shorter time and 50 percent stay longer.

Pure Genius!

A Family Option for Long-Term-Care Coverage

If you're considering alternatives for shifting assets so that you might qualify for long-term-care benefits through Medicaid, let me suggest a more ethical option.

One of the primary reasons for "hiding assets" to qualify for Medicaid is so that the money you've accumulated isn't depleted—thus leaving nothing to the next generation.

I have found that many retirees' children are more than willing to share in the monthly costs associated with paying for a long-term-care insurance policy so that your wealth can remain preserved and in your control.

Remember shifting assets out of your name means giving up control of *your* money. You'd be very surprised to learn how interested your children may be in helping preserve your legacy by assisting with some up-front costs for the purchase of a long-term-care policy now.

Average length of stay was fourteen months. Since the median is only five months, this means that those staying longer often stay a *much* longer time.

We all know someone who has been in a nursing home for much longer than the averages, and like I mentioned in previous chapters, national averages include the entire spectrum of Americans. Nevertheless, buying a long-term-care policy that requires coverage for more than four to five years may be both cost prohibitive and more expensive than necessary.

What about Cognitive Ailments Such as Alzheimer's and Parkinson's Disease?

Both Alzheimer's and Parkinson's diseases are very real illnesses and in most cases don't lead to quick deaths. As such, they can keep an individual in a nursing home for a very long period of time. If this trait is prevalent in your family, it may be wise to consider coverage that is unlimited. But beware. The costs will be extraordinary.

How Can I Hide Money So I Can Qualify for Long-Term-Care Benefits through Medicaid?

I may strike a nerve with readers, but I really frown on people who believe that they have the right to hide money from the government so they can qualify for Medicaid (welfare) benefits. Medical costs in America are out of control already, and expecting to have the government extend its welfare program (cutely disguised as Medicaid) so that families can cry after they've hidden the money they've earned is disgraceful.

Don't get me wrong. We need to care for those who can't care for themselves, but when we try to beat the system so that other taxpayers can foot our bills, it creates an unhealthy—and unpatriotic—attitude.

Most of us (not all) have opportunities that allow us to plan for the costs of long-term medical care. It's incumbent on each and every one of us to figure out a way to *not* be a burden on the state and instead provide adequate resources and/or insurance to protect what we've accumulated.

To Summarize...

- The world today is different from the world of your childhood. Embrace it. Enjoy it. You'll be amazed at how much fun you'll have.
- Have a good night's sleep tonight. The issues that keep you up can be addressed, and in most cases, a rational solution can be achieved. Trust in yourself.
- Endeavor to have "money" conversations with your adult children. They need to know that you are not a bank; nor are you an unlimited source of money.
- Long-term-care insurance is a wealth-preservation tool—and should be explored by retirees.

Chapter 21

Should Probate Be Feared? Can It Be Avoided?

In This Chapter...

- Strategies for avoiding probate
- The real costs of probate
- The role of the executor
- Should a trust be part of your estate plan?

Most retirees don't understand the probate process. Nor do they understand which assets are subject to probate and which are not. You may be surprised to learn that many of your investment, retirement, and insurance accounts could already be exempt from probate altogether.

Similar to most pieces of advice concerning your financial life, you need to tread carefully when taking guidance from friends, neighbors, and relatives. When it comes to how your assets will be divided, distributed, taxed, and inventoried, it's important that you rely on your sense of genius.

Should You Avoid Probate?

Many retirees elect to establish trusts for the sole purpose of avoiding probate. For that reason alone, a trust may be a solution for you. Yet did you know that it's possible to avoid probate altogether without having to establish a trust at all? You may want to pull out your net worth statement as you read along in this chapter. It will be a helpful resource, I assure you.

What Is Probate?

The word "probate" derives from the Latin word *probare*, "to prove or make valid." Under the probate process, all of a decedent's assets that did not have some form of beneficiary or contingent owner designation, such as "payable on death" or "joint with rights of survivorship," must be reviewed and proven that they are indeed part of the deceased's estate.

Probate is a court-supervised process of locating and determining the value of the assets owned in the individual name of a deceased person (referred to as a "decedent"); paying the decedent's final bills, estate taxes, and/or inheritance taxes (if any); and then distributing what's left of the decedent's assets to the heirs.

Most of us have heard that it's wise to avoid probate court, but we don't necessarily know why. In a nutshell, there are some big problems with probate:

- It can tie up assets for months, sometimes more than a year.
- It's expensive. In some states, attorney and court fees can take up to 5 percent of an estate's value. In other states, attorneys simply bill by the hour. But let's be honest, the attorney knows the value of your estate and what you can afford. Worst of all, you're not there to argue the attorney's fees.
- It is a very public process. Your will becomes a public document to be read by anyone who cares to pay the clerk of the court the fee to copy it.

Steps Involved with Probating and Estate

Most of what happens during probate is clerical. In most cases, there's no conflict and no contesting parties. Probate rarely calls for a lawyer's adversarial skills.

The probate attorney, or the attorney's secretary, fills in a small mountain of forms and keeps track of filing deadlines and other procedural technicalities. In some states, the attorney makes a few routine court appearances. In others, the whole procedure is handled by mail.

Each state will have specific sets of laws to determine the maximum costs (keep in mind, even these are negotiable) and probate process. In general, they'll require the following steps to settle an estate:

1. Appoint a personal representative (or executor). If you have yet to notify the person dubbed personal representative (usually your spouse or oldest child), I'd recommend letting the "chosen" person know while you're still alive.

2. Locate the decedent's assets. An executor is first charged with gathering and listing all of the decedent's assets. These might include an individual checking account, stock certificates, a brokerage account, a car, personal property, and real estate, as well as any other assets that name "the estate of..." as the beneficiary.

3. Gather date-of-death values. This can be accomplished by looking through statements, capturing historical prices via the Internet (bigcharts.marketwatch.com/historical), and gathering appraisals of personal property and real estate.

4. Identify known creditors. The executor is responsible for ensuring that all outstanding debts get reported as part of the probate process and that plans are arranged to settle outstanding debts and obligations..

5. Publish a notice in the newspaper. If your estate is subject to probate, you must notify the local newspaper to report your plans to probate the deceased's estate.

6. Pay bills. A bank account and checkbook must be created for "the estate of..." The executor is responsible for paying all of the decedent's final bills, settling with creditors, and issuing distributions to beneficiaries. It is very important to keep impeccable records and rationale for all dollars in and out.

7. File income tax returns. The decedent's final income tax return, and any estate income tax returns, must be filed and reviewed.

Consider Rewarding Your Executor

The role of an executor can be exhausting, time consuming, and thankless.

Executors do have a right to draw a fee from the estate for serving in this important capacity, but in most cases (unless the executor is not a family member), I see one child from the entire family work tireless weeks, months—sometimes up to a year. As steward of the family, the executor doesn't seek compensation for these efforts while the other siblings periodically pester the executor and stand on the sidelines waiting for the inheritance to land in their pockets.

Consider stating a fee, or special allocation, to your executor so that your chosen representative feels both honored to serve your estate and rewarded for honoring your wishes.

Perspiration

If the deceased is over age 70½, the executor should ensure that a minimum distribution was taken during the year of death. If the deceased did not take a distribution prior to death, one must be taken and included in the deceased's estate.

8. Determine estate tax liability. Unless your estate is in excess of $5.34 million in 2014 (adjusted for inflation), the decedent likely won't owe a federal estate tax (not to be confused with income tax). However, many states have their own rules concerning estate taxes.

9. Pay any estate taxes and/or inheritance taxes. If any estate taxes (federal and/or state) or inheritance taxes will be due, raise the cash necessary to pay the taxes and then pay them in a timely manner (usually within nine months of the decedent's date of death).

10. Distribute the remaining balance to the beneficiaries.

A Job Description for the Executor

The following checklist will give you a sense of the responsibility and tasks involved for being the executor. Think of who you selected to serve as your executor. Is this person capable of both physically and mentally handling this important role?

Executor Checklist

Immediate Tasks

- ❑ Find the will
- ❑ Apply for an Employer Identification Number (EIN) from the IRS
- ❑ Appraise assets, if needed
- ❑ Arrange to publish a "notice of probate" in local newspapers
- ❑ Determine whether probate proceedings are needed
- ❑ Protect/manage assets until turned over to beneficiaries
- ❑ Collect money owed to the estate (e.g., wages, insurance benefits, rents, etc.)
- ❑ Pay bills
- ❑ File final income tax returns for deceased
- ❑ File estate taxes, if necessary
- ❑ Notify inheritors and beneficiaries
- ❑ Distribute assets

Businesses and Agencies to Notify

- ❑ Banks
- ❑ Credit card companies
- ❑ Utility companies
- ❑ Post office
- ❑ Doctors or other health care providers
- ❑ Employer and former employers
- ❑ Investment firms
- ❑ Insurance companies
- ❑ Landlord and/or tenants
- ❑ Pension payers
- ❑ Service providers (e.g., landscapers, trash haulers, etc.)
- ❑ Social Security Administration
- ❑ State health/welfare departments
- ❑ Department of Veterans Affairs

Documents You'll Need to Locate

- ❑ Bank statements
- ❑ Birth certificates (both deceased's and minor children's)
- ❑ Brokerage account statements
- ❑ Business co-ownership agreements
- ❑ Checkbooks
- ❑ Child support documents
- ❑ Credit card statements
- ❑ Disability-related documents
- ❑ Divorce papers
- ❑ Health insurance policies, statements, or bills
- ❑ Immigration and citizenship document
- ❑ Investment records
- ❑ Life insurance policies and premium payment records
- ❑ Marriage license
- ❑ Military service records
- ❑ Pension records
- ❑ Prenuptial agreement
- ❑ Real estate deeds and tax records
- ❑ Registration papers for vehicles or boats
- ❑ Retirement account statements
- ❑ Social Security records
- ❑ Form W-2 showing wages for the current year
- ❑ Workers' compensation paperwork

What Does Probate Cost?

Both the lawyer and your executor are entitled to fees from your estate. However, it is common for the executor to waive the fee, especially if he or she inherits a substantial amount of your property.

Attorney Fees

In many states, probate fees are what a court approves as "reasonable." In some states, fees are based on a percentage of the estate subject to probate, and in others, it may be an hourly fee. No matter what state law says, you can always negotiate the fee. It generally isn't set in stone.

One big mistake of many personal representatives is to automatically go to the attorney who wrote the will. A personal representative does not need to go to the decedent's attorney for probate assistance. We often recommend interviewing at least three attorneys to compare competence, fees, and compatibility.

Accounting Fees

These fees will vary depending upon the overall value of the estate and the types of assets owned. If you have an estate that owns two properties, twenty-five different mutual funds, stocks and/or bonds, and three annuities, you may actually generate more accounting fees than a larger estate that owns just a primary residence, a bank account, and a CD. Of course, if the estate is taxable at the state and/or federal level, then the accounting fees may include the preparation and filing of the state and/or federal estate tax returns if the attorney for the estate doesn't prepare and file the returns. Thus, as you approach retirement, simplifying your financial affairs isn't just a time saver during retirement; it can also save money at death for your heirs.

Appraisal and Business-Valuation Fees

These fees will be necessary to determine the date-of-death values of real estate, personal property (including jewelry, antiques, artwork, boats, cars, and the like), and business interests. Appraisal fees for personal property can range anywhere from a few hundred to a few thousand dollars, while business-valuation fees will run several thousand dollars.

Miscellaneous Fees

These are the nickel-and-dime costs that drive your heirs nuts. These fees can include the cost of postage (to mail notices to the executor and beneficiaries and mail documents to the court and taxing authorities), the cost of insuring and storing personal property, the cost of shipping personal property, the cost of moving personal property, and the cost of courier services to deliver documents.

Can You Reduce Probate Fees?

One way to reduce probate fees is for your executor to handle the probate proceedings without an attorney. But, as a practical matter, I don't advise it. Rather, look to have your estate positioned to avoid probate in advance of your death.

Managing Probate on Your Own

You can find "do-it-yourself books" on just about any subject, but when it comes to the settlement of your estate, and the implications that go along with distributing your assets to various people in your life, it's best to rely on professionals.

Without help, learning one's way through the challenges of probate laws is likely to be difficult, but it's not impossible. Your executor can get forms and instructions from an attorney's practice guide. These books are usually available at public law libraries, and many people have successfully used them.

You can also try to get an attorney to agree to do your probate for less than the usual fees. You cannot, however, legally bind an attorney to such an arrangement. In fact, you don't have the power to select the attorney at all. The law gives this authority to your executor.

Avoiding Probate Altogether

It makes more sense to see if you can avoid probate altogether. At the very least, consider reducing the amount of property that will be subject to probate. This will reduce fees and ensure that your beneficiaries get some of their inheritance faster.

Strategies for Avoiding Probate

The only assets that are subject to probate are those where there is no beneficiary named on an account. As such, unless your beneficiary designation on an account is "the estate of…," the following assets would avoid probate:

- Assets owned as joint tenants with rights of survivorship (JTWROS) or tenants by the entirety (TEN), which is available only to spouses
- Retirement accounts, including 401(k), IRA, Roth, 403(b), and retirement plans
- Annuities
- Life insurance
- Individually owned assets that list a transfer on death (TOD) or payable on death (POD)

So think about it. Take a look at your net worth statement. Are there any assets you own individually and without any beneficiary designation? Are your beneficiary designations up to date? Those assets may include real estate, a business, automobiles, investment accounts, stock options, etc. If it is your intent to prevent these assets from passing through probate, you may want to explore establishing a revocable trust.

What Is a Trust?

It seems that every estate planning attorney in America espouses the rationale for owning a trust—even when they have no idea the size of your estate. While these legal documents serve a very important purpose, they are not necessary for everyone.

A trust is a legal document that is just another way to "own" assets and serves as an extension of your and your spouse's wishes. This legal agreement allows a trustee (which can be you) to hold, and manage, assets on behalf of beneficiaries. Sound confusing? It really isn't. In most cases, you maintain control over the assets, you have access to the assets, and you can even make changes to the trust at any time prior to death, including beneficiaries and how the assets are distributed prior to your death. But, most importantly, you can dictate how your assets will be distributed and to whom.

Can I Use a Fill-in-the-Blanks Trust Template?

Absolutely not. A trust should be written by an attorney, not a fill-in-the-blanks solution that you can pick up at your local office supply store. Each state has different rules about how your assets are to be settled upon your death. If your trust is written in one state and you move to another, it may be prudent to have an attorney in the new state review not only your trust but all your estate documents as well. You want to be certain that your trust document has the ability to provide flexibility. Just imagine that you wrote a trust in 2012, a few years prior to your retirement. Then, in 2018, you decided to move across the country. Chances are, the last thing you'll be thinking about is whether or not your current trust document will work in the state in which you'll be living in soon.

How Does a Trust Help Me Avoid Probate?

Trusts can help you avoid probate, streamline the process of passing assets to heirs, and offer an instruction manual for trustees and beneficiaries to ensure your wishes are maintained—even after you've departed this world.

Think about your individual checking account for a moment. It's in your name alone. If you die, who gets the money? Since it's registered in your name only, the likely course of action would be for the account to go through probate. An estate account would need to be established and an executor appointed, and then the probate process would ensue. Only then would the executor look to the last will and testament for direction. This could take months, and perhaps more than a year, to simply transfer your account to your heirs.

Revocable versus Irrevocable Trusts

Generally, trusts fall into two different categories:

- Revocable. You have the ability to make changes to the trust during your lifetime.
- Irrevocable. In most cases, changes can't be made once the trust is funded.

All revocable trusts become irrevocable upon the death of the grantor (the person funding the trust).

Explaining the Revocable (Living) Trust

A revocable trust is often referred to as a living trust. You and your spouse can each have a trust of your own, or you can create a "family trust" that holds both of your assets.

A living trust generally uses your Social Security number(s) for income tax purposes. It can include either or both of you as trustees, and you can (if you so choose) be the beneficiary of your own trust during your lifetime.

The primary reason for maintaining a living trust is to avoid probate. If you die (and I guarantee—you *will* die!), someone needs to know where to distribute your assets. If your assets are in a trust, the answer is predetermined. You will have named beneficiaries in your trust. One of those beneficiaries may be your spouse, but if you're the second to die, it would also name "successor beneficiaries" (i.e., your children) as the recipients of your assets. If you die with assets in your name and no beneficiary is named (think about your personal checking account or individual brokerage account), your assets would pass through probate and then be distributed under the direction of your will.

When you draft a revocable trust, it is important that you reregister all the accounts that you wish to be owned by the trust. Neglecting to do so could make your decision to establish a trust a waste of time.

Once assets are in the trust (and these can include real estate, securities, cash assets, and business interests), you can feel confident that these assets will avoid probate. Instead, upon your death, the survivor trustee will follow the directions of the trust document and distribute the assets as instructed. It's actually pretty simple. It just takes a little time to draft the document and fund the trust.

How Real Estate Can Make Probate Maddening

If you own real estate in different states, you may be leaving a mess of nightmarish proportions for your executor (the person who oversees and distributes your assets when you die). The court-supervised process, called probate, ensures the orderly accounting and transfer of your wealth according to your will. If you own property in multiple states, your executor will have to go through the probate process in each state where you owned property. Not only is the probate process different in each state, but it costs money and takes time (sometimes years). The lake house you own in Michigan and your residence in Virginia will most likely mean your executor must initiate probate proceedings in both states.

However, with a little estate planning, you can greatly reduce the headache. One common solution is to transfer ownership of the property to a revocable living trust.

Other Reasons Trusts Make Sense

If you have an estate worth over $5.34 million in 2014 (adjusted for inflation), you may want to establish trusts to avoid having to pay estate taxes. There are multitudes of estate planning strategies that utilize trusts to accomplish the wishes of the super rich. This book isn't designed to address these issues.

However, if you're among the 22.5 million mass affluent baby boomers, you'll be interested to know that there are some very important reasons you should consider a revocable trust. Situations may include the following:

- Providing income to a special-needs individual
- Addressing the complexities of asset distribution for second- and third-marriage couples
- Controlling the needs of spendthrift beneficiaries
- Managing money for minor children
- Avoiding estate taxes

The Surprise of a Lifetime

Jerry and Gillian had been married for fifty-three years. They had three children. Tom, aged forty-six, was married and had three children. Cheryl, forty-two, was engaged to her life partner. And Scott, forty, was divorced and recently released from a rehab facility. Upon their deaths, Jerry and Gillian had plans to distribute their assets, which totaled about $1.8 million, but they wanted to be sure that Scott's share would be distributed to him slowly so that he wouldn't waste the money. His tendency to give money away, use it unwisely, and purchase narcotics and alcohol with it caused great strain among the family.

Jerry and Gillian had a simple will. It simply stated that upon the death of the second of them, money would be split evenly to the children in thirds.

With all that had occurred in Scott's life, Jerry and Gillian decided to visit with an estate planning attorney to establish a trust for their assets. It was their primary objective to name Tom and Cheryl as trustees for Scott's money and to have the account pay him a stipend each month—as well as additional funds when they felt Scott had cleaned up his act. Tom and Cheryl were initially reluctant to take on the role, as they imagined heated arguments with their brother. Yet, after some pleading, and wanting to ensure that their parents' wishes were met, they obliged.

On October 4, 2012, Jerry and Gillian signed their new trust documents.

On February 14, 2013, while traveling to Philadelphia for a Valentine's weekend, Jerry and Gillian's car was hit by a drunk driver. They both died on impact.

Almost immediately after the funeral, Tom and Cheryl were bombarded with

Be Sure to Fund Your Trust

A trust is a legal entity, or "person." It can own real estate, stocks, bonds, bank accounts, and any manner of personal property, such as stamp collections, paintings, furniture, and online accounts. Each trust operates according to the terms spelled out in the trust document—as determined by the person who creates the trust. To fund a trust, you must transfer the ownership of an asset from yourself to the trust.

If you've made the decision to establish a trust, it's important that you do more than just sign the trust document. Having a trust and *funding* a trust are two important but separate steps.

To change the ownership on your accounts into the name of the trust, notify your banker, financial planner, real estate attorney, etc. Send each a copy of your trust, and they will prepare paperwork for your signature so that your assets are registered appropriately.

IMPORTANT!

questions from Scott, wondering when he would have access to his parents' share of the money.

The children learned that their parents never reregistered their accounts into the names of the trusts. In fact, the folder that held the signed trust documents appeared to be in the same place they left it on the day they brought it home from the attorney's office. Both Cheryl and Tom tried to convince the attorney to let them place a third of their parents' assets into a "spendthrift trust," as had been documented in the trust document, but he couldn't. Since Jerry and Gillian's assets remained in individual names and the retirement accounts still named the three kids as beneficiaries, the attorney had no choice but to simply distribute the family's estate into three equal shares, with Cheryl, Tom, and Scott each retaining total control of their own allocations.

Just two years later, Scott found himself on the wrong side of the law. He binge drinks, buys fancy cars, and is living the lifestyle that his parents hoped they could prevent. Cheryl and Tom feel enormous guilt for not ensuring that their parents funded the trusts properly.

To Summarize...

- Probate can be a time-consuming, arduous process. Work to find ways to minimize or eliminate the need to subject your assets to probate.
- Carefully select your executor. Recognize the importance of the role as well as the time and energy needed to settle your estate.
- Many people elect to use revocable trusts as a means for avoiding probate. Yet without funding your trust, the expense of drafting a trust will have been wasted.
- Not everyone needs a trust.

Chapter 22

All Good Things Must Come to an End

In This Chapter...

- Estate planning documents every retiree should hold
- The importance of actually reading your documents
- The final years
- A personal reflection

No matter the size of your estate, there are critical legal documents that you should have at your disposal. As you age, you may be limited in activities, become partially disabled, or even be unable to communicate. No, it's not the life you want—but you're still living.

Who will you want to make decisions on your behalf? Who will you want to "legally" sign your name when you can't? And, most importantly, how will you ensure that your legacy and your wishes are fulfilled?

Your Life Is Important, Even When You're Not in Control

There is a fifty-fifty chance you have a will. Yes, that's right. More than 50 percent of Americans don't have the simplest estate planning document around. For many, the reason is simple. You believe that as a married couple, if one of you dies, the other will inherit the other's assets. That may be true, but not always. What happens if this is a second marriage for either of you? What happens if your children, an ex-spouse, a nosy neighbor, or long-lost relative wants a piece of your estate after your death? Without a last will and testament, your estate could face some legal battles that you never imagined could occur.

Furthermore, what happens if you die without a will and you don't have a spouse? Who will inherit your money? Do you want to leave it to state law or perhaps a judge to decide? And if you're married, what if you die in a common accident? How will your assets be split? Who will administer the distribution of your estate? All these questions are addressed in a will.

Is Your Will Current?

Take a look at your most recent last will and testament. If you still have guardians named for your children (and they are now in their thirties and forties), it may be time to update your documents. Also, review who you've named as executor of your estate and who the executor should be if the primary one is unable to perform those duties. If you've named an attorney, bank, or trust department to serve in a fiduciary capacity following your death, make sure that you're still comfortable with your decisions.

Laws around estate planning change on a regular basis. You want to be certain that your wishes meet current federal and statutory rules.

Who Conducts the Reading of the Will?

The movies have made such huge fanfare around the family gathering from far and wide to meet up at the stodgy law firm. Brothers, sisters, mistresses, business partners, and the rest of the motley crew pack into the oak-paneled office of the executor/attorney to find out what they've inherited.

Uninspired

Read Your Will—Don't Just Sign It

When we engaged the Fredricksons to establish a financial planning relationship, we had already known each other for a number of years. Through activities in the community, our paths had crossed quite a few times. A couple of years back, Noah Fredrickson had a mild stroke. Though he had recovered completely, the family wasn't so certain early on.

As part of our overall financial planning review, we were given the opportunity to review the Fredricksons' legal documents. About five years ago, they had met with a respected estate planning attorney who drafted wills, health care proxies, and powers of attorney on their behalf. They expressed great relief in having these documents—especially after going through Noah's health scare.

While the estate planning documents for Noah's wife, Ilana, appeared to be in good order, my heart sank when I read Noah's. In the course of analyzing his overall estate plan, I realized that his will was essentially *blank*. What I mean is that wherever the document required a person's name, address, beneficiary name, or executor name, all that appeared was a blank space. His will was essentially a template without any of the details filled in. What was worse was that each page had been initialed by both Noah and Ilana. The attorney had notarized the document, and witnesses had signed it. As such, the will appeared to be in good order and paid for in full. Yet it lacked any direction or authorization.

When I shared the information, Noah began to tremble. After all, he knew how close to death he had come when he was dealing with his stroke. Noah became furious. He stormed out of my office and headed to the attorney's office. She redrafted the will at no cost, of course. Nevertheless, it was a lesson I'll never forget—and one that I hope you'll always remember.

Read your legal documents! If you don't understand them, ask!

Chances are that in the case of your family, if you've planned appropriately, there won't be a reading of the will. Instead, your wishes will be fulfilled simply—and in an organized, efficient manner.

Don't Procrastinate—Draft/Update Your Will

My guess is that if you don't have a will, you probably know you need one but just haven't gotten around to it.

You can't use that excuse any longer. After you've finished reading this chapter, I want you to contact an estate planning attorney. Understand?

But wait. There's more. No matter your estate's size, it's important to have more than just a will. A power of attorney, health care proxy, and even a revocable trust are, in many cases, essential legal documents that you need. You may also want have the attorney prepare a living will, which is a document that expresses your wishes to be taken off of life support if there is no reasonable chance for your recovery.

Why You Need a Power of Attorney

A power of attorney gives someone comprehensive permission to act on your behalf in matters of business and financial dealings when you are unable to act on your own. When you're well, it's hard to imagine that you wouldn't be able to sign your name—especially in this day and age of digital signatures. But, trust me, there will come a time—probably later in life—when you may no longer be able to sign a check, a contract, a birthday card, or your tax return.

When giving someone the power of attorney, you'll obviously want to choose someone you can trust. But even more so, you'll want to be certain that person will act in a fiduciary capacity, placing your interests first.

Can You Limit Powers?

Yes. Yes, you can. A limited power of attorney specifically names areas where someone can and cannot act on your behalf. You can also issue limited powers. These instructions would come into effect only with your explicit authorization or if you become incapacitated or unavailable.

A power of attorney document terminates upon your death or your revocation.

The Health Care Proxy or Medical Directive

If you're in your sixties or older, chances are that you've either faced having to make a medical decision on behalf of a loved one or known someone who's been burdened with the task. A health care proxy isn't a document that just gives "do-not-resuscitate" directives; it can also be a tool that conveys your most private and personal end-of-life wishes. It may include instructions

Pure Genius!

An Ethical Will

More often than not, family members wonder about the wishes of an ill family member that extend beyond "medical care." Perhaps there is music that you'd like to have played in your hospital room. Maybe there are prayers you'd like recited each night. You may have a favorite blanket, photograph, or fragrance that will make your last days as pleasant as possible.

But how will your family know what you want?

Five Wishes is a booklet designed by The Robert Wood Johnson Foundation. It will help answer questions to some very personal issues:

- Who will be the person you want to make care decisions for you when you can't?
- What kind of medical treatment do you want (or not want)?
- How would you want to be kept comfortable?
- How would you want people to treat you?
- What you want your loved ones to know?

Like it says in the booklet, "There are many things in life that are out of our hands. It's an easy-to-complete form that lets you say exactly what you want."

You can order yours at agingwithdignity.org.

pertaining to organ donations, authorization for access to HIPPA-protected documents, and locations where you'd like to receive long-term medical care if necessary.

Which Estate Planning Documents Should You Consider?

Below is a summary of common estate planning considerations across varying wealth levels:

The American Taxpayer Relief Act of 2012 (ATRA) helped create more certainty around the federal estate planning laws for investors and planners alike. The table below is designed to help you understand the various estate planning concepts available to investors of all sizes.

Keep in mind that various concepts and strategies may or may not be appropriate for investors of all sizes. Many additional factors, such as state of residence, client preferences, longevity, etc., can make various concepts appropriate when they otherwise might not be (and vice versa).

Estate Planning Strategy	Less Than $1 Million	$1–5 Million	$5–10 Million	More Than $10 Million
Basic documents (wills, powers of attorney, health care proxy)	✓	✓	✓	✓
Establish/fund revocable trusts to avoid probate	✓	✓	✓	✓
Asset titling review	✓	✓	✓	✓
Plan to minimize state death taxes (estate and inheritance)	✓	✓	✓	✓
Transfer assets to charitable entities via donor advised funds	✓	✓	✓	✓
Establish/fund credit shelter trusts (CST)		✓	✓	✓
Establish/fund spousal limited access trusts (SLAT)		✓	✓	✓
Hold life insurance outside of estate to provide liquidity at death		✓	✓	✓
Maximize gifting strategies (529 plans, outright gifting, etc.)			✓	✓

Estate Planning Strategy	Less Than $1 Million	$1–5 Million	$5–10 Million	More Than $10 Million
Advanced estate planning techniques (GRTs, FLPs, etc.)			✓	✓
Establish/fund charitable trusts (CRTs and CLTs)			✓	✓
Establish/fund dynasty trusts for perpetual legacy transfers				✓
Establish/fund family foundations for charitable giving				✓

What Is a Homestead Declaration?

In some states, it makes sense for a homeowner to file a "homestead declaration" for a primary residence. This legal statement claims that your "dwelling" is your primary place of residence. By doing so, you may be able to protect against a loss from creditors. But one of the major reasons that couples file a homestead declaration is so that it can stay protected against a forced sale. This could happen if one spouse needed to be confined to nursing home care while the other spouse was well enough to stay at home. With a homestead declaration in place, the "well" spouse would be able to remain in the home without fear of being forced to sell. It is important that you check with an attorney to see whether a homestead filing is applicable in your state.

The Slowdown Years

I'm in my late forties and have already begun to experience my eyes weakening. I remember joking with my father when he had to hold a menu out at arm's length so he could read it. Now I find that that's me. Getting old, as I'm sure you know, stinks. But it's also a part of life. It's something you can complain about, or you can make the best of it. I'm an optimist, and I'm sure that when I approach my "senior years," I'll try to squeeze the life out of everything I touch. I hope you will too.

Yet there does come a time when your physical ability can become a hazard to others.

When to Take Away the Keys

Driving is a privilege. Yet, for most of us, we've taken advantage of how lucky we are to escape regular testing of our brains and reflexes. I've always been a proponent of testing drivers every ten years. I find it incredulous that earning a driver's license at sixteen years old (or whatever it is in your state) is a single milestone for achievement that requires no further continued education or sensory testing. If you have aging parents, you well know how quickly the mind can wander.

One of the toughest decisions for any aging retiree is the decision to stop driving. For some, it's like taking away a badge of honor. For others, it's an opportunity to be chauffeured. It's all in how you look at life.

In retirement, life will throw you curves. You can choose to be the miserable old man who complains about what's wrong in the world, what aches and

Inspiration

Finding Dignity

My mom recently passed away. For more than thirty-five years, she battled multiple sclerosis. But even in her last months, she refused to let the disease get the best of her. My mom was an optimist, a fighter, and an inspiration to those she met. However, she knew that the impact of her disease would soon limit her physical abilities.

After realizing that her foot reflexes weren't agile enough to drive, she gave up her license. "I'll just let your father drive," she said. But when she was no longer able to walk without a cane, she fought with us over the idea of using a motorized scooter. Despite the fact that her legs were getting weaker, and the sensitivity to the bottoms of her feet was severely diminished, she worried that people would look at her differently if she was "in a chair."

It took all of two days for my mother to find pure joy, freedom, and independence unlike she'd ever felt before. The motorized scooter allowed her to visit places previously unattainable. She went to Disney World with all of my kids, and she found true pleasure driving the grandkids around the park and letting them honk the horn.

pains are nagging you, and how no one visits anymore. Or you can decide that you'll look at life differently—that you'll make the most out of every moment. That you'll view hearing aids, walkers, nonglare sunglasses, and even adult diapers as opportunities rather than drags on your life.

I also hope that you'll consider the safety hazard you could pose by driving when your sight isn't the best and your reflexes are limited. No one wants to turn over the keys, but could you imagine living with the knowledge that your stubbornness about driving took away the life of, or severely injured, another human being?

The Final Years

Some of the toughest years of any retiree's life are watching a loved one decline due to illness or disease. Finding strength to care for a life partner is both emotionally and mentally draining. While medical science has extended our lives, it hurts nonetheless to watch when the color, energy, and clarity diminish from someone over time.

It's during these years that financial costs begin to simplify. The idea of traveling, filling your day with errands, and maintaining an active lifestyle with the grandkids slows down. Preparing meals and doing the laundry becomes a chore—especially if you're the one who has to do it all while the other spouse is needing more and more medical care. Personal care begins to take a backseat, and the management of medications and doctor visits becomes of great importance.

With any hope, you'll have family members to call upon. After all, you gave so much to them.

Watching a Loved One Die

Watching my mother die slowly was not easy. After years of fighting her illness, the disease finally won. I believe my mom is at peace, and I know that she'd be very proud of this book. Yet in the final weeks of her life, I learned something. Death doesn't happen on your dime. As hard as it is to watch someone die, and see in their eyes that they'd like to be set free, there's simply nothing we can do. We watch. We wait. We stroke their hair, hold their hand, sing them a song, and tell a story. It is out of our control.

The Magic of Hospice

My mom was in a wonderful hospice facility in southwest Florida called Joanne's House. The place was amazing. The inside felt like an Italian villa with private rooms for each patient. Unlike a hospital where doctors, nurses, and other personnel are rushing frantically through the halls, this respite was just the opposite. Serene, comfortable, a sense of home. For more than six weeks, my mother slowly faded. I could visit her only periodically from Boston, but we had the opportunity to Skype and exchange phone calls.

The last day I saw her, about two weeks before she died, she told me that she had no regrets—that she didn't have any enemies. I thought that was amazing.

Preparing for Your Final Days

If you were in a similar situation, would you have any regrets? Do you have any skeletons in your closet that you want to share? Are there any existing open wounds that still need healing? Don't wait until it's too late. Pick up the phone, buy a plane ticket, send an email, or simply knock on someone's door. After all, if you want to live your retirement to its absolute fullest, you owe it to yourself to be at peace when it's time to close the book.

To Summarize...

- Be sure to revisit and update your will, power of attorney, health care proxy, and other estate planning documents.
- Check with your attorney to see if a homestead declaration can be made on your primary residence.
- Find opportunity when physical challenges become part of your life in retirement. You'll be so happy you did.
- Be honest with yourself. Avoid placing others in danger when your abilities begin to diminish.
- Have no regrets!

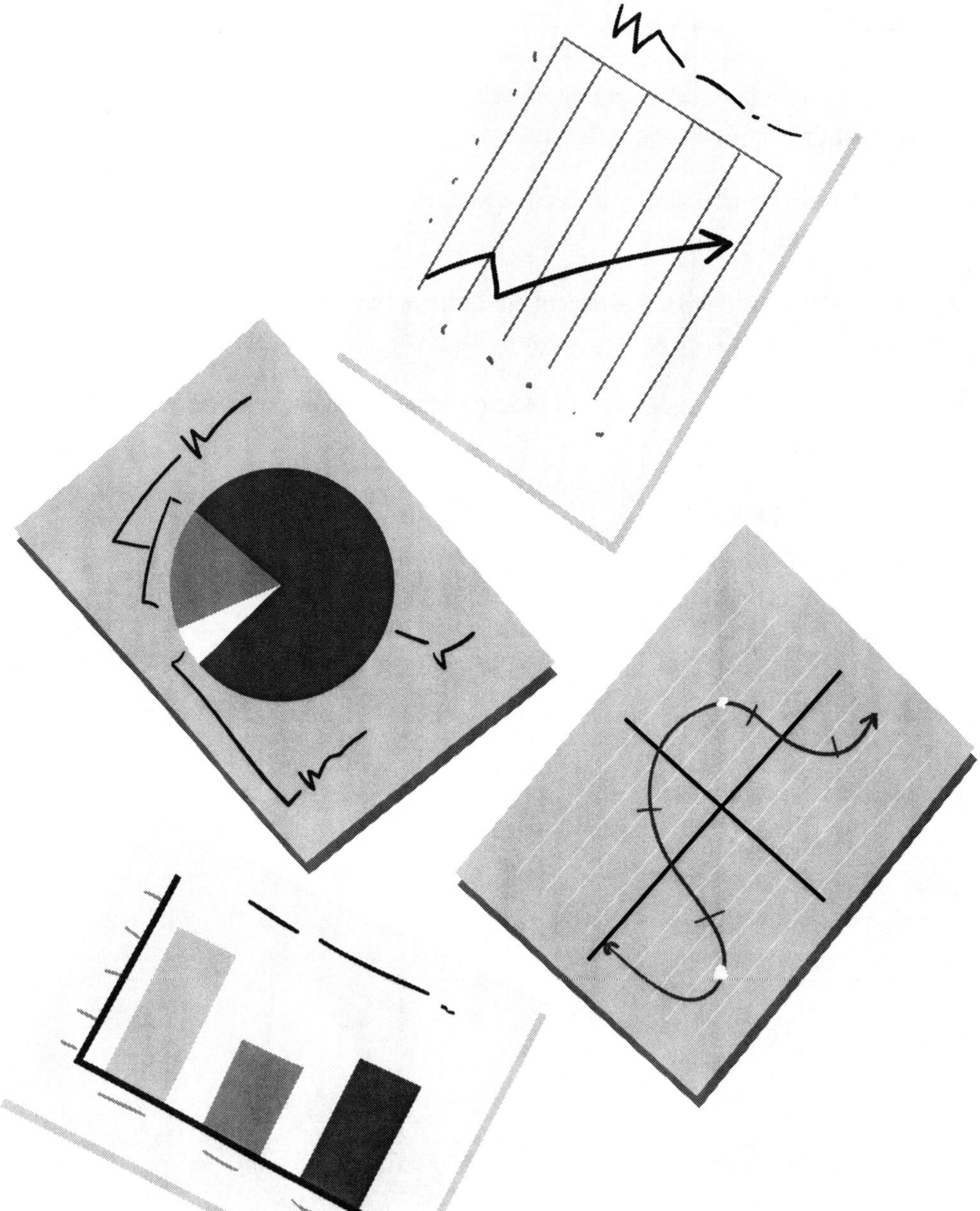

Part 4

Tools, Templates, and Time-Tested Advice

Everyone loves cheat sheets, summaries, and checklists. This final section provides a compilation of writings, ramblings, and instructions that I've provided to hundreds of retirees. The world has become inundated with "rules of thumb" and "quick-fix solutions." You need better than that. You deserve ideas and concepts that will lead to better conversations with loved ones. If you're considering a visit to a financial planner, you need ammunition so that you don't feel intimidated or overwhelmed.

Chapter 23

Ideas to Ignite Your Retirement Plan

In This Chapter…

- Ten myths that still exist in retirement planning
- Ten timeless retirement planning strategies
- Ten reasons it's time for a retirement plan do-over
- What it means to be rich

If you've made it this far, you're probably on information overload. So let's lighten up the reading. Everyone likes lists and tidbits that reinforce what they've learned.

In the pages that follow, you'll find light bulb ideas that might just give you the kick in the pants to turn your "want to dos" into "need to dos." More importantly, you'll be reminded that retiring with confidence doesn't require a degree in economics, finance, or even brain surgery. Yet sometimes, through no fault of your own, distractions get in the way. Perhaps you've made decisions based on myths, heard voices in your head, or watched an influential presentation on television. This chapter is will help you ignore the temptations of emotions. Instead, you'll be placed on a path that's filled with rational advice.

Ten Myths That Still Exist in Retirement Planning

Some myths become legend, and once they reach that level of status, it's tough to shake them from their perch. The world of retirement planning is no different, but as much as rules of thumb, old wives' tales, and lessons from our parents have become the training wheels that got us all started on our financial planning journeys, the rules have most definitely changed.

The Important Things in Life

The love of family and the admiration of friends is much more important than wealth and privilege.

Charles Kuralt

Quote

Myth 1: The Most Important Pieces in Constructing a Puzzle Are the Corners

Try viewing this myth from the perspective of retirement planning and everything you've learned from the previous pages. When it's time to build a puzzle, what are the most important pieces? You may be thinking it's the corners, the last piece, or the edges. But when it comes to retirement planning, the most important piece… is the cover of the box.

Think about it. In order to build a plan that meets your situation, it's important to avoid guessing and instead refer to the cover of the box to find answers. In doing so, you're forced to keep looking at "the whole picture."

Myth 2: Don't Touch the Principal—Live Off the Interest

It's been more than two decades since retirees could comfortably consider retiring off the interest they earned at the bank. Life today is different. You need to take a more sophisticated look at your overall financial life, and you can. If not, you'll find yourself living a life of scarcity when your retirement life could be filled with abundance.

Consider taking a total-return approach as a mechanism for creating an income stream (**Chapter 15**). Consider using some of the equity in your home, reassessing the need to maintain investment property, or simply reevaluating how much of a legacy you really want to leave to the next generation.

Myth 3: Only the Rich Have Access to "Real" Retirement Planning Advice

Not true! By virtue of purchasing this book, I think you'll admit that it's more than the rich who have access to retirement planning advice. From websites to personal financial programs, retirement planning books, and courses at community colleges, advice is available to everyone—and at an affordable price. However, we sometimes need individualized attention. Advice that is specific to *our* needs, not the general populace. You can find help. Visiting CFP Board's website, letsmakeaplan.org, or Financial Planning Association's website, plannersearch.org, is a great start.

Myth 4: The More a Financial Plan Weighs, the More Valuable It Is

When my father first started in this business, he joked that financial planning was delivered by the pound. Financial institutions would battle over who

Inspiration

What It Means to Be Rich

Arthur, also known as "Tutsy," knew how to make a buck, but he didn't know how to invest it, grow it, and keep it safe. Over time, with the help of a Certified Financial Planner professional, he built a secure financial foundation for his retirement. This allowed him to buy a dream beach house in Maine for the whole family to enjoy (ten people and a dog) and to winter in sunny Florida. When he died after a prolonged illness, he left his finances in excellent shape so that his wife, Myra, didn't have to worry about money.

Tutsy had many lifelong, dear friends and a wonderful family that loved him. He used to say, "What else could a man want in his life? The love of family and friends is better than all the riches in the world." And he wasn't afraid to show his emotions and tell them how much he loved them. He told us every day.

Arthur did not measure his wealth by his balance sheet or net worth statement. He measured the richness of his life by the love of family and friends. By that measure, he lived a rich life and died a very wealthy man.

Story contributed by Marci Soreff Lerner, MBA and CTP.

had the most attractive, heaviest, most premium leather binder to provide a client. But in truth, most pages were boilerplate filler and many of the "data pages" were supplemented by "artificial intelligence" that emerged based on the parameters of the client's financial situation. Make no mistake, the report looked impressive. It had heft. It made you "feel" like you'd just received incredibly comprehensive personalized advice. But if you're like most people who've had advisers prepare such reports, it ended up on your bookshelf collecting dust rather than delivering advice.

Today's financial plans are living documents. Generally, they are introduced with a three- to five-page executive summary that highlights your strengths, weaknesses, opportunities, and threats. The report is supplemented with eight to twelve pages of high-level analysis and reports. The last page of your plan features an "action plan" that lists steps you should consider taking to better position yourself for retirement success. All this data is then made available through a cloud-based software system where you (and, if necessary, your adviser) can monitor the progress of your plan and keep you on track.

Your Living Retirement Plan

A retirement plan remains successful when you have the opportunity to monitor your progress and identify where goals and objectives have changed—and when you have the tools available to help you make adjustments to your plan.

Websites such as quicken.intuit.com, mint.com, aarp.org, and others have programs to assist your basic planning needs. If you wish for something more sophisticated, look to the Financial Planning Association or to CFP Board of Standards' website (cfpboard.net) for resources and tools.

Inspiration

Myth 5: My Life Is Simple and I Have a Will—That's All I Need

I'm always amazed by how unprepared people are when a loved one (especially a spouse or parent) passes away. Without proper planning, the days following a death can be disastrous and not the way the deceased had planned. No, I'm not talking about the division of assets and who inherits which jewelry. It starts with someone, other than the deceased, knowing where any instructions are pertaining to the funeral, cemetery, and final wishes.

Many people elect to keep end-of-life instructions in a safe deposit box. Yet if you haven't given anybody instructions on where to find the key and/or who has authority to open the box, your wishes may not be fulfilled.

Does someone you know have instructions on where you'd like to be buried? Who would you like to officiate at your funeral? Are you an organ donor? Do you want to be buried or cremated? How long would you like to be mourned, waked, etc.? Does someone have access to a checking account or your credit card to pay funeral bills?

No matter how simple a life you lead, or how basic you'd like your funeral to be, it's important that your instructions be clearly noted and that someone knows where those notes exist. Finally, I recommend having your personally written wishes notarized.

Myth 6: A Surviving Spouse Will Honor the Way the Deceased Spouse Managed Money

If you're nodding your head in agreement, I hope you're not serious. With you gone, your spouse's life will change. For a short time, your spouse may wonder "What would Irving do?" or "How did Sylvia handle all the bills?" but soon that will fade. A surviving spouse's life adapts and changes to the new environment.

What's even scarier is the thought that your spouse never learned how to handle the checkbook, pay bills, purchase a car, upgrade cell phone plans, make decisions on extended warranties, or plan a vacation. Your spouse is going to need to rely on a trusted companion, family member—or, God forbid, an unsuspecting predator.

Make certain that you are both familiar with day-to-day money management skills, or build a relationship with someone to serve as a trusted adviser for the surviving spouse who you feel will place your interests first.

Myth 7: I Can Trust Anyone Who Holds a CFP Designation? After All, That's the Industry Gold Standard

As a CFP professional myself, I'd be lying to you if I said I believe in the statement above. There are close to seventy thousand CFP professionals in America, yet by all accounts, fewer than 20 percent of them actually offer personalized financial planning advice. (Yes, you read that correctly.)

All too many people seek to gather professional designations with the intent of building a resume and use it as a marketing tool to attract business. With that being said, there is a *huge* difference between professionals who *have* a CFP mark and those who *are* CFP professionals. Although there are differences in how CFP professionals practice, it is probably better to deal with someone who has the CFP mark than someone who doesn't. In the next chapter, I'll provide you with some interview questions that will help you distinguish between the two.

Myth 8: When I Retire, I Need to Dramatically Shift My Investment Portfolio Away from Stocks and into Bonds

You've probably heard the myth "Invest your age in bonds and the rest in stocks." This is another old wives' tale that has gone the way of the encyclopedia. (Yet, like this myth, we still insist on keeping those hardbound volumes on the shelves in our homes.) Everyone's personal financial situation is unique. In retirement, you might find a need to *increase* your stock allocation, especially if the bulk of your retirement income comes from non-inflation-protected pensions.

Even more importantly, you should view your overall investment allocation by including all your investable assets. This might include money in the bank, annuities, the cash value of life insurance, personal investments, retirement accounts—and, yes, even the present value of your pension and Social Security. With all this data, now you can build an asset allocation that truly reflects your retirement income needs.

Myth 9: Most Individuals Need Life Insurance in Retirement

If I hear one more person tell me that he or she needs to keep a life insurance policy "so you can bury me," I'll scream. That may have been the case when all retirees had for assets was a pension, a couple of dollars in the bank, and a home. Today, retirees generally have adequate dollars, that's easily within reach (in most cases) to pay for a funeral and cemetery plot.

If you really think about it, the day you die, the funeral director wants to get paid. How long do you think it will take for your beneficiaries to collect the death benefit on the life insurance policy? Probably months. I assure you that there isn't a team at MetLife, New York Life, and other insurance agencies scouring the daily obituaries looking to see who died today and comparing those names with their lists of insured clients.

There are a few reasons to continue owning life insurance late in retirement. They include your desire to have the following items paid for upon your death:

- The mortgage
- Your children's college education
- A continued income stream to the surviving spouse
- A replacement of the assets used to pay estate taxes

In the last case, though, unless your estate is in excess of $5 million, I see no need to maintain life insurance.

Myth 10: A Financial Planner Provides Only Investment Advice

It is true that many professionals who hold themselves out as financial planners provide only investment advice, but that's because they are simply looking to sell you something. They do both you and my profession a disservice. They should more fairly refer to themselves as investment advisers. Those who hold themselves out as financial planners should seek to understand more about you than the money you wish to invest.

A financial planner should spend the first meeting asking *you* questions and learning more about *your* overall goals and objectives. A financial planner should insist on gathering data about how each asset and liability impacts your overall life. Then the financial planner should take the time to examine every component of your financial life prior to ever offering any recommendations. Lastly, a great financial planner will charge you a fee for objective financial planning advice—and will put it in writing. The advice should come from the financial adviser, not a boilerplate program.

Finally, and only then, should a financial planner suggest how you might implement strategies.

Ten Timeless Retirement Planning Strategies

As we look to the future, there are many lessons we can learn from our past. The following ten strategies are lessons that prevail whether economic climates are erratic or calm. Allow them to serve as the foundation for your financial plan.

Strategy 1: Maintain an Emergency Fund

Always maintain a reserve account in an FDIC-insured bank equal to three to six months' total expenses. The interest rate doesn't matter.

The Trifecta: Truths about Investing

1. Investing isn't hard.
2. Active trading is a loser's game.
3. Rebalancing your portfolio is most important.

Pure Genius!

Never consider investing money prior to fully funding your emergency fund. It is critical to always have easily accessible cash on hand.

Never view your investment account as your emergency fund.

Strategy 2: Examine Your Expenses

Continually find time to revisit your *needs* versus *wants*—sometimes referred to as fixed expenses versus discretionary (fun) expenses. Your mortgage, utilities, food, insurance, auto expenses, etc., are fixed costs. Dining out, vacations, manicures, lawn service, club memberships, lottery tickets, and electronics purchases are items that can be rationed if needed. When money is tight, consider limiting the "fun stuff" for a while.

Strategy 3: Safeguard Your Short-Term Income Needs

If you're at a stage in your life where you're drawing money from investments to supplement your spending needs, consider positioning three years of distributions from your investment account into a highly liquid, low-risk cash investment, such as a money market account or very-short-term liquid bond fund.

For instance, if you rely on $2,000 per month from your $500,000 investment portfolio, consider liquidating $72,000 ($2,000 x 36 months) from investment risk and secure this money in a safe, highly liquid investment, such as a laddered certificate of deposit, money market funds, short-term bond funds, etc. Your remaining portfolio should continue to participate in a balanced collection of stock- and bond-based investments.

Strategy 4: Rebalance Your Portfolio

Revisit your existing investment accounts at least annually to ensure that the current asset allocation remains in line with your overall risk tolerance and time horizon.

Committing to a rebalancing plan keeps you focused on buying low and selling high. If you leave investment decisions to your emotions, you're bound to do just the opposite.

Strategy 5: Manage Tax Losses versus Gains

No one knows what tax rates will look like in the years to come, yet there are times when you can control the tax liability on your investments by offsetting realized gains with realized losses. You could have a large tax-loss carryforward still sitting on your tax return due to selling investments at a loss over the past couple of years. A run-up in the stock market can create large gains in your portfolio. Perhaps there is an opportunity to offset gains against losses.

Also, in good years, many mutual funds can pay capital gains distributions. If you own these funds in a nonretirement account, you may want to review the implications that this "special distribution" could have on your overall tax situation (**Chapter 8**).

Strategy 6: Avoid Speculation—Stay the Course

Never try to recoup losses with quick-fix investment strategies. Investing is a long-term proposition. Avoid the temptation of get-rich-quick seminars and razzle-dazzle software programs. Think about it. If speculative trading is so easy, why isn't everyone already doing it?

Strategy 7: Invest in the Stock Market

Rather than trying to time the market, if you have cash available, begin building positions through an asset-allocation strategy using well-managed, highly regarded mutual funds designed to manage risk while achieving long-term returns.

If you're wondering whether *now* is the time to invest in the stock market, ask yourself this simple question: "Do I believe that the stock market will be higher five years from now or not?" If your answer is yes, then consider investing. If it's no, then consider another strategy.

However, if you need access to your money in six months, one year, or two years, don't allow the temptations of the stock market to lure you into making a decision you may regret.

Strategy 8: Don't Give Up on Your 401(k)

"Free money!" Did someone say "free money"?

This employer-sponsored pretax investment account remains one of the best investment opportunities for working Americans. You are able to place a portion of your hard-earned money in an account that has the potential to grow over time—without having taxes withheld prior to making the investment. If you're about to place one hundred dollars per week into a 401(k) plan and can avoid having twenty of those dollars deducted to pay federal, state, FICA, and Medicare taxes, you've just retained some extra money to grow for free for your retirement. Yes, when you withdraw the money, much later in life, you'll have taxes due on the distribution, but until then, that money gets to work for *you* and not sit in the coffers of the government.

In fact, contrary to popular belief, you should wish for the stock market to head downward during your "working years" so that you can buy shares of mutual funds at lesser and lesser prices. If you believe that investments will recover over time, never abandon your systematic investment strategy in down markets.

Strategy 9: Review Beneficiary Designations

Challenging economic conditions offer rare opportunities to reflect and rethink about our life today—as well as the legacy we hope to leave behind. Be sure that you review both your primary and your secondary beneficiary designations on retirement accounts, life insurance policies, and annuities.

Don't be surprised if your mother, ex-husband, or sister are still listed on an old account. You have the ability to change beneficiaries. Do it now if necessary.

Strategy 10: Seek Professional Guidance

Now more than ever, consumers are seeking the independent, objective advice of a Certified Financial Planner professional. Yes, you will pay for advice, but in the end, I suspect that after meeting with someone who is both ethical and independent, you will wish that you sought help sooner. To find a Certified Financial Planner professional in your community, visit letsmakeaplan.org or fpanet.org.

Pure Genius!

Beneficiary Designations: Pro Rata versus Per Stirpes

Assume you have three children—Stella, Robert, and Eva—and you wish to leave your retirement account equally to the kids. Stella has three children (your grandchildren), and Robert and Eva each have none.

Under either the pro rata or the per stirpes designation, the three children would split your assets evenly (Stella one-third, Robert one-third, and Eva one-third) upon your death.

However, if Stella predeceased you, would you want your three grandchildren to inherit what would have been Stella's share? Or would you prefer to skip them over and just leave the money to Robert and Eva evenly (fifty-fifty)?

If you selected pro rata, Robert and Eva would split the money—and the grandkids would get nothing.

If you selected per stirpes, your grandchildren would split Stella's share (one-third) evenly among the three of them. Robert and Eva would get their one-third each.

You may be surprised to know that most brokerage firms use pro rata as the default instruction when the beneficiary designations are assigned to a retirement account. What's even scarier is that most financial advisers aren't aware of it.

Ten Reasons It's Time to Revisit Your Financial Plan

The following ten ideas will lend pause as you think about whether it's time to revisit your current financial plan.

Reason 1: Your Last Financial Plan Is Collecting Dust

If you're like many people, the allure of a "free financial plan" was just the medicine you needed to alleviate your financial worries. Unfortunately, it's likely that the leatherette binder with the fancy gold embossing is now buried on your bookshelf and hasn't been updated to reflect your current situation. If you're serious about financial planning, pay for the advice. After all, when it's free, you should expect to get what you pay for. Your plan should be easy to follow, monitored regularly, and filled with personalized advice—not cookie-cutter strategies.

Reason 2: New Baby, New Spouse, New Job, New Transition in Life

Financial planning is a fluid process that requires change over time. Think back five or ten years. Ask yourself how different your life looks today. Does your financial plan reflect today's outlook on life or what you hoped it would be? The decisions you make today are likely to change. New financial questions will arise in your life all the time. Make sure you find an objective individual who will listen to changes in your hopes and dreams and lend guidance with readjusting your retirement plan to reflect what *you* want.

Reason 3: You Know That Now's the Time to Get Your Financial House in Order

Do you know where everything is and what it's worth? If you don't know, you should. If you want to know, you can. **Chapters 3–5** will give you the skills to build the net worth and cash flow that's reflective of your situation.

Reason 4: You're Actually Considering Financial Advice from Strangers

Walk into most pizza parlors, dry cleaners, or barber shops today, and you're likely to see the talking heads on television making stock recommendations and offering tactical strategies. While it makes for entertaining television, their advice does not have your specific interests in mind. How can it? They know nothing about your personal financial goals and objectives. The best advice—the kind you should follow—needs to come from people who know your situation and can offer advice that's just for you, not just a generalization.

Reason 5: It Was Fun for a While, But Now It's Time to Get Serious

Perhaps you elected to do financial planning on your own, or worried about putting all your eggs in one basket, so you spread your money among several financial advisers to see who could make you the most money. But times have changed, and you need to build a strategy that isn't fragmented anymore. You need to consolidate your financial life and find someone who will view your retirement plan as seriously as you do. The days of chasing hot stocks are over. It's time to be prudent.

Reason 6: You're Unsure Whether You're on Track to Achieve Your Goals

Just because the market fluctuates, or your 401(k) plan drops in value, that doesn't mean you have a greater or lesser chance of achieving your goals. That's only one piece of a financial plan. A financial plan integrates the impact of your employment income, spending patterns, major expenses, current savings, lifestyle, etc. Do you or your current financial adviser(s) have a mechanism for tracking your progress? How can you tell whether you're on track?

Reason 7: Your Financial Planning Review Is Limited to Analyzing the Performance of Your Investment Account

Financial planning is not a slice in the proverbial pie. It *is* the pie. Investments are just the slice. When you have a comprehensive financial plan, you are able to recognize that cash flow, taxes, insurance, estate issues, and major expenses are integral parts of your financial plan. If you aren't including *all* the pieces, perhaps it's time for a new look at your retirement plan.

Do You Need a Financial Planner?

Choosing a financial planner is a personal decision, analogous to choosing a doctor. You should feel exceedingly comfortable, and willing to share personal issues surrounding money, with your planner. After all, if you truly want to achieve your financial goals and objectives, you need to draft a map that is prepared to encounter roadblocks, detours, cobblestones, and potholes.

Perspiration

Reason 8: You Still Think US Savings Bonds Will Double in Value in Seven to Ten Years

Amazingly, people continue to purchase US EE savings bonds as gifts for children and grandchildren with hopes they can use them to help pay for college costs. The "Rule of 72" is a calculation that allows someone to determine when an investment will double in value. Today's EE savings bonds will reach face value in twenty years. So if you thought you were buying these bonds to help pay for college, think again. It's more likely that the beneficiary will use them to pay off some student loan debt.

> **The Rule of 72**
>
> If you've ever wondered how long it will take for money to double, you need not wait any longer. The Rule of 72 is a well-regarded mathematical formula. All you need to do is take the number of years that you would like your money to double and divide it by seventy-two.
>
> For example, if you'd like your money to double in ten years, simply divide seventy-two by ten:
>
> 72 ÷ 10 years = 7.2 percent
>
> If your investment grows at 7.2 percent for the next ten years, your account will double in value.
>
> Want to know what percentage you'd need to triple your money? Use the number 144 in place of 72.
>
> Definition

Reason 9: You Don't Know How Your Financial Adviser Gets Paid

Advisers can charge you a number of ways to help with your financial planning and investment needs. Commissions, fees, retainers, and servicing fees from financial institutions are some of the more popular approaches.

When you are working with Certified Financial Planner professionals, if you ask, they are required to tell you how much they made for giving you advice and/or for any products that you bought. Whether your financial adviser is a CFP professional or not, a financial adviser who is not willing to fully disclose compensation is probably someone you don't want to deal with.

Reason 10: You Wonder Whether You Are Still Your Financial Adviser's Ideal Client

Your life has changed and so too has your financial adviser's. Do your financial planning needs reflect the services and advice that fall into your adviser's "sweet spot?" Never asked before? Go ahead. You have a right to do so. Ask your financial adviser to describe what a "typical client" looks like in your financial adviser's office. If you don't measure up, it may be time to rethink the relationship.

Working with a financial planner can be among the best decisions a retiree ever makes, but it can also be among the most dreadful. It's no wonder people have such strong feelings about whether to work with one or not. If you think it's time to revisit your financial plan, the next chapter will give you the skills and talking points to begin that journey.

To Summarize...

- The financial myths you've learned from generations before have changed dramatically. When it comes to your money, you need to decide what's best for you, not what "they" say.
- A smart retirement strategy is grounded in a sound plan and an honest vision of your goals and objectives. Relying on an investment strategy alone is a path filled with pricks and thorns.
- Chances are that your old financial plan (if you even have one) is outdated and not reflective of your current financial situation. It's time for a refreshing new glimpse into your current state of financial affairs—and a bright, shiny lens of what the future can hold.

Chapter 24

Finding an Adviser Who Makes Sense for You

In This Chapter . . .

- The truth about how advisers get paid
- Seeking fair value for the fees you pay
- Uncovering trust and transparency in advisers
- Conventional and unconventional interview tips when considering a financial adviser

There are millions of statistics that have framed the public's perspective on retirement planning. Some are spot on, and others are exceedingly misleading. Yet one statistic that retirees struggle to accept is the fact that they can make more informed, rational retirement decisions when working with a Certified Financial Planner professional who is dedicated to placing their interests first.

In the pages that follow, I want to give you tools so that when the time is right, you can find a planner who will serve your needs best.

It's Time to Get Serious

How many times have you gone to Home Depot expecting to buy all the right parts so you can fix an issue in your house only to discover later that you didn't do the task the right way? Something's still leaking. There are extra pieces. Now you're stuck spending money again to hire a professional to do it right. In the end, did you save money?

Have you done the same thing with your finances? Have you tried to do it yourself? Perhaps you've given small pieces of business to a bunch of different professionals with hopes that you can act as general contractor and manage the big picture?

As you approach retirement, it's time to get serious about your financial future.

You may find yourself managing your family's finances in your spare time, only hoping that you made the smartest decisions for your financial future. If the markets head upward, you feel like a hero. Yet when they retreat, you second-guess your actions.

Hiring a financial planner means allowing yourself to begin transferring the emotions surrounding your retirement life to someone willing to manage your expectations and offer a rational perspective during emotional times. As many clients tell me, most great planners are as much therapists as they are coaches, money managers, and life-skills Sherpas.

How to Find a Retirement Planning Expert

In today's world of finance, all too many people can hang a shingle indicating that they can provide you with retirement planning advice. The alphabet soup of financial designations is so abundant that it's tough to sift through the noise.

Below are just a few of the designations that may be found on the business cards of financial professionals today:

> AAMS, AEP, ATP, CCRA, CEA, CEBS, CEP, CFM, CFA, CFP, CFS, CHFC, CIC, CIMA, CIMC, CISP, CLTC, CLU, CMA, CMFC, CPA, CPC, CPCU, CPhD, CRA, CRC, CRPS, CSA, CSTSA, CTFA, EA, JD, LLM, LUTCF, MBA, MST, PFS, QFP, REBC, RFA, RFP, RIA, RHU, RR

Can you identify the quality ones from those that simply require watching a one-hour video and taking an online test?

As baby boomers turn sixty-five years old at a clip of ten thousand per day, there are all sorts of financial predators interested in making money from you. Your retirement deserves advice from a competent, ethical financial planner who has been tested in areas that are most important to your financial needs. In addition, you deserve a professional who has taken not just an examination but who is also held to a code of ethics and a fiduciary standard. You should seek someone who was required to have actual experience in the field before adhering the designation to a business card—and who continually needs to gather continuing education credits to keep that designation current.

I believe that the CFP mark is the "gold standard" and should be a *minimum requirement* when seeking the advice of a professional to help with your retirement needs.

A Distinguishing Characteristic of a Great Financial Planner

A financial planner dedicated to helping you achieve retirement planning success should never ask you to invest money or make changes to your portfolio prior to understanding your overall financial situation. As such, you will likely pay a fee for a comprehensive analysis of your financial situation first. This allows the planner to provide unbiased, independent advice, in writing, that comes from a place of understanding your overall financial goals and objectives. It should include recommendations that you can implement *anywhere* you see fit. When financial planning is offered for free, chances are the adviser has an ulterior motive.

Inspiration

When It Comes to Retirement Planning, Don't Be an Impulse Shopper

Hiring a financial planner isn't an impulse purchase. A great financial planner should be interested in working with you only when you're willing to share everything about your financial life. A less confident planner will accept a piecemeal relationship and hope to earn your trust through small victories, like positive investment performance in one account. It's important that you have clarity around your expectations prior to attending any meeting.

Seek to build a lifelong relationship together. Make sure you've made a decision that's best for *you*. Don't agree to a relationship because you feel bad for the adviser or you think the adviser could really use the business!

Your planner should be receptive not only to the financial aspects of your life but also the emotions, influences, and distractions that require serious conversations and guidance.

Keeping Track of Your Relationship

When meeting with a new planner, ask how the planner keeps records of conversations that you have, both in person and over the phone. Ask how emails you send back and forth are secured and recorded.

If the financial adviser doesn't have a contact management system that maintains records of all your conversations, interactions, letters, reports, and performance reviews, you should be concerned.

Retirement Planning Tip

The key to finding the right planner for you is preparation.

If you walk into a financial planner's office unprepared and uneducated, you could be guided down a path that doesn't make sense for your financial future.

You need to be harnessed with questions—tough, probing questions—so that you can interview your planner. After all, they intend to ask tough questions of you.

Perspiration

Your relationship with your financial adviser is private and confidential. Maintaining your relationship on sticky notes, yellow pads, and random notes leaves your privacy open for exposure. Not to mention the fact that a fire or other catastrophic event in the planner's office could leave your data either destroyed or in the hands of others.

Interview Questions That You Should Ask of Every Planner

I would suggest that you weave the questions below into the "typical questions" posed on CFP Board's website (letsmakeaplan.org). In fact, there is nothing wrong with sending these questions to your prospective financial planner in advance of your first initial consultation. After all, most planners ask you to prepare for the meeting by having you bring along information about yourself. Why not ask the planner to prepare for the meeting as well?

Here are the questions you should ask:

- *It is my understanding that Certified Financial Planner professionals are required to obtain thirty hours of continuing education credit every two years. How do you go about obtaining these credits, and do you generally focus on a particular area of specialization?*

  Many CFP professionals focus exclusively in one area of financial planning (estate planning or investments, for instance). If you're seeking broad financial planning advice, make sure your CFP professional is staying on top of changes in the industry that affect your situation.

- *Where do you turn when you need help finding answers to questions?*

  Cross your fingers and hope the first answer isn't Google. If it is, you might wonder if you're really paying for professional expertise. The best financial planners have access to a network of colleagues, investment companies, associations, research entities—and, yes, Google too.

- *To what extent are you involved in the development of my personal financial plan? Who is responsible for updating, maintaining, and charting its progress?*

  Depending on the size of the firm you engage, certain tasks are delegated and sometimes even outsourced. If nothing else, you want to be sure you know who will be held accountable for the advice provided to you. And don't forget, you want all of your advice in writing.

- *Do you rely on outside managers, or do you handle investment decisions within your office? Why do you choose one strategy over the other?*

  This will help you understand the day-to-day involvement your planner has with your investment portfolio. There really isn't a right or wrong answer here. Seek to find someone who makes you feel at ease with the response.

What is the profile of your "ideal" client? What percentage of your client base represents this group?

This is a critical question. You need to understand the adviser's "sweet spot" or what marketers call "target market." If you're about to build a long-term relationship, wouldn't you feel more at ease if you knew your situation was part of the adviser's bull's-eye rather than in the periphery?

Will I be surprised by any charges for transaction fees, custodial fees, wire transfers, trading costs, etc.?

Transparency is a key relationship-building tool with an adviser.

Besides investment management services, what other services can I expect?

Many financial advisers maintain practices where they charge you a fee (ranging from 0.5 to 2 percent) to manage your assets under an advisory relationship. For instance, if you place $800,000 with a financial adviser who charges you a 1 percent fee (or $8,000 for the year), what type of advice will it buy? Will it be limited to investments only? You deserve a comprehensive answer to that question.

What professional associations do you belong to? Do you volunteer your time in any leadership roles?

If you're interested in making sure that your retirement plan is current with changes in the regulatory world, the economic environment, and the most appropriate planning strategies in the nation, your adviser should be an active member of one of the leading industry organizations. This may include the following:

- Certified Financial Planner Board of Standards (cfp.net)
- Financial Planning Association (onefpa.org)
- The National Association of Personal Financial Advisers (napfa.org)
- Investment Management Consultants Organization (imca.org)
- Financial Services Institute (financialservices.org)

- American Institute of CPAs (aicpa.org)
- Any other number of reputable organizations designed to advance the body of knowledge for the profession

How does your firm help clients deal with "nonfinancial issues"?

If the adviser is positioned as a financial planner, there should be a wide array of services provided to you. As you know by now, money isn't the only issue that hits at the heart of a successful retirement. If you'd like to learn more about addressing nonfinancial issues in retirement, you'll be thrilled with **Chapter 25**.

How often do you deal with clients dying or needing long-term-care services?

Chances are that if your planner is new to the business, there hasn't been the opportunity to address the emotional and technical roles needed to support your family in the event of death or long-term-care disability. Many advisers are advocates of selling life insurance and long-term-care policies, yet fewer than 15 percent of all financial advisers have actually helped a surviving spouse, family member, or trustee with the filing of claims or provided advice on probate, estate settlements, and the transfer of assets. Seek someone who leans on experience, not book knowledge alone. For instance, in my office, we handle nine to twelve deaths each year. I'll admit that's high, but remember that my father started our firm in 1968.

Finding a financial planner is a personal decision. It is critical that you feel exceedingly comfortable and willing to share personal issues surrounding money with your planner. After all, if you truly want to achieve your financial goals and objectives, you need to draft a map that is prepared to encounter roadblocks, detours, cobblestones, and freeways.

Why the CFP Mark Is the Gold Standard in the Industry

Mary Beth Franklin is a nationally recognized journalist in the financial services world. She provides thoughtful and pragmatic guidance to both consumers and financial professionals. Recently, after thirty years of journalism, she decided to take the CFP exam. After learning that she passed, she posted a column that I thought would be of great value to you (on the facing page).

How Do Financial Planners Get Paid?

When hiring a financial planner, clarity and transparency are the keys to a successful relationship. Depending on the size of your overall financial net worth, certain compensation styles may work better for you. Below are some of the most common.

Commissions

Upon the purchase of an investment, the sales representative earns a commission. Disclosure is the key element in this relationship. You may or may not see the commission deducted from your investment. It's all a function of the "type" of investment you purchased. Generally, mutual funds carry a commission that starts at 5.75 percent and can be lower based on amount of money invested. Advisers who sell mutual funds may also receive a "servicing fee" from the investment company equal to about 0.25 percent of the value of the account.

When you purchase stocks, the commission cost can run as high as 2.5 percent to buy or sell a security. When buying individual bonds, the commission is built into the price. It's tough to find. Make sure your adviser discloses the amount of compensation.

Fee Only

The term "fee only" is defined as a fee earned for services rendered. It can also be a fee charged when assets are placed under management. For instance, if you elected to hire a financial planner to produce a retirement planning analysis and were charged a fee of $3,000, it would mean to me that you "paid a fee... only" for objective advice. However, if you agreed to invest $1 million through a financial planner and you both agree on a fee of 1 percent to be charged on an annual basis and paid quarterly, would that be a "fee-only" arrangement? Some say yes. I personally think the term is misleading.

I Passed the CFP Exam

(But you can't call me a certified financial planner and probably never will)

By Mary Beth Franklin

I was notified Dec. 20 that I passed CFP Board's certification exam.

As the national pass rate for the November 2013 CFP exam was a mere 63 percent, I felt it was an enormous accomplishment that culminated three years of study and a substantial financial investment.

But unfortunately, you can't call me a certified financial planner—and probably never will.

The congratulations letter announcing my exam results also noted that "passing the CFP certification examination does not entitle you to use the CFP marks." The form letter sent to all successful CFP candidates noted: "Only those individuals who have completed all of CFP Board's requirements are authorized to use the CFP marks."

Those requirements include a bachelor's degree. I graduated cum laude from American University with a degree in communications in 1975. Check.

Completion of a college-level financial planning certificate program. University of Virginia, 2013. Check.

According to the board's website, a total of three years of full-time qualifying experience, or the equivalent of 6,000 hours, is required to satisfy the work experience requirement.

Experience must fall within one or more of the six primary elements of the personal-financial-planning process, which includes: establishing and defining the relationship with the client, gathering client data, analyzing and evaluating the client's financial status, developing and presenting the financial planning recommendations, and implementing the and monitoring those recommendations.

Acceptable work experience can be satisfied through one or more of the following ways: personal delivery to individual clients, supervision of personal delivery to individual clients, direct support of personal delivery to individual clients, teaching courses at a CFP Board-registered program or finance-related courses at a university, or through internships or residency programs.

I have readers, not clients. And apparently 30+ years of award-wining personal-finance writing and appearances on numerous radio and television programs doesn't hold a candle to three years of qualifying work experience.

There's a reason the CFP designation is considered the gold standard in the financial advice industry: It sets the highest standards and accepts nothing less. I admire the board's mission to foster professional standards and ethical conduct in the delivery of financial advice to the public. It's their game and they are entitled to set their own rules.

This is a portion of a letter that appeared on December 26, 2013, in the InvestmentNews *daily.* InvestmentNews *is the leading news and information source for financial advisers.*

Fee Based

When an adviser charges a fee based on assets under management, I think that the logical term for the adviser's compensation would be "fee based." After all, the adviser's earnings are based on a fee that is deducted from the assets that have been placed under the adviser's management. In fact, many financial advisers also provide ongoing financial planning advice included as part of the fee collected on the assets under management. You may think I'm splitting hairs here—but, trust me, this is a thorny subject among financial advisers.

Fee Based and/or Commission

You will find that roughly 65 percent of all financial advisers work under this approach. After all, there are times when a particular investment and/or insurance solution makes sense for you that can be sold only on a commission basis. There are also other times when the best solution that the adviser has to offer you is a fee-based relationship. I happen to believe that this option delivers the best of both worlds to a retiree. Yet, like I said above, make certain that your adviser is very clear in explaining all of your costs and how your adviser is compensated.

Retainer

Some retirees with a large net worth elect to pay a flat retainer fee to a financial adviser. This fee provides you with an open array of services and benefits by the firm. Many of these firms have tiered services that deliver certain features and benefits based on the size of your estate. You will generally find retainer-based firms accepting clients with $3 million or more in assets.

Hourly as Needed

This approach is becoming more and more popular for people who elect to do much of their retirement planning on their own but simply seek a second opinion periodically.

Using the Internet to Learn about Financial Advisers in Your Area

Not all financial planners are the same. To find the one that's right for you, visit the planner's website. You can find answers to questions about the following:

> **You Deserve Transparency**
>
> Regardless of the type of financial adviser or financial institution you work with, if someone is not willing to *fully* disclose his or her compensation *in writing*, it's time to find another financial adviser.
>
> **IMPORTANT!**

- Titles, financial designations, educational background, and work experience
- Professional affiliations
- Licenses held to sell certain financial products, such as life insurance or securities
- Basic approach to financial/retirement planning
- Minimum net worth or income requirements
- Whether a free consultation is offered and how often clients meet with the planner
- How the planner is paid for services and an idea of typical charges

Finding a financial planner should take some effort. You should spend more time researching and selecting a planner than you did planning your last vacation.

The Match Game

Find a financial planner who specializes in serving your retirement needs and financial situation. Aside from being familiar with the circumstances you are facing, a financial planner can also serve as a resource, guiding you to new opportunities and ways to connect with people who have similar interests.

For example, in 1995, we established our Client Advisory Council. It was an opportunity for us to gather candid feedback from our clients and explore new programs, events, and services. It also provided unexpected benefits to a couple of clients who participated. Ray and Jim both retired from different industries and were among our initial group of advisory council members. During the first meeting, they struck up a conversation that led to monthly talks over coffee, a train excursion to the Mayan pyramids in Mexico, and endless outings and laughs. It's a friendship that's still going strong today, and it exemplifies the strong connections our clients have—not just with us but also with each other.

What Should You Expect for the Fee You Pay Your Adviser?

Investment management services are certainly an important part of the value you should receive from a fee-based or fee-only adviser. However, you should seek an alternative relationship if you're not receiving much more than the following:

IMPORTANT!

The Free Initial Consultation

The mass affluent baby boomer should never have to pay for an initial consultation with a financial planner. If a fee is required, it may mean that the planner already has too many clients and is simply using the fee as a means of collecting money for time spent in the event you don't meet the financial planner's "minimums." Stay away from those planners.

When you schedule your complimentary initial consultation, the planning firm should do the following:

- Send you an information kit to help you prepare for your meeting (or make it available to you online).
- Schedule an appointment time that is convenient for you. Your meeting will likely run about one hour.
- Recommend that you visit at the planner's office. My personal feeling is that planning for your retirement is as important as visiting your doctor. If a meeting was held at your home, there could be a number of distractions to pull your attention away from a fully engaged conversation about your money.
- Contact you a day or two before the meeting to confirm your appointment.

If the adviser doesn't have a means of communicating with you that is custom to the firm, wonder how much personal attention you'll receive after you become a client.

- A well-constructed investment portfolio
- Periodic rebalancing of your portfolio
- Monthly statements
- An annual review

When you work in an environment where you are paying for ongoing advice from your planner, your fee should also provide you with many of the following items.

Financial Planning Advice

Your adviser should always deliver the same depth of analysis and reporting that was developed for your initial financial plan. On an ongoing basis, make sure that your adviser updates the progress of your goals and that fresh recommendations are proactively presented to you as needed. In addition, your planner should be aware of changes in your financial life and, as such, should be ready, willing, and able to provide service (at no additional cost) in the following areas:

- Advice and analysis on large-purchase considerations, such as a home, boat, or car. In fact, some advisers are known to visit auto dealerships with widowed and single clients so that the "sales" process doesn't seem so intimidating.
- Advice and analysis on refinancing and mortgages
- Advice on reallocation and review of retirement plans held with your current employer
- Analysis of corporate benefits, such as stock options, deferred compensation plans, executive bonus plans, etc.
- Ongoing review of your homeowners, automobile, and umbrella policies
- Continued analysis of life, disability, and long-term-care insurance
- Ongoing conversations pertaining to estate issues, such as legacy planning, tax planning, charitable giving, and more

Client/Planner Review Meetings

The number of meetings/reviews that you'd like to have with a planner should be your choice—not your adviser's. During the first year of a relationship, you may find it necessary to meet three or four times, yet as time passes, you should feel that one to two times should be more than adequate for reviewing your retirement plans.

Online Access to Your Accounts and Financial Plan

Not all retirees utilize the Internet, but many do.

It's very common for planners to provide their clients with cloud-based software that allows you to view your overall net worth on a single page and to have all your financial data updated automatically on a daily basis. In addition, you should also be able to easily navigate to investment reports, financial planning progress, and realized gain and loss statements—and snapshots of your insurance and liabilities are accessible at your fingertips.

Many of these programs now offer you the ability to upload private documents, such as wills, trusts, insurance policies, deeds, and more to your own secured online vault. (And, like I said earlier, this should all be an additional value-added service provided as part of the fee you pay.)

Performance Reporting

When you engage with a planner, the performance reporting should be maintained from the day investments were placed under the planner's management. Each calendar quarter, you should receive a performance report of your portfolio either in the mail or online. If your planner is producing performance statements from Excel spreadsheets or on a yellow pad, beware!

Tax Planning

As changes occur in your financial life, it is important to compare and contrast the impact taxes will have on your decisions. Many financial planning firms offer tax-planning (not preparation) services. By having access to your previous year's tax return, your financial planner should be able to run what-if scenarios on planning software and, thus, create pro forma tax statements that can better prepare you for the future.

Family Meetings

As you age, it's not uncommon to bring your children into the discussion surrounding your money and your thoughts on how you'd like your assets handled after you're gone. This is a growing trend in the financial planning community. Planners are skilled at facilitating conversations around some of life's most delicate and personal financial issues. As moderators, they help communicate your intentions and wishes in an informal environment with the whole family present. Oftentimes, families use this time to discuss their choice of executor, special instructions, or personal wishes.

Review Meetings

Each time you visit an adviser for a review of your retirement plan, make sure that you spend time revisiting your goals, discussing live events that have occurred since the last meeting, and exploring all the areas you initially discussed in your planning meetings. The time spent reviewing your investment portfolio should take no more than 25 percent of your review meeting. If it takes longer, you may want to ask yourself whether you have an "investment relationship" or a "planning relationship" with your adviser.

WATCH OUT!

Client Advisory Council

Earlier in the chapter, I shared a brief story from our firm's client advisory council. Today, many established firms maintain an advisory council on behalf of their client base because they all recognize how hard it is to give themselves haircuts.

An advisory council shouldn't be a test kitchen for soliciting new products that the adviser wants to sell. Instead, it's an opportunity to gather feedback and ideas on communications plans, reporting capabilities, event ideas, and more. An advisory council generally reflects the demographics of the planner's client base. One great idea I collected from our advisory council was to establish a program that would help our clients and their children talk to one another about money.

Client-Only Events

Does your adviser host events exclusively for you? Client-appreciation events, educational programs, computer tips and techniques seminars, and antique road show events are among many of the benefits that fee-based clients receive from financial advisers. These events should be free of charge and, surprisingly, are often social gatherings of friends, neighbors, and coworkers who had no idea that they too were working with your adviser.

A Customized Newsletter

It's impressive when a financial planning firm can send out a custom newsletter on a weekly, biweekly, or monthly basis. Yes, it's easy for an adviser to subscribe to cookie-cutter newsletter systems. Yet when an adviser can deliver a publication that's set squarely on the needs of the market served, you get "news you can use" in your retirement life every day.

A Real Voice

Beware of the financial institution that doesn't have a real voice answering the phone when you call. A machine answering the phone during regular business hours is an indication of one of two things: (1) your call really isn't important, or (2) the institution doesn't have the financial resources to hire a person to answer the phone and build a personal, genuine rapport with you.

There's Genius in You—Told You So!

Well, you made it. You've reached the end of this book. I hope that you've found the advice to be genuine, honest, and straightforward. From the onset, it's been my goal to present retirement planning advice to you in a language you can understand. I hope you feel that I delivered on that promise.

I'd be delighted to hear what you thought of the book—and how any of the advice I provided gave you the incentive or inspiration to make your retirement a success. Until then—you genius, you—spend wisely, invest rationally, and enjoy the greatest years of your life.

To Summarize...

- Never feel intimidated by a financial planner. If you find yourself making a decisions because you don't want the adviser to get mad, reassess the relationship.
- When seeking a financial planner, take your time. Do some research, develop questions, and imagine you're interviewing someone you'd like to have as a trusted member of your family.
- Make sure you're exceedingly clear on how your adviser will get paid. You should never be surprised by any costs.
- Retirement is a major decision in life. You don't need to approach it alone. There are lots of professionals prepared to guide you. When you're seeking help, make sure at the very least that you look for someone who maintains a Certified Financial Planner designation.

Chapter 25

The Most Important Question of All

In This Chapter…

- Time with family: the retiree's soft spot
- Reconnecting with friends
- Self-care: Isn't it time for *you* time?

Bonus chapter! Years ago, I met with a potential client who was preparing to retire after thirty-five years with the same company. He was a bit skeptical about financial planners, so he grilled me with questions. But one question he asked was so compelling that I decided to write a booklet to answer it.

This question is on the minds of every retiree, yet sometimes the "money conversation" shields what may be the most important question of all: "How will I prepare for nonfinancial issues in retirement?"

The Heart of the Matter in Retirement Planning—The Real Concern for Retirees

Toward the end of our initial meeting, the client made the following comment: "I'm fairly comfortable that you'll be able to give me the assurances I need so that I can approach retirement with financial comfort—but you'll truly earn your stripes if you can advise me on my biggest concern."

> **The Essentials**
>
> *Retirement is wonderful if you have two essentials: much to live on and much to live for.*
>
> Author Unknown
>
> Quote

I asked him to elaborate, and he confided that his biggest worry was what to do after retiring.

"How can you help me adjust to the *non*financial issues pertaining to my retirement?"

After working at the same job, socializing with the same colleagues, and keeping the same schedule for thirty-five years, he worried how he and his wife would handle the sudden freedom of their new lifestyle.

"I'm not even sure what my interests are, let alone my wife's," he said. "Can you help?"

That simple question led me toward developing *The Retirement Resource Booklet.*

Designed primarily as a starting point for retirees begin to identify activities, volunteer opportunities, lifelong learning programs, and health living resources in and around the community where I live, the booklet has become a home-run resource, and it's my pleasure to share it with you.

How to Use This Guide

Retirement is a little like a really long road trip. Part of the fun comes from the unexpected pleasures you'll find—and the chance encounters along the way that lead to new hobbies, new friendships, and even new lifestyles. But like any good trip, a certain amount of planning has to be done before you can relax enough to enjoy the unexpected. I created this guide to help you get started. It's organized into three simple sections:

- Family
- Friends and Fun
- Fitness and Health

Each section contains ideas, stories, and websites for more information. We hope you find it helpful as you set out on your own journey into retirement.

Family: The Retiree's Dream

One of the most frequent comments I hear from mass affluent baby boomers, whether retired or not, is that they want to spend more time with their family. For some, that may mean reconnecting with their spouses. For others, it may mean getting to know their children as adults and/or enjoying their grandchildren.

Before retirement, it's a good idea to start "checking" with your spouse, discussing your dreams and how you plan to achieve them. You may be surprised with what you come up with.

Rebecca and Bill always wanted to start their own business, but they had three children to educate and good jobs with the state of Massachusetts that provided secured pensions and lifelong health insurance. Going out on their own just felt too risky. When they retired, we helped them use their resources to establish a delicatessen in central Florida. They're living their dream, working together, and enjoying a happy "retired" life.

The Truth about Planning for Retirement

If there's anything I've learned, it's that financial planning done well leads to lifelong rewards and the achievement of hopes and dreams. Yet integrated planning must also incorporate the intangible "nonfinancial" issues to fully achieve the life you want.

Pure Genius!

Not everyone is as fortunate as Rebecca and Bill. Sometimes after years of focusing on jobs and children, spouses have difficulty reconnecting. They have problems agreeing on how to spend their time. A husband may be retiring just as a wife becomes busier at work or with her volunteer organizations, and conflicts may arise. Increased time together may reveal long-standing cracks in the relationship that were easier to ignore when both partners were busy working and raising a family.

If you're trying to minimize conflict with your spouse early into retirement, you might want to make sure you each have separate activities outside of the marriage that you enjoy. For instance, one person may belong to a birding club, while the other spends time gardening or woodworking. Even an informal activity, such as meeting friends once a week for coffee, can help reduce the strain on a marriage by providing individualized social outlets. After all, before retirement, you didn't expect your spouse to fulfill all of your social needs. That shouldn't change now.

At the same time, find new interests you can share that will energize your relationship. Try asking what your spouse would like to do for fun. The two of you may come up with a whole new hobby.

Location, Location, Location

A recent survey by real estate developer Del Webb revealed that 55 percent of baby boomers intend to move out of their present home during retirement. Some may be planning on downsizing to a condo or retirement community. Others may want to live closer to family—or try out a vacation destination full time. Whatever the reason, moving can be a huge source of stress if both partners aren't fully on board with the decision.

Despite having a desire to move, the Del Webb study also explains that 55 percent of all Americans choose to live retirement less than fifty miles from where they grew up.

Start talking about this decision well before you retire. In some cases, particularly if there's conflict, I recommend that you rent rather than buy a second home in the new location and try living there part time first.

Reconnecting in Retirement

One way to cut down on problems is to communicate clearly and often about your expectations—ideally before retirement takes place. Ask these questions to one another once you're both out of the workforce and settled into retirement.

Who will be responsible for housework? For yard work? For preparing meals? For keeping up with social and family commitments?

Perhaps there are some shared responsibilities that you could enjoy together.

In some cases, hiring outside help to take over some of these chores can make a big difference in a marriage. In other cases, spouses may decide to take on a rotating task list of chores to make the work more equitable. Whatever you decide, making sure both partners are happy with the results can reduce friction.

Pure Genius!

Remain Considerate of Other People's Hectic Lives

If you are moving (or staying) to be closer to family members, be realistic about how much time you can expect to spend with them. Adult children are often in the peak years of child raising or are fully engaged in their careers. Grandchildren may be active with school, sports, or other activities. Connecting with them may involve some juggling. Conversely, adult children who are parents may expect more in terms of babysitting or child care than you are willing to give. Flexibility and good communication on both sides are key.

Connecting with the Grandkids

To build a relationship with grandchildren, try finding a hobby you can share. Get your grandchild's sports schedule and show up at games. Or for a birthday or holiday, give a gift certificate for a special activity—a trip to the museum and lunch, for example, or tickets to a sporting event and dinner after. The memories will last much longer than any toy or clothing you could give.

Another way to reconnect is with a family vacation. It's a chance to bond on a special trip, without the pressures of daily life getting in the way. One trend we're seeing is adventure vacations, where families bond while tackling a challenge together. It's a trip that will be remembered for years.

Fast Fact

Twenty-two percent of travelers between eighteen and thirty-four took their parents and/or grandparents on their most recent soft (less strenuous) adventure vacation.

Source: Adventure Travel Report

Observation

Worried about the responsibilities involved in traveling with children? Consider going in a special group designed just for families. It's a chance to meet new friends who share similar life situations, and it gives grandparents (and parents!) a little more freedom.

And, of Course, There's Always Disney

Disney, to this day, is among the happiest places on earth. It remains a special place for many people—and for one of our clients in particular.

A Dream Comes True

After discussing the three questions (as explained in **Chapter 11**), we learned that at age sixty-eight, Rosalyn's dream was to take her extended family (twenty-two people in all) on a weeklong trip to Disney World. But she and her husband were living on their combined Social Security income and a quarterly dividend from just one stock—the company where she had worked for over thirty years.

As a way to help Rosalyn envision her dream, we had a local travel agency create a proposal to take the whole family to Disney World. When Rosalyn saw the price tag—$35,000—she cried.

"That's just too expensive for us," she said. "We won't have enough money to meet *our* needs if we take everyone on the trip." But Rosalyn was wrong. When she realized that her sole investment was spinning off too small of a dividend, she began to reevaluate her loyalty to that one company. Over time, we helped Rosalyn and her husband pare back this position and reallocate the money among several asset classes.

Not only does Rosalyn reflect daily on the amazing family vacation in Florida, but she and her husband loved it so much that they became Florida residents and look forward to hosting children and grandchildren in the Sunshine State. Each year, Rosalyn writes us a note and always includes a picture of her family.

Celebrating Your Friends and Having Fun

Finding a new network of friends once you've retired can be challenging. If you've been working at the same company for many years, if you've recently moved, or if you've retired when many of your friends are still working, it can get a little lonely at times.

The good news is that there are lots of ways to find other adults with similar interests—and lots of reasons to do so. For starters, a recent study published in the *Journal of Gerontology: Psychological Sciences* tracked 1,669 adults aged sixty and over. The study found that friendships were more important than family relationships in predicting good mental health. Those whose social contact was limited to family members were more likely to suffer from symptoms of depression (probably because the kids always seem to be busy). Another study linked loneliness to increased blood pressure in older Americans, which could increase the risk of stroke, heart disease, or death.

Successful Transitions

Our clients are awe inspiring in their range of interests. Robert S., for example, parlayed his love of learning into friendship by joining a peer learning group. He enjoys sharing stories with us of how he has taught lectures (sometimes dressed in period costume), participated in discussion groups, and attended field trips with others in the club.

> **Fast Fact**
>
> Having close friends can help protect against Alzheimer's disease, according to a study done by physicians at Rush University Medical Center in Chicago.
>
> Inspiration

Julia, on the other hand, amazes us because she is so active. At age seventy-eight, she belongs to a tap dance troupe. These women—many of whom are in their seventies and eighties—visit senior centers, nursing homes, and other venues to display their skills and their celebration of life.

You may not be a history buff or a dance enthusiast, but it's likely that you have common interests with others. If you're nervous, start small. Many houses of worship hold weekly or monthly social hours after services. Make plans to attend, and offer to either bring refreshments or help clean up after. Having a task to perform gives you something to focus on and can help relieve any anxiety you may feel.

> **Fast Fact**
>
> Eighty percent of all individuals who have ever lived to age sixty-five are *alive* today!
>
> Inspiration

To find other seniors, check with your town hall to see if your community has a senior center. These centers offer classes, trips, and educational activities on a regular basis. They also provide a chance to connect with other seniors informally.

Or, if you've had a long-neglected hobby or passion, consider joining a club or taking lessons. To get started, look in the calendar section of your local newspaper, check the bulletin board at your grocery store, or search online for area activities.

Social Media for Seniors

A few years ago, my wife, Laura, and I purchased iPads. We attended a "Meet your iPad" session at the local Apple Store and were surprised to find that we were the youngest people at the meeting. Seniors were all eagerly awaiting guidance from the Apple "Genius" on how to send emails, view pictures, download games, and access the Internet.

Technology—and social media in particular—is not just for the kids. It's for everyone. The ability to find friends through Facebook, communicate with grandkids via Skype, send "selfies" to your pals through Snapchat, or simply curl up on the couch to read about current events on your electronic device is mainstream for everyone.

If social media scares you, don't fret. There are many retirees highly proficient in teaching you tricks and tips. Guess what? You don't have to rely on your eleven-year-old grandson anymore.

Volunteering

One of the best ways to meet people is to volunteer. It's an activity that makes you feel good, helps others, and connects you with like-minded individuals. There are plenty of opportunities. Consider helping out at the schools in your town, at the local hospital, or at a senior center. If you want to combine adventure with helping others, look for a "working vacation"—a trip that lets you explore a new area while volunteering and meeting people.

Whatever venue you choose, remember that friendships take time to develop. Just as you didn't accumulate your retirement savings in one day, friendships take time to grow. It may require several club meetings or volunteer sessions before you feel comfortable—and several more before you feel you've been accepted. Don't give up. It's an investment well worth making.

Feeling Fit and Healthy

One of the most important steps you can take to ensure that your retirement years are extraordinary is to protect your health. Being fit and healthy makes traveling, pursuing hobbies, and even simply playing with your grandchildren much more enjoyable.

If you've been balancing your career and family, it can be difficult to find time to take care of yourself. Starting an exercise program or changing the way you eat can seem overwhelming. The secret to success? Avoid radical diet or exercise plans. Setting unrealistic goals can leave you feeling frustrated and discouraged. Instead, start small with modest changes that you can maintain, and then build on the results.

Eating Healthy

Try gradually cutting back on processed foods—chips, cookies, crackers, white bread, etc.—in your diet over the course of several weeks. Replace them with healthier snack foods, such as fruits, vegetables, and whole-grain breads. If you drink soda, replace one or two servings a day with water. (To make it more palatable, add a splash of fruit juice.) Look at labels when you shop. A good rule of thumb is to buy only those foods with ingredients you can easily pronounce!

Exercise at a Smart Pace

Start gradually and work more movement into your normal routine. Try parking a few spots farther away from the grocery store than you normally would. Walk to the mailbox instead of driving. At the mall, park at the opposite end from the store you plan to visit, walk there, and then work your way back toward the car. When the grandkids visit, go for a walk instead of watching television.

> **Fast Fact**
>
> A great way to try healthful eating is to change your shopping pattern at the supermarket. Try sticking to buying foods that line the perimeter of the store. It's where you'll find most fruits, vegetables, dairy products, meats, and more. Zigzagging up and down the aisles may be a more colorful adventure, but be aware that the items on these shelves tend to be less healthy.
>
> **Pure Genius!**

After a few weeks, add more changes. Try having one or two meatless meals a week, with the focus on healthful foods—filling salads made with dark, leafy greens, whole-wheat pasta dressed in a simple tomato sauce, ripe fruit drizzled with a dab of chocolate for dessert. Experiment. Add fresh herbs to your meals to boost taste without calories, or sample a new fruit or vegetable.

To boost your fruit and vegetable intake even more, consider joining a community-supported agriculture (CSA) program. CSA members pay up-front fees, usually several hundred dollars, directly to a local farmer. They then receive a share of the harvest each week during growing season. CSAs are a wonderful way to focus on healthful food and support the local economy at the same time.

Stepping Up the Pace

If and when you decide you are ready to start a formal exercise program, consider these steps:

- Check with your doctor. Make sure you're cleared for an exercise program, and discuss any concerns you might have. If you have a bad back or sore knees, for example, ask what types of exercise can help you avoid putting strain on those body parts.

- Find a buddy. It can be easier to stick to an exercise program when you are in it with someone else. Enlist your spouse, a friend, a former coworker, or a neighbor. Some gyms also offer bulletin boards where members can find exercise buddies.

- Look for a facility or program that is qualified. Ask what types of certification the staff has. Do personal trainers have college degrees in some type of physical education or sports medicine? Is the degree from a college you recognize? If not, is it recognized by the US Secretary of Education? Is the trainer also certified by a qualified agency, such as the Aerobics and Fitness Association of America, the American College of Sports Medicine, or the American Council on Exercise? The goal is to find a trainer who has completed a serious course of study, not someone who received certification from a weekend Internet program.

- Avoid facilities or trainers who want to sell you supplements or special foods. Their focus may be more on making money than providing solid services. (And talk with your doctor before taking *any* supplements. Some can interact with prescription medications in negative ways.)

- Pick a program that will help you build strength and avoid falls—both good goals for seniors. Tai chi, for example, is a martial arts form that can help you improve your balance and build flexibility when practiced regularly.

- Find a class you'll enjoy. If it's fun, you're more likely to stick with it. Ballroom dancing, pool aerobics, and yoga can all be good choices.

- Don't forget hospitals and senior centers. They frequently offer affordable, well-run exercise programs.

- Remember that you don't have to pay to play. Walking, biking, gardening, or exercise tapes are all effective, affordable alternatives to a gym.

So there you have it. Retiring with confidence is achievable. You don't need to be a rocket scientist. (Told you so!) The next step is up to you. What parts of this book will you implement? All? Some? Will you attempt to build and maintain your retirement income strategy on your own or by partnering with a Certified Financial Planner professional?

Will you take the time to reconnect with your spouse, your children, and others who are important to you? How will you achieve the retirement of your dreams and exceed your expectations? It's my sincerest hope that this book has given you the inspiration, motivation, and determination to fulfill your life's dreams. Enjoy your retirement. You've got so much to look forward to.

To Summarize...

- Life in retirement is more than dealing with financial issues.
- You have an opportunity to maximize time with your children in retirement. Make it fulfilling to you.
- Reconnect with friends from the past—and create new kinships in the surrounding community. You'll find shared interests and perhaps even a new hobby or travel companion.
- Find time for self-care. All your life, you took care of others. Now's the time to find time for you. Eat healthy, stay active, and live your life to its fullest.

Appendix A

The Fact Finder

Personal Information	Spouse Information
Name:	Name:
Home address:	Home address:
Date of birth:	Date of birth:
Social Security number:	Social Security number:
Home phone:	Home phone:
Occupation:	Occupation:
Employer:	Employer:
Work address:	Work address:
Work phone:	Work phone:
Email address:	Email address:
Cell phone:	Cell phone:
Mother's maiden name:	Mother's maiden name:

Sources of Income	Spouse Income
Base salary:	Base salary:
Expected bonus:	Expected bonus:
Social Security (annual):	Social Security (annual):
Pension:	Pension
Other:	Other:

Children		
Name:	Name:	Name:
Social Security number:	Social Security number:	Social Security number:
Date of birth:	Date of birth:	Date of birth:
Annual cost of college:	Annual cost of college:	Annual cost of college:
First year of college:	First year of college:	First year of college:
Earmarked funds:	Earmarked funds:	Earmarked funds:
Percentage you'll pay:	Percentage you'll pay:	Percentage you'll pay:

Planning Objectives Ranking			
Client Categories	Client Ranking	Spouse Categories	Spouse Ranking
Reduce income tax		Reduce income tax	
Build wealth		Build wealth	
Retirement comfort		Retirement comfort	
College funding strategy		College funding strategy	
Reduce estate taxes		Reduce estate taxes	
Adequate life, long-term-care, and disability insurance		Adequate life, long-term-care, and disability insurance	
Purchase a home		Purchase a home	
Leave a legacy to my children		Leave a legacy to my children	
Other (specify)		Other (specify)	

Investment Experience

What percentage do you consider to be a reasonable rate of return on a long-term investment portfolio?

If your investment dropped in value, at what percentage would you be concerned?

What investments would you consider? (Check all that apply.)

❑ CDs ❑ Stocks ❑ Mutual funds ❑ Bonds ❑ Annuities ❑ Partnerships
❑ Other (please explain):

What is the best investment you ever made?

What is the worst investment you ever made?

If you are considering changing your current investment adviser, please explain:

Estate Planning

Do you have a will?	Does your spouse have a will?
Who is the guardian for your children?	
Who is the executor under your will?	Who is the executor under your spouse's will?
If your will contains a trust, who is the trustee?	
Who, if anyone, have you exchanged powers of attorney with?	
Do you have current health care proxies?	
If you have any trusts, why did you establish them?	

Assets			
Bank/Money Market Fund Names	Ownership	Current Value	Interest Rate (%)

Certificate of Deposit—Bank Names	Ownership	Current Value	Maturity Date	Interest Rate (%)

Brokerage Account Names	Ownership	Current Value	Stocks (%)	Bonds/ Cash (%)

Mutual Funds	Ownership	Number of Shares	Cost Basis	Current Value	Dividends Reinvest? (Y/N)

Stocks/Bonds Held by You (Description)	Ownership	Number of Shares	Cost Basis	Current Value	Dividends Reinvest? (Y/N)

Assets					
Stock Options (Indicate Owner)	Date Vested	Option Price	Number of Shares	Current Value	ISO or Nonqualified
Limited Partnership (Description)	Owner	Total Cost	Purchase Date	Annual Income	Write-Offs or Tax Credits?

Retirement Issues	
At what age do you plan to retire?	At what age will your spouse retire?
How much in annual income, in today's dollars, will you want in retirement?	
Do you plan on working after retirement? ❑ Yes ❑ No	
Earnings per year:	
How many years will you work?	
Have you verified the status of Social Security benefits? ❑ Yes ❑ No	Has your spouse? ❑ Yes ❑ No
Monthly benefit:	Monthly benefit:
Do you expect to have any debts in retirement? ❑ Yes ❑ No	
Explain:	
Do you have any aspirations to make seasonal location changes (i.e., winters in Florida)? ❑ Yes ❑ No	
Explain:	

Retirement Plans—Client					
Type (IRA, Roth IRA, 401(k), 403(b), Pension Plan, Profit Sharing, SEP, Simple IRA, etc.)	Where Invested	Current Value	Your Annual Contribution	Employer Contribution	Percentage Vested in Plan

Retirement Plans—Spouse					
Type (IRA, Roth IRA, 401(k), 403(b), Pension Plan, Profit Sharing, SEP, Simple IRA, etc.)	Where Invested	Current Value	Your Annual Contribution	Employer Contribution	Percentage Vested in Plan

Any specific information you would like to add?

Real Estate Property			
Property Category	Home	Other 1	Other 2
Address			
Describe vacation home, investment property, etc.			
Owner			
Month/year purchased			
Purchase price			
Cost of improvements			
Current market value			
Mortgage amount			
Mortgage date			
Interest rate/years remaining			
Monthly payment (principal and interest)			
Annual property tax			
Homeowners insurance			
Co-op or condo fee			

Rental Property		
	Property 1	Property 2
Monthly rental income		
When do you intend to raise the rent?		
How much will you raise it?		
When did you last raise rent?		
Management fees you pay		
Repairs and maintenance costs		
Utilities paid by you		

Potential Real Estate Purchases
Do you have plans to change your residence in the near future? ❑ Yes ❑ No
Explain:
Do you have long-term plans of owning a vacation home? ❑ Yes ❑ No
Explain:

Personal Property (Other Than Real Estate)					
	Car 1	Car 2	Furniture and Jewelry	Collectibles	Other (Describe)
Owner					
Estimated value					

Liabilities (Not Real Estate)				
All Loans and Debts (Auto, School, Credit Cards, etc.)	Amount Due	Monthly Payment	Estimated Payoff Date	Interest Rate

Equity Line of Credit					
Bank Name	Credit Limit	Outstanding Balance	Original Date	Interest Rate	Form of Payment

Financial Advisers			
	Name	Address	Phone Number
Accountant			
Attorney			
Banker			
Casualty insurance agent			
Financial planner			
Life insurance agent			
Stockbroker			
Trust officer			

Business Information
Name of business:
Estimated book value:
Percentage ownership:
Is there a buy/sell agreement?
Notes payable to business?
What are the terms?

Original Amount	Length of Note	Interest Rate	Original Date	Payments (Monthly, Annual)

Insurance				
Life Insurance	Policy 1	Policy 2	Policy 3	Policy 4
Company name and policy number				
Face value				
Policy date				
Cash value				
Annual premium				
Policy type (whole life, term, universal life, group, etc.)				
Insured				
Owner				
Beneficiary				
Amount of loan due				
Interest rate				

Please bring policies and/or company benefit statements as well as your most recent premium notice. (Attach another sheet if insufficient space.)

Insurance		
Disability Insurance	**Client**	**Spouse**
Name of insurance carrier		
Monthly benefit		
Annual premium		
Through company or personally owned		
Waiting period and length of benefits		
Medical Insurance	**Client**	**Spouse**
Name of insurance carrier		
Annual deductible		
Annual premium		
Auto Insurance	**Client**	**Spouse**
Name of insurance carrier		
Amount of deductible for collision/comprehensive		
Annual premium		
Homeowner's Insurance	**Client**	**Spouse**
Name of insurance carrier		
Amount of deductible		
Annual premium		
Amount of umbrella coverage/premium		
Replacement value (yes or no)		

Committed Expenses (Expenses That You Cannot Readily Reduce)			
	Average Monthly Expense	Estimated Annual Cost	Anticipated Change (Y/N)
Rent (not mortgage)			
Renter's insurance			
Gas, oil, auto repair			
Utilities, water, sewer			
Telephone			
Online expenses			
Medical, dental			
Other insurance premiums			
Groceries			
Clothing, dry cleaning			
Personal care			
Alimony/child support			
Support for relatives			
Education/day care			
Job-related expenses			

Please choose either monthly expenses or annual costs.

Discretionary Expenses (Expenses That Are Possible to Reduce if Needed)			
	Average Monthly Expense	Estimated Annual Cost	Anticipated Change (Y/N)
Annual vacation(s)			
Entertainment (theater, sports, outdoor activities)			
Dining out			

Discretionary Expenses (Expenses That Are Possible to Reduce if Needed)			
	Average Monthly Expense	Estimated Annual Cost	Anticipated Change (Y/N)
Cable television			
Gifts			
Babysitter			
Kids' activities			
Hobbies			
Subscriptions			
Pocket money			
Charitable contributions			
Lawn care/snow plow			
Home improvement			
Other			
Planning any major expenses or unusual fluctuations in your expenses?			
Is there anything else we should know about your expenses?			

Please choose either monthly expenses or annual costs.

Your Thoughts
This Space Is Reserved So That You Can Prepare Any Questions You May Have for Us

Your Thoughts
This Space Is Reserved So That You Can Prepare Any Questions You May Have for Us

Below are some notes that you should use as a reference if you have trouble completing the "fact finder."

Ownership

Identifying who owns what asset/liability is a critical component when building a net worth statement.

You should identify ownership as follows (for now):

- P1 (person 1). This is you. You can use your name if it's simpler.
- P2 (person 2). This is your spouse, partner, companion, etc.
- JT (jointly owned). This indicates that more than one person owns the item.
- T (trust)—This indicates trust assets.

Maturity Date

If you know the maturity date of a particular CD, bond, or other interest-bearing investment, be sure to write that in the appropriate column. This will be particularly helpful in the planning phase, as you'll want to know what money is coming due so that you'll be prepared when the item matures.

Contribution Amounts to Retirement Plans

While this information isn't quite needed for your net worth statement, it's likely listed on your most recent retirement plan statement. This is a good opportunity to capture the percentage of your pay, or the flat amount for each pay period, that you contribute to your retirement plan. If your employer provides some form of matching contribution, a profit-sharing amount, or combination of the two, you might want to write these numbers down in the space allowed. You'll need to gather it later on.

Liability Info

The amount of your outstanding mortgage or current credit card balance is an important part of a net worth statement. However, items such as interest rate, term of the loan, and monthly payment aren't included in your net worth.

What's So Important about Cost Basis?

Your cost basis is the amount of money you paid for an investment plus any reinvested dividends and/or capital gains on which you paid taxes in past years. Knowing your cost basis will allow you to make smarter planning decisions when it's time to review the investments in your portfolio. Generally, cost basis applies in nonretirement accounts. That's because most retirement accounts are fully taxable when they're withdrawn.

If you've bought securities (stocks, mutual funds, bonds, etc.) in the past few years through a brokerage firm, it's likely that your cost basis is captured on your statement.

Gathering Insurance Information

The questionnaire asks a lot of questions about insurance, such as the owners, the insured, the beneficiary, premium payments, and more. Your annual statement typically has most of that information. If you can't find it, take a look at your policy. You'll find the details of your policy on the first two pages, and beneficiary designations and more in the back. It should also contain a copy of the application you completed.

Appendix B

Net Worth Statement

Name: Ilana and Noah Fredrickson

As of : ______________

Assets	Noah	Ilana	Joint	Total
Bank Account(s)				
Crown Bank checking	$	$	$	
Crown Bank CD (due 10/18/15)				
National Bank savings				
Babson Credit Union				
Subtotal				
Nonretirement Account(s)				
LPL Financial				
Charles Schwab				
US EE bonds				
Subtotal				
Insurance Assets				
MetLife (cash value)				
Subtotal				
Business Assets				
Jerrycadabra Enterprises				
Subtotal				
Retirement Assets				
Majestix 401(k) plan				
City of Peabody 403(b)				
Pineapple Bank and Trust Roth IRA				
Topix 401(k) (previous employer)				
Bank of Kansas IRA CD (due 1/6/17)				
Subtotal				
Personal Assets				
54 Corey Circle (home)				
2104 Acura MDX				
2010 Honda Accord				
Jewelry and personal property				
Subtotal				
Total Assets	$	$	$	$

Liabilities (the Stuff You Owe)	Noah	Ilana	Joint	Total
Mortgage—54 Corey Circle	$	$	$	$
Home equity—Crown Bank				
Auto loan—Acura				
Credit cards				
Total Liabilities	$	$	$	$
Net Worth				$

Add additional rows or columns as needed.

Appendix C

Preparing for Emergencies

Your Personal Information

Name: ____________ Social Security number: ____________

Birth date: ____________ Passport number: ____________

Driver's license: ____________ Vehicle license plate number: ____________

Employer name: ____________ Employer address: ____________

Supervisor's name: ____________ Phone number: ____________

Supervisor's email address: ____________

Primary care physician: ____________ Phone number: ____________

Medical plan name: ____________ Member ID number: ____________

Blood type: ____________ Allergies: ____________

Medications: ____________

Spouse/Partner's Information

Name: ____________ Social Security number: ____________

Birth date: ____________ Passport number: ____________

Driver's license: ____________ Vehicle license plate number: ____________

Employer name: ____________ Employer address: ____________

Supervisor's name: ____________ Phone number: ____________

Supervisor's email address: ____________

Primary care physician: ____________ Phone number: ____________

Medical plan name: ____________ Member ID number: ____________

Blood type: ____________ Allergies: ____________

Medications: ____________

Children's Information

Name:

Cell phone number:

Social Security number:

Teacher:

Phone number:

Day care:

Phone number:

Physician:

Phone number:

Blood type:

Allergies:

Medications:

Name:

Cell phone number:

Social Security number:

Teacher:

Phone number:

Day care:

Phone number:

Physician:

Phone number:

Blood type:

Allergies:

Medications:

Name:

Cell phone number:

Social Security number:

Teacher:

Phone number:

Day care:

Phone number:

Physician:

Phone number:

Blood type:

Allergies:

Medications:

Name:

Cell phone number:

Social Security number:

Teacher:

Phone number:

Day care:

Phone number:

Physician:

Phone number:

Blood type:

Allergies:

Medications:

Pet Information

Name: ______ Name: ______

Veterinarian name: ______ Veterinarian name: ______

Phone number: ______ Phone number: ______

Medications: ______ Medications: ______

Investment Accounts

Firm name: ______ Financial adviser name: ______

Phone number: ______ Email address: ______

Address: ______

Account type: ______ Account number: ______

Account type: ______ Account number: ______

Account type: ______ Account number: ______

Account type: ______ Account number: ______

Other Professional Services

Attorney: ______ Phone number: ______

Address: ______

CPA/tax professional: ______ Phone number: ______

Address: ______

Banking Information

Bank name: ______ Phone number: ______

Address: ______

Checking account number: ______ ATM: ______

Savings account number: ______ Other account number: ______

Bank name: ______ Phone number: ______

Address: ______

Checking account number: ______ ATM: ______

Savings account number: ______ Other account number: ______

Insurance Information

Automobile insurance provider:

Policy number: Phone number:

Cars insured (license plates):

Homeowner's insurance provider:

Policy number: Phone number:

Umbrella insurance provider:

Policy number: Phone number:

Life insurance provider:

Policy number: Phone number:

Disability insurance provider:

Policy number: Phone number:

Long-term care insurance provider:

Policy number: Phone number:

Credit Card Information

Credit card company:

Account number: Phone number:

Credit card company:

Account number: Phone number:

Credit card company:

Account number: Phone number:

Credit card company:

Account number: Phone number:

Mortgage Information

Institution name: Phone number:

Account number:

Institution name: Phone number:

Account number:

Consumer Loans

Home equity loan provider: Phone number:

Account number:

Car loan provider: Phone number:

Account number:

Emergency Contact List (Make Sure One Contact Is from Out of State)

Emergency: 911 Police department:

Hospital: Fire station:

Name: Address:

Home phone number: Cell phone number:

Name: Address:

Home phone number: Cell phone number:

Name: Address:

Home phone number: Cell phone number:

Emergency Meeting Places

Within the Neighborhood

Address:

Landmark: Phone number:

Outside the Neighborhood/Out of Town

Address:

Landmark: Phone number:

Miscellaneous Information

Index

D

E

F

G

H

I

J

K

L

M

N

O

P

R

U

V

W

Z

CPSIA information can be obtained at www.ICGtesting.com
Printed in the USA
BVOW06s1633230714

359879BV00009B/4/P